Reading the Bible with Horror

Horror and Scripture

Series Editors: Brandon R. Grafius, Ecumenical Theological Seminary,
and Kelly J. Murphy, Central Michigan University

Horror and Scripture publishes monographs and edited volumes examining biblical and theological themes and texts in the light of contemporary horror theory and monster theory, along with theory of "terror management," trauma, and moral injury. The series also examines the reception and remixing of biblical themes in subsequent cultural, literary, and cinematic genres characteristic of horror.

Recent Titles:

Reading the Bible with Horror, by Brandon R. Grafius

Reading the Bible with Horror

Brandon R. Grafius

LEXINGTON BOOKS/FORTRESS ACADEMIC
Lanham • Boulder • New York • London

Published by Lexington Books/Fortress Academic
Lexington Books is an imprint of The Rowman & Littlefield Publishing Group, Inc.
4501 Forbes Boulevard, Suite 200, Lanham, Maryland 20706
www.rowman.com

6 Tinworth Street, London SE11 5AL

Copyright © 2020 by The Rowman & Littlefield Publishing Group, Inc.

All rights reserved. No part of this book may be reproduced in any form or by any electronic or mechanical means, including information storage and retrieval systems, without written permission from the publisher, except by a reviewer who may quote passages in a review.

British Library Cataloguing in Publication Information Available

Library of Congress Control Number: 2019949957

ISBN: 978-1-9787-0168-7 (cloth)
ISBN: 978-1-9787-0170-0 (pbk)
ISBN: 978-1-9787-0169-4 (electronic)

Contents

Acknowledgments	vii
List of Abbreviations	ix
Introduction	1
1 Reading with Horror	15
2 Monsters, Monster Theory, and Us	29
3 Hauntings of the Hebrew Bible	55
4 Haunted Spaces	77
5 "The Calls Are Coming from Inside the House!": The Monstrous Within the Community	101
6 The Monstrous YHWH	125
Conclusion	143
Bibliography	147
General Index	167
Scripture Reference Index	171
About the Author	175

Acknowledgments

Writing and research are solitary endeavors, but they can only happen with the support of family, friends, and community. The support I've received, from so many places, during the writing of this book has been overwhelming, and the gratitude I can express in these acknowledgments is only a small part of what is due.

Some of these chapters were presented, in significantly different form, at meetings of the Midwest Society of Biblical Literature; a version of chapter 5 was presented at the first "Gods and Monsters" conference, hosted by Texas State University. Thanks is due to Natasha Mikles and Joseph Laycock for organizing this conference, which will hopefully be the first of many. I have deep admiration for my colleagues at Ecumenical Theological Seminary, who have continued to support my rather nontraditional approach to biblical studies. In addition, I am grateful for the students who have studied with me through the writing of this book, particularly in courses on the book of Job and biblical interpretation. The richness and depths of our classroom discussions are due in large to the particular nature of Ecumenical Theological Seminary, whose students have a diversity of religious and life experiences that is truly unique.

Kelly Murphy, the coeditor on this series with me, has been a support since the very early stages of this project; her insights on all things monstrous have been indispensable in helping me develop my own thinking. The anonymous peer reviewer offered challenging and cogent critiques that led to more focused and tightly constructed arguments. And thanks are due to my editor Neil Elliott, who not only accepted this proposal for publication but proposed that we launch the *Horror and Scripture* series of monographs. I'm excited to see where this series will lead in the coming years.

My family has been an unwavering source of support. My parents, Edward and Ellen Grafius, helped me to learn the importance of critical thinking from an early age and instilled in me the value of following ideas wherever they may lead. My children, Fenton and Reece, have grown along with this book to the point where we can discuss the jump scares in James Wan's films together. I am so grateful for their presence in my life. And my wife, Kate Simon, has so graciously allowed my scholarly needs to set the evening film agenda and is always ready to challenge and deepen my ideas with precisely the right question. I feel lucky every day to have her as a life partner.

Biblical quotations are my own translations, unless otherwise noted. When discussing a particular Hebrew word or phrase, I have included the Hebrew consonants, as well as a rough transliteration to aid non-Hebrew readers.

List of Abbreviations

AB:	Anchor Bible
AIL:	Ancient Israel and its Literature
ArOr:	*Archiv orientální*
AYBRL:	Anchor Yale Bible Reference Library
BBR:	*Bulletin for Biblical Research*
Bib:	*Biblica*
BibInt:	*Biblical Interpretation*
Biblio:	*Biblotecha Sacra*
BJS:	Brown Judaic Studies
BJSUCSD:	Biblical and Judaic Studies from the University of California, San Diego
BZAW:	Beihefte zur Zeitschrift für die alttestamentliche Wissenschaft
CBQ:	*Catholic Biblical Quarterly*
CBQMS:	Catholic Biblical Quarterly Monograph Series
CurBR:	*Currents in Biblical Research*
D:	Deuteronomist Source
E:	Elohist Source
EANEC:	Explorations in Ancient Near Eastern Civilizations
FAT:	Forschungen zum Alten Testament
H:	Holiness Source

HALOT:	*Hebrew and Aramaic Lexicon of the Old Testament*
HAR:	*Hebrew Annual Review*
HBM:	Hebrew Bible Monographs
HBT:	*Horizons in Biblical Theology*
Heb:	Hebrew
HSM:	Harvard Semitic Monographs
HTS:	Harvard Theological Studies
HUCA:	*Hebrew Union College Annual*
ICC:	International Critical Commentary
J:	Jahwist Source
JBL:	*Journal of Biblical Literature*
JE:	Jahwist/Elohist Source
JETS:	*Journal of the Evangelical Theological Society*
JFSR:	*Journal of Feminist Studies in Religion*
JHS:	*Journal of Hebrew Scriptures*
JSOT:	*Journal for the Study of the Old Testament*
JSOTS:	Journal for the Study of the Old Testament Supplement Series
JSPSup:	Journal for the Study of the Pseudepigrapha Supplement Series
JTI:	*Journal for Theological Interpretation*
LAI:	Library of Ancient Israel
LHBOTS:	Library of Hebrew Bible/Old Testament Studies
LNTS:	Library of New Testament Studies
MT:	Masoretic Text
NICOT:	New International Commentary on the Old Testament
NIDB:	*New Interpreter's Dictionary of the Bible*
NSBT:	New Studies in Biblical Theology
OBO:	Orbis Biblicus et Orientalis
OBT:	Overtures to Biblical Theology
OTL:	Old Testament Library
P:	Priestly Source
RBS:	Resources for Biblical Studies

SBL:	Society of Biblical Literature
SemSt:	Semeia Studies
SJOT:	*Scandinavian Journal of the Old Testament*
STr:	Scriptural Traces: Critical Perspectives on the Reception and Influence of the Bible
TBN:	Themes in Biblical Narrative
TynBul:	*Tyndale Bulletin*
UCOP:	University of Cambridge Oriental Publications
VT:	*Vetus Testamentum*
VTSup:	Supplements to Vetus Testamentum
WBC:	Word Biblical Commentary
WJK:	Westminster John Knox
YAB:	Yale Anchor Bible
ZAW:	*Zeitschrift für die alttestamentliche Wissenschaft*

Introduction

GETTING UNDER OUR SKIN

At twelve, I wasn't afraid of dying.

But I was afraid that my life wasn't my own and that authority figures were always exerting control in ways that left me feeling stifled, limited, and small. At times, I remember feeling that this was what life was always going to be like—never in control, never making my own decisions, all the outcomes predetermined. I would continually be shuffled from room to room at the ringing of a bell, trying to squeeze in a visit to my locker in the three minutes I had to get to the next class. Dying seemed far away and impossible. The experience of adults controlling my life was always with me.

It was around this time that I first watched *The Omen*, a movie I found on the shelf of the local video store and grabbed because there wasn't anything that looked better. Watching it in my living room that night, I was enraptured, completely under the movie's spell for reasons I couldn't quite understand. I didn't sleep well that night and kept thinking about it throughout the next day. I think I rented it three more times in the next month.

Of the horror movies to come out in the 1970s, *The Omen* is far from the most accomplished, in spite of its pedigree. (The film starred A-list actors Gregory Peck and Lee Remick and featured highly competent directing from Richard Donner, who would go on to direct Hollywood blockbusters such as the first two *Superman* movies and all four of the *Lethal Weapon* films.) Although very polished and technically sophisticated, it was just another one of the demonic child movies that flooded the marketplace in the wake of *The Exorcist*.[1] But it got under my skin in a way that nothing had before.

It's the story of a well-to-do couple who's been trying to conceive for a long time. Their baby is stillborn, but before the wife finds out, the husband swaps it out for another baby who's mother had just died. This turns out to have been a very poor idea, as this baby is, in fact, the antichrist. A variety of creepy protectors gather around baby Damien as he grows into a supremely creepy child, and anyone who gets too close to uncovering his secret is dispatched through an unfortunate accident.[2]

The part of the film that wouldn't leave me alone for weeks afterwards was the subplot concerning a photographer by the name of Keith Jennings (played with a doomed sense of foreboding by David Warner), who suspects that something isn't right with the young boy. So, because he's a photographer, he starts taking pictures, both of young Damien and of the people around him. After developing these photographs, he notices a series of black lines—lines that correspond to the deaths of the people in the photograph. A young priest who was skewered with a lightning rod (yes, it's as silly as it sounds) has a jagged black line running through his body. A young woman who was found hanged to death has a black line across her neck. And the coup de grace comes when Keith develops a proto-selfie photograph, taken in a mirror, and sees a black line running across his own neck. Shortly thereafter, a pickup truck carrying sheets of glass crashes, sending one of the glass sheets hurtling towards David, who is decapitated in slow motion (and from several different angles).[3]

What haunted me as a twelve-year-old was less the gory death itself. It was the photograph, and the black line, and this photographer looking at the photograph of himself and knowing with a certainty the message it was conveying to him. These other people had been marked in the same way, and they had all died a violent death. He was next.

Now, my middle school mind didn't worry that I had somehow been marked for death, that the bully who tormented me on the school bus was actually the antichrist and that I was on some infernal hit list. But there was something under there that tapped into a fear that was real for me. All these years later, I think I've figured it out.

GROWING UP WITH HORROR

When people find out that part of my academic work involves studying horror films, I usually get one of two responses.

The first goes something like this: "Ugh, I can't watch that stuff. Too much blood." It's usually followed up by a story about being exposed to some horror movie or another at far too young an age and spending the next three months being unable to sleep out of fear of the monster in their closet. I remember a student telling me a story about sneaking out of his room at six years old, finding his parents watching something on TV, and hiding behind the couch to watch for a little while. It turned out to be *Nightmare on Elm*

Street; this poor six-year-old was too scared to come out from behind the couch and ended up watching the whole movie, about the spirit of a child-killer who has returned with the power to kill teenagers in their dreams, in a state of abject terror. He hadn't watched a horror film since.

When I hear stories like this, I usually make a few polite statements about how horror is like roller coasters; that some people like it and some people don't, and it's hard to say why. And that there's a lot more to horror than blood, that my favorite horror films aren't actually very bloody at all,[4] but that it's still not everyone's thing. I'm fine with that—I don't have a need to make converts, or try to convince people who aren't horror fans that they should be.

I also hear another response that goes more like this: "Man, I remember watching *Something Wicked This Way Comes* when I was five, and I couldn't get enough of it. I watched it over and over until the VHS tape wore out. And I've loved horror ever since." For some of us, horror gets in our bones in just the right way, at just the right time, and it's something we never let go of. Most horror fans can think of one title that really stands out from their childhood as being a revelation, as opening up a window into the world of adult fears that they kept wanting to return to.

THE PLEASURES OF HORROR

There's been a lot of theoretical work done in the last couple of decades as to why horror produces pleasure, stemming from a basic question: These are experiences that would be extremely unpleasant in real life, so why do we enjoy watching them on screen? Why do audiences seek these experiences out?

Mary Beth Oliver and Meghan Sanders have surveyed a wide range of audience responses to horror films and found the enjoyment of horror arises from many different sources and is not easily reducible to a single cause. For example, they explore the premise that horror is a form of "sensation seeking" and suggest that this seems to hold true but does not serve to distinguish horror from other adrenaline-fueled entertainment, such as action-adventure films.[5] They observe that horror films can serve as a form of social bonding (particularly for adolescent audiences), or even a coping strategy.[6] But in the end, the studies, which center on surveys of audience responses, are able to point to a number of factors that allow audiences to participate in the enjoyment of horror, but they are unable to pinpoint precisely which factor distinguishes horror from other forms of entertainment or draws particular audiences to the experiences. These questions require the assistance of philosophical approaches.

Noël Carroll, in his oft-cited work *The Philosophy of Horror*, argues that horror films produce an emotion that is distinct from actual feelings of horror and terror, which he terms "art-horror." He finds this emotion to combine feelings of attraction and repulsion; the pleasures of the horror genre have to do with this paradox.[7] Cynthia Freeland offers a response and suggested revisions to Carroll's proposal, offering the theory that the appeal is in "the genre's unique presentations of evil and human struggles with it."[8] In Freeland's view, audiences intuitively understand the presence of evil in the world and want to wrestle with why it exists and how it might be overcome. Both of these views help to distinguish horror from the more mundane evil that is found in action-adventure films; while they may not answer the question of "Why horror?" precisely, they provide a foundation for reflection on the question and give a starting point for further exploration. They move from helping us understand why some audiences prefer horror to the question of what horror can mean and how it functions as a genre.

I wasn't afraid of dying. But I was painfully aware of the experience that my choices didn't matter, that my life was an endless cycle of adults telling me what to do. And that's exactly what I was seeing dramatized in *The Omen*, through the photographer who began to realize that his own fate had already been sealed, the end of his life had been determined by powers much larger than he, and there was nothing he could do about it. While I couldn't have named this at twelve, I think that my middle-school brain somehow intuited it and felt a connection. Here was one of my worst fears being laid out before me and put into narrative form.

The best horror movies work that way. It's not the crazy guy with the knife we're afraid of, at least not mostly. We're afraid that what this narrative seems to be telling us about the fragile state of the modern family might be true, and maybe we're thinking about the fragile state of our own family. We're not afraid of the ghost, not really—we're afraid that we, too, have left things undone in the past, and that this is a past we can't keep outrunning much longer. Maybe we're afraid of the witch who lives in the woods, but our deeper fears are that we're like the patriarch of that movie, trying to hold our family together against impossible odds, with no one to help us when everything goes wrong.

And I think this is what causes audiences to keep returning to horror movies. While the action on the screen involves psychopathic axe murderers, creepy ghosts, or decaying zombies, the best horror movies tap into fears we have for our own lives, or fears we have for our society, or maybe even fears about the meaning of life itself. We see other characters wrestling with these fears on the screen and trying to defeat them, usually with at least some degree of success (at least until the sequel). And even if the characters aren't successful, there's some comfort in seeing someone else struggle against the same thing we struggle against, and come up short, just like we experience ourselves as coming up short time and time again in our own lives.

Many theorists and philosophers, going back at least as far as Søren Kierkegaard, have made a distinction between the emotion of horror and the emotions of anxiety or dread. The difference is that horror consists of a direct, definable threat; both anxiety and dread, in contrast, doesn't have a specific object attached to it. At least not one that can be easily named. Freeland, for example, has written about the "subtle and lingering" horror of films of the late '90s and early 2000s, such as *The Sixth Sense* and *The Blair Witch Project*, as tapping into our deep sense of dread, as opposed to more overt terrors of slasher films and monster movies. "Instead of witnessing deeds of a central monster, we experience a vague sense of impending doom and disaster. Instead of ever more developed gore and special effects, we see only fog and shadows."[9] I'd suggest that it's not just the understated horror films that Freeland discusses, along with their predecessors in Val Lewton's films of the 1940s, that work this way. When horror is most effective, it's because it connects with this sense of anxiety and dread that we experience in our lives, whether it's through an atmosphere of unease or a photograph that spells out a character's imminent demise. Even when there's horror on screen, what I'm most attracted to as both a scholar and viewer is the dread that waits underneath.

Of course, every horror movie doesn't succeed at this. The vast majority of them are disposable, cliché-ridden affairs, without anything much to say about our lives. (Even so, for real horror fans like myself, even bad horror movies have their pleasures!) But in most years a handful come out that, either through the insightful intention of the writers and directors or just blind intuition (or maybe even random luck), tap into something in our culture. Often, it's something that we're afraid to say out loud because we're worried that not everyone feels that way or it's something we don't want to be true. This is one of the real gifts of the genre of horror—the ability to uncover what is usually kept hidden, to give voice to what is usually silenced.

A TURN TO SCRIPTURE

So, what does all this have to do with the Bible?

Many modern readers have trouble with the Bible, particularly with the Hebrew Bible. Part of it is the stilted language, particularly for people who grew up with the King James Version and feel like that's the only version that they're authorized to read. Part of it is the huge distance between our culture and ancient Israel, such that when modern readers read about their laws and customs they seem so foreign that there's no way to relate to them, no way to cross the immense gulf from the modern world to theirs. And part of it is just that the Hebrew Bible is a book written against the backdrop of a thousand years of history, a history which seems completely inaccessible. All of these problems are real.

But even more than these, there's the problem of the violence of the Hebrew Bible—for a multitude of reasons, the violence in the New Testament is sometimes easier for readers to screen out.[10] God as portrayed in the Hebrew Bible is not warm and fuzzy, as our images of Jesus are. (But ask the Syro-Phoenician woman, or the money lenders in the temple, if Jesus was warm and fuzzy.) When God gets angry or disappointed, God often lashes out indiscriminately, killing hundreds of Israelites in the wilderness, or a pair of priests for what seems like a small and insignificant ritualistic infraction. And there are wars after wars, with the Israelites running amok throughout the book of Joshua, tribal skirmish after bloody tribal skirmish in the book of Judges, and more wars from kings Saul and David. And that's even before we get to the dour prophets with all their detailed descriptions of destruction, doom, and woe. It's a dark, bloody place.

We have a right to be disturbed, a right to protest when the text lifts up violence as a solution. Like Abraham bargained with God when God was getting ready to smite Sodom and Gomorrah, or like Job argued against God's fairness in the midst of his tribulations, and like the dozens of unnamed psalmists who cried out to God for hope, we have the right to hold the text accountable when it doesn't live up to God's standards of justice. This is the approach modeled by Eric Seibert in a pair of recent monographs; for Seibert, the way to deal with troubling texts is to hold them up against the hermeneutic of nonviolence, which he believes is the dominant hermeneutic in the Bible as a whole.[11] By using this as the standard against which texts are measured, we are able to critically engage texts that fall short of this ideal.

This hermeneutical approach is very helpful, but also incomplete. When overused, it can quickly shut down many readings of the text. As soon as a text produces discomfort, it can be dismissed as a text borne out of violence, and then talked back to before it has actually been heard. Reading these texts through the lens of horror starts with this process of listening. For the most horrifying texts often reveal the fears and anxieties of the individuals and the culture that produced them. And readers willing to listen might find an echo of these same fears in contemporary experiences, a recognition that the fear underlying the surface of the text is not a dusty relic of history, but a fear that is alive and well today. Often, in spite of the enormous distance across time and space, the anxieties of a biblical text can bear remarkable similarities to our own.

Learning from the Darkness

When I was eight, I had just started reading chapter books like many kids my age. At first, I tore through Hardy Boys books, sucked in by the promise of some deep mystery that was waiting to be uncovered at the lighthouse, or the secret room that held answers to long-buried questions. For my young brain, the first chapters of these books were always full of suspense and anticipation, as hints of whatever secret would be unveiled were slowly put into place. But by the end, I was always disappointed, as it always turned out to be some variation on Mr. Docker scaring everyone away from the room where he made counterfeit money. There was never any real secret, just a mildly unpleasant person who was trying to scare everyone into leaving him alone. Every book was a letdown. Yet, I kept coming back for more for a long time, because I continued to hold onto the hope that the next book would deliver on its promise. The next time, there will be an actual threat; this time the mystery that the young detectives are unravelling will be something that actually matters. Looking back, what I wanted was a book that didn't hold my hand, something that took me seriously as a reader. I wanted to be treated like a grown-up.

Many of us have a similar experience with all different types of stories, whether on the printed page or on the screen. An action movie might enthrall its viewers by the dangerous situation the hero finds himself in and produce some tension over how John McClane is going to finally beat up the bad guys. There's enjoyment in these tensions, and in seeing the ingenuity in how everything gets worked out. But in the end, the expectations of the genre dictate that the problems will be solved, and the world will go back to the way it was before the villains showed up with their dastardly plot du jour. The world, at its heart, is a good place—the job of the hero is to restore everything to this state of goodness. Watching a romantic comedy might cause audiences to smile along with the star-crossed couple as they move through a world of obstacles, but in the end things will work out for them because all of the barriers in their way are just the world's way of testing to see if they truly are made for each other. Once they've overcome whatever has been put in their way, they live happily ever after.

While many people enjoy these kinds of entertainment, others feel that on some level they're insulting. Because the world isn't like this. Our own personal worlds are worlds full of workplaces where we're not appreciated, spending our days performing jobs where we feel undervalued, for a paycheck that never quite seems to be enough. It's a world of worrying about whether we'll have enough to pay our bills at the end of the month or, if we're lucky, whether we're saving enough for our kids' college. It's a world where our relationships sometimes break, and fixing them is much more complicated than two people finding each other on the Empire State Building's observation deck. Sometimes things break, and we can't fix them.

To be sure, there are times in our lives when we want to have the basic goodness of the world reaffirmed. Sometimes, we respond to tragedy, or even just frustrations and feelings of incompleteness, by wanting to smile again and experience a vision of the world in which our daily struggles are simply small challenges to be overcome on our way to a beautiful life. Or sometimes, we just want to spend ninety minutes doing something other than thinking about the shortcomings of our lives. That's okay—I wouldn't wish for a world where horror films were the only kind of cinema being made. But other times, this can strike us as false. Sometimes, we might want to experience a cinematic world that lines up more closely with the experiences of the challenges and struggles of our own lives.

This is something that horror (at least good horror!) and the Bible share: they both experience the realities of life too deeply to tell us that everything is okay when it's not. For the most part, horror is the only mainstream genre that takes this reality seriously. In the world of horror, the monster doesn't arrive into a perfect world; the monster comes to show us what's been wrong all along, all of the ugly truths we've been trying to ignore. Even if the monster is defeated at the end, we've seen a darker underbelly to the world, and the sunlight that we return to doesn't seem quite as bright as it used to. And in the same vein, the Hebrew Bible tells us that we can receive God's blessing, that we can reach the promised land, but that it's a long, hard road to walk, that not everyone will make it there (even Moses!), and that there will be hardships we can't imagine. And that even when we make it through, it won't be long until the armies of Babylon are knocking on Jerusalem's gate, and we'll need to struggle and hope for God's deliverance again.

In a paradoxical way, this can actually make us feel better about our own lives and about the state of the world because we've had our own experiences confirmed and have found someone else who has experienced the world in the same way. Watch too many romantic comedies and you start to feel like it's your fault that the world doesn't look that warm and radiant to you. (Of course it's a matter of personal taste, but for me romantic comedies are the prosperity gospel of film.) But after a horror movie, you know that the darkness in your own life is real, and that it's okay. Because other people see the world the same way, and somehow, they endure.

Too often, our religion, particularly as experienced during Sunday morning worship, is one designed to make us feel good about ourselves and the world around us. If we have sinned, we are forgiven. If our world is broken, we pray for its healing. And in the end, we are sent out into the world in peace, with good courage. Too often, this involves an act of repression, both of the true horrors of our lives and of the world. And even of the text itself. Just as Robin Wood has famously suggested that horror is "the return of the repressed,"[12] these biblical texts are trying to call our attention back to what can be repressed in our own lives. Too often, we respond by suppressing the texts in turn. But there is another way. We don't have to suppress these texts; we can listen to them.

For me, it doesn't feel calming to jump straight to the texts of affirmation. When I read Psalm 23, I need to think about what the shadow of the valley of death means before I'm ready to spend time in the beautiful green fields. And I don't just want to read the end of the psalms where God's faithfulness is affirmed. The journey is important. Most of our lives are spent on that journey, the journey through the wilderness on our way home. Sometimes, God seems a long way off, both in our world and in our individual lives. Wrestling with the horrors of scripture can help us as we walk on this same journey, through our own shadows of the valley of death.

RELIGION AND BIBLE IN HORROR

Religion is a major theme in a surprisingly large number of horror films. Perhaps even more surprisingly, a large number of horror films are largely sympathetic to the religious experiences of their characters and the yearning for God, even if they remain critical of institutional structures.

The Exorcist is a classic example. We might think of young Regan, spitting out pea soup and obscenities while her head spins around, but Father Damien's subplot takes almost as much screen time and is at least as crucial to the film.[13] Father Damien (yes, another Damien!) has studied as both a priest and a psychologist; he has one foot in the world of the spiritual and one foot in the world of modern science. As the film opens, he has been tasked with working with troubled priests at Georgetown University. Damien complains about how difficult this task is, and what spending so much time with all of these struggling people is doing to him. "I think I'm losing my faith," he confesses. Shortly afterwards, he sees a homeless man at the subway station, who asks Father Damien for some spare change. "I was an altar boy," the man says to Damien, "I'm a good Catholic." Father Damien turns away without a word.

When Damien first encounters Regan, the demon inside of her rubs Damien's face in this failure, quoting the words of the homeless man back at the stunned priest. The demon also tries to get under Damien's skin by forcing him to recall his recently deceased mother, claiming that the afterlife is a less-than-pleasant place for her. The demon seems to sense that Father Damien is struggling with his faith and exploits this struggle. The demon cannot be vanquished as long as one of the priests performing the exorcist is wrestling with these questions of doubt.

The demon is only subdued when Father Damien demands that it leave Regan and enter into him instead. The demon obliges, but Father Damien is able to maintain his clarity long enough to throw himself out of the bedroom window, dispelling the demon and killing himself in the process. The resolution of the supernatural conflict of the film is also the resolution of Father Damien's faith crisis: he is able to triumph over evil through an act of self-sacrifice. In this action, he returns to the heart of the Christian faith, and demonstrates that faith can, indeed, triumph over evil.

Similar examples abound in the history of horror films, though few are as effective as *The Exorcist*. (Its status as a horror classic is well-deserved.) But even when it is less explicitly handled than in *The Exorcist*, the horror genre is frequently used to raise questions about the existence of evil in the world, and whether the world is as benevolent as we like to think of it as being. Even if God is never mentioned, it's not a large step from those questions to questions of theodicy.

Religion is used in broadly thematic ways, through characters and plot structures of horror films. But the Bible shows up as an important object with a surprising frequency. Steve Wiggins's monograph *Holy Horror* explores some of the ways that the Bible features in horror films, either as a sort of talisman against evil, a signifier of a character's moral worth, or foreshadowing when it gets dropped on the ground or otherwise mistreated.[14] As Wiggins points out, horror films repeatedly turn to the Bible to make a simple point: this icon, and the teachings contained within it, should protect us from the forces of evil. But they don't. Frequently, the Bible is ineffective or, even worse, twisted until it becomes a tool for evil itself.

The Horrors of Scripture

The writers of the Hebrew Bible wrestled with more than a few horrors of their own. Some of them are obvious, like the monstrous Leviathan that swims around the edges of the text, the great chaos monster who threatens to break into the God-ordered world at any moment. Less obvious might be the hauntings that appear at various points in the text, including the ghost of Samuel and the ghosts of the other gods whom Israel can't quite seem to leave behind. And then there are the haunted spaces of the Bible, including the wilderness and the House of David.

Frequently, the texts work to turn outsiders into an object of horror, a monstrous presence who marks the boundary of the Israelite community. In many places, the text uses foreigners to serve this function; in other places, the Israelite women serve as an abject presence within the community. Perhaps most provocatively, the text often positions YHWH as the greatest of all monsters, hunting down Moses on the road and striking down the Israelites for seemingly minor breeches of ritual protocol. And most dramatically,

YHWH, who defeated the chaos in the creation story, brings chaos into the world himself through the flood of Genesis, the Sea of Reeds in Exodus, and even in his speech from the whirlwind at the climax of the book of Job. Throughout the Hebrew Bible, this monstrous side of God is never too far from the surface.

Too often, religion shies away from the broken spaces in our lives and in our world, offering instead a vision where God's love and Christ's forgiveness makes everything right.[15] Recently, the prosperity gospel movement has been the most vocal and obvious purveyor of this kind of theology, but subtler versions have permeated much of our worship life across many denominations.[16] This type of worship offers praise without lament, the resurrection without the crucifixion. It's a religion of shiny surfaces and powerful promises, but also a religion that often leaves people feeling empty. Empty, and needing to consume more.[17]

However, there are many voices in the Hebrew Bible that offer a different perspective. In its dark corners, the Hebrew Bible reaches both hands into the anxieties that all of us carry around every day, and pulls them out for us to look at. It puts us face-to-face with these horrors, often in a way that's much less comforting than we may have been brought up to believe religion should be. But the Hebrew Bible shows us these horrors so that we can wrestle with them, so that we can reduce their power by naming them. When we take our fears and insecurities and trap them in a story, they can't hold onto us quite as tightly. And we find that there are, indeed, green pastures. But sometimes we have to walk through the shadow of the valley of death to find them.

NOTES

1. Quite a bit has been written about the genre of exorcism or possession films, often from a perspective involving questions of gender. See, for example, Carol Clover, *Men, Women, and Chain Saws: Gender in the Modern Horror Film* (Princeton, NJ: Princeton University, 1992), 65–97; Tanya Kryzwinska, "Demon Daddies: Gender, Ecstasy, and Terror in the Possession Film," in *Horror Film Reader*, eds. Alain Silver and James Ursini (New York: Limelight Editions, 2000), 247–267. And in this same monograph series, see the forthcoming volume by Steve A. Wiggins, *Nightmares with the Bible: The Good Book and Its Demons* (Horror and Scripture; Lanham, MD: Lexington Books/Fortress Academic, 2020), which explores how the biblical texts have influenced the popular understanding of demons in films such as *The Conjuring*.

2. In her brief discussion of this film, Carol Clover makes the interesting observation that, in spite of the film's seeming focus on Damien as the product of a possessed female, the mysterious, unspoken center of the film's plot is the never-revealed identity of Damien's mother. See Clover, *Men, Women, and Chain Saws*, 75. Clover seems to dance around the revelation, but the film hints that Damien's biological mother was a jackal; these are the bones uncovered when the protagonists unearth the mother's grave. The precise meaning of this image is still difficult to determine.

3. Steve A. Wiggins, *Holy Horror: The Bible and Fear in Movies* (Jefferson, NC: McFarland, 2018), 130–134, discusses the biblical imagery in *The Omen*, including reading Keith's death as a reference to John the Baptist.

4. Blair Davis and Kial Natale have surveyed a broad range of horror films from 1998 to 2007 and attempted to quantify the amount of gore in them. Interestingly, they note that "By far the goriest American film of the last ten years, however, is one that was not included in our sample of one hundred films . . . Mel Gibson's *The Passion of the Christ* (2004)" (50). "'The Pound of Flesh Which I Demand': American Horror Cinema, Gore, and the Box Office, 1998–2007," in *American Horror: The Genre at the Turn of the Millennium*, ed. Steffen Hantke (Jackson: University of Mississippi, 2010), 35–57. More recently, *A Quiet Place* drew massive audiences to the theaters and reportedly had adverse effects on concessions sales, as theater-goers did not want to be heard munching on popcorn in the midst of the film's intense silence. Even with a somewhat bloody childbirth sequence, the film is still well within the boundaries of the PG-13 rating.

5. Mary Beth Oliver and Meghan Sanders, "The Appeal of Horror and Suspense," in *The Horror Film*, ed. Stephen Prince (New Brunswick, NJ: Rutgers University, 2004), 242–259.

6. Ibid., 249–250.

7. Noël Carroll, *The Philosophy of Horror: Or, Paradoxes of the Heart* (New York: Routledge, 1999), esp. 158–195.

8. Cynthia Freeland, "Horror and Art Dread," in *The Horror Film*, ed. Stephen Prince (New Brunswick, NJ: Rutgers University, 2004), 189–205; quote from 190.

9. Freeland, "Horror and Art-Dread," 189.

10. For an interesting and slightly different view, see Dan W. Clanton, Jr., "The Divine Unsub: Television Procedurals and Biblical Sexual Violence," in *The Bible in Crime Fiction and Drama: Murderous Texts*, eds. Caroline Blyth and Alison Jack (LHBOTS 678/STr 16; New York: T&T Clark, 2019), 125–148. In his experience, "students—both undergraduate and adult learners—often dismiss or explain away the sexually violent images and actions in the Bible because they consider the Bible to be 'sacred,' and therefore beyond criticism." For Clanton, this presents an opportunity to discuss the violent content of television shows in comparison with the Bible as a means of entering into a more honest critique of the violence of the Bible. While I find Clanton's method to be very helpful in encouraging readers to think of the Bible in new ways, I've found that students, including graduate students and adult learners in a church context, are quick to condemn the violence of the Hebrew Bible, but firm in their defense of the New Testament.

11. See Seibert's *Disturbing Divine Behavior: Troubling Old Testament Images of God* (Minneapolis, MN: Fortress, 2009) and *The Violence of Scripture: Overcoming the Old Testament's Troubling Legacy* (Minneapolis, MN: Fortress, 2012). For a conservative response, accusing Seibert of Marcionism, see Paul Copan and Matthew Flanagan, *Did God Really Command Genocide?: Coming to Terms with the Justice of God* (Grand Rapids, MI: Baker, 2014), 38–46. I discuss Seibert and other views of the violence of scripture in my monograph *Reading Phinehas, Watching Slashers: Horror Theory and Numbers 25* (Lanham, MD: Lexington/Fortress Academic: 2018), 1–33.

12. While frequently reprinted in anthologies of essays on the horror film, one convenient place to find Wood's seminal essay on horror as "the return of the repressed" is in his volume *Hollywood From Vietnam to Reagan . . . and Beyond*, revised and expanded edition (New York: Columbia University Press, 2003), 63–84.

13. Much has been written on the themes of religion in *The Exorcist*; see, for example, Marsha Kinder and Beverle Houston, "Seeing Is Believing: *The Exorcist* and *Don't Look Now*," in *American Horrors: Essays on the Modern American Horror Film*, ed. Gregory A. Waller (Chicago: University of Illinois, 1987), 44–61; Clover, *Men, Women, and Chain Saws*, 85–90; Leo Braudy, *Haunted: On Ghosts, Witches, Vampires, Zombies, and Other Monsters of the Natural and Supernatural Worlds* (New Haven, CT: Yale University Press, 2016), 63–70. Carol Clover's analysis is still highly relevant. Clover observes that in *The Exorcist*, as well as in most of the possession films to follow, the female body is used as a battleground for the male protagonist's personal struggle; see *Men, Women, and Chain Saws*, 85–97. Rhiannon Graybill, *Are We Not Men?: Unstable Masculinity in the Hebrew Prophets* (New York: Oxford, 2016), 49–69, uses this insight to place possession films such as *The Exorcist* in conversation with the book of Hosea, in which Gomer is also used as a plot device for the theological discussion between the prophet and YHWH.

14. Wiggins, *Holy Horror*. Hint: It doesn't go well for the characters who drop the Bible.

15. While far from horror theory, Walter Brueggemann has discussed the need for open and honest expression of pain in the church in "A Shape for Old Testament Theology II: Embrace of Pain," in *Old Testament Theology: Essays on Structure, Theme, and Text*, ed. Patrick D. Miller (Minneapolis, MN: Fortress, 1992), 22–44.

16. Katie Bowler, *Blessed: A History of the American Prosperity Gospel* (New York: Oxford University Press, 2013), provides a thorough history of the prosperity movement, placing it in the context of American religious history.

17. The connection between American culture, feelings of emptiness, and consumption has been a theme of Walter Brueggemann's writing for decades. For a recent example, see his *From Whom No Secrets Are Hid: Introducing the Psalms*, ed. Brent A. Strawn (Atlanta: WJK, 2014), 8–14.

Chapter One

Reading with Horror

It's no secret that hermeneutical approaches have multiplied in the field of biblical studies at a rapid pace in the last several decades.[1] In this, biblical studies mirrors the broader field of humanities, though biblical studies seems to trail behind by a decade or so. Starting with feminist criticism and the new literary criticism in the '70s and '80s, the field has expanded to include a dizzying array of methodological approaches, drawing from such diverse fields as social science, post-colonial theory, queer theory, and disability studies.[2]

In previous generations of scholarship, the goal was to find a singular "method," an almost scientific set of steps to be undertaken in order to arrive at an irrefutably correct reading of a passage. The goal was to find the one (and only one) true reading of a passage, variously understood as aligning with the author's intention or with how the passage would have been read in its original context.[3]

More recently, many scholars have rejected the idea of identifying a singular method for reading and the assumption that a given text has one correct meaning that can be uncovered. Instead, the goal is to uncover readings that generate meanings and to explore what can be found within the text that might speak to a reader, whether or not this is what was intended by the author. In many of these approaches, the text sets the parameters for interpretation—we are still reading texts, after all—but there is a wide latitude for an individual reading within those parameters. Meanings multiply and inform one another, rather than competing for supremacy.[4]

So horror theory isn't intended to provide a methodology, or even an interpretive strategy. It's simply one particular lens through which to view the text, one way of reading and noticing details, themes, and connections that might otherwise go unnoticed, or at least have less emphasis placed upon them. Horror theory provides a way to gather a set of texts under one umbrella, then gives us a vocabulary for talking about them. Simply put, this monograph looks at biblical texts and horror films and tries to see what can be gained from reading these two sets of texts together.

This monograph is intended to serve several purposes: in addition to providing readings of some scripture passages through the lens of horror theory, the hope is that this monograph will also serve as a primer for scholars interested in using horror theory in their own work. It will also seek to blend more traditional forms of scholarship with horror theory in order to demonstrate, for example, that reading Job with monster theory is an outgrowth of previous studies on Job's use of the *Chaoskampf* motif, rather than a complete break from the history of scholarship. Traditional historical critical models and horror theory can play nice together in the sandbox, at least on occasion.

Throughout the monograph, horror films will serve as dialogue partners. While only a few examples exist to this date of biblical scholars using horror films as exegetical tools, there is significant literature on the intersection between film and the Bible. Frequently, this involves a symbolic approach, in which themes from the biblical text are recognized as being given either direct or indirect representation through films.[5] Some horror movies do directly reflect on theological concerns.[6] But this isn't the primary interest of this monograph. Instead, I will follow the methodological lead of scholars such as Larry Kreitzer and George Aichele,[7] who argue that it can be more profitable to "reverse the exegetical flow,"[8] allowing for films and the Bible to read each other, rather than simply using films to offer "an exegetical depiction of a biblical text."[9]

Aichele argues that many examples of film and Bible study simply use a particular film as a vehicle for the theological principle the scholar has already determined exists in a given text. Aichele writes, "The Bible (as it is understood in such studies) is allowed to critique the movie, but the movie is not allowed to critique the Bible."[10] In studies of this nature, films are only used to support what the scholar has already determined the meaning of a particular biblical text to be. There is little dialogue between film and the Bible; a film is used merely as a means of illustrating something from a biblical text.

This monograph hopes to use films differently. Horror films will not be used to buttress preexisting theological claims, but will serve as means by which the claims, methods, and narrative structures of the biblical text can be examined. By placing biblical passages into conversation with horror movies, this monograph hopes to reveal the inner workings and underlying anxieties of biblical texts. Few of the films under discussion will deal with biblical texts directly; indeed, many of them fall into the category of "poor taste," which Laura Copier notes is a category frequently shunned by biblical scholars.[11] But bringing these films into the conversation, both on the level of narrative and on the level of film,[12] will help us to expand our understanding of the biblical text and the fears that lie beneath it.

While subgenres of horror film and their particularities (with resources specific to the individual subgenres) will be discussed in the following chapters, it will prove helpful at the outset to offer a brief overview of horror theory, and what it means to study horror films.[13] In the pages that follow, I will attempt to outline some of the major discussions surrounding horror films in hopes of providing a framework for the more detailed readings to follow.

MONSTER AS METAPHOR (IN MOTION)

Noël Carroll has gone as far as to propose that horror requires the presence of a monster.[14] If we understand "monster" broadly, such that the category could include monstrous humans such as Norman Bates or Hannibal Lecter, then Carroll seems to be on solid ground.[15] But in the pages that follow, I hope to expand this definition to include not only entities, but also events and emotions that we might deem monstrous.

One of the foundational premises of the study of horror is that monsters are always signifiers.[16] They might signify a "category crisis," in the phrasing of Cohen,[17] in which the boundaries of the world that were previously understood as fixed and reliable are called into question. They might signify a part of ourselves that we try to deny—frequently, aggression and the need for dominance. Or they might signify a problem within our culture, which the monster is able to draw attention to. Paying careful attention to both the construction of the monster and how the monster functions within the narrative can allow us to "read" both the monster and the narrative in which the monster is embedded.

In this fashion, monsters can be seen not as static metaphors, but as metaphors in motion. At times, the discipline known as "monster theory" can place too much emphasis on the construction of a particular monster, as if the monster existed in isolation. But along with the construction of the monster, we must read the role of the monster within the narrative to produce a more complete picture of the rhetoric at work in a given horror narrative. The analysis will focus less on individual figures than on events and relationships. Matt Hills, as an example, has suggested that scholars should move away from "an analysis of fiction entities" and toward an "events-based" exploration of horror.[18] This would open up a space for films such as Danny Boyle's *127 Hours* (2010) to be understood as participating in the horror genre; in spite of its absence of a monster, the film can be profitably seen as participating in the subgenre of "body horror," and its effect on the audience is most certainly horrifying.[19]

A frequent example of an events-based approach to horror theory is found in the scholarship on slasher films, the rather disreputable cycle of predictably gory and misogynistic films that flooded both the theaters and home video markets in the early- to mid-80s, following the template established by John Carpenter's surprise box-office smash *Halloween* (1978).[20] By himself,[21] the slasher is a blank slate. Usually scarred (figuratively or literally) from a childhood trauma of some sort, the slasher kills the unsuspecting teens who are unfortunate enough to cross his path. But it is within the construct of the narrative, including the treatment of the victims, the shifting audience identifications, and the role of authority figures in the film, that the symbolic value of the slasher becomes clear: he represents the reactionary response to the cultural liberalism of the 60s and 70s, the Reagan revolution made enraged flesh. He kills the transgressing youth, whom more traditional authority figures have lost control over.

Whether it's slashers, ghosts, zombies, or some other type of monster, a well-crafted horror narrative allows the audience to read the monstrous figure as a representation of something else. Even when the monster is central, the richest interpretations of these malignant beings include a reading of the monster within the narrative, interacting with the characters, themes, and cinematic techniques of the film. Through the interaction of these elements, we can read the monster is a living embodiment of our anxiety, whether universal or cultural. But most importantly, the monster is a figure to be read. And it is in this reading that the ideology of the horror narrative can be uncovered.

HORROR AS ANXIETY: UNIVERSAL AND CULTURALLY SPECIFIC

As briefly discussed in the introduction, the emotion that most frequently dominates the horror genre is that of anxiety. While fear may be present, this emotion (along with disgust) is usually secondary. Fear is the reaction to a particular object or situation that poses a threat to the individual's well-being. Anxiety, on the other hand, is a response to something that is unknown. When we are afraid, we can identify precisely what is functioning as the cause of our fear. When we are anxious, we have a feeling of unwellness, a deep-seated sense of worry, but nothing we can blame this feeling on. At its best, the horror genre takes these nontangible anxieties and wraps them in the figure of a concrete, physical terror. While horror movies make us fear for the physical safety of the characters on the screen,[22] they also connect to more pervasive anxieties about our lives and the state of our world, anxieties that we might not even be able to name exactly.

So while the monster on the screen might be frightening, the monster itself is not what really arouses our emotions and follows us home from the theater at night. It's what the monster represents symbolically, the latent anxiety that the monster activates, that keeps us awake at night.

Freud, wearing his hat of literary critic, was the first to explore the connections between the representation of the monster and the unconscious anxieties the monster taps into, at least in anything approaching a systematic manner. In his essay "The Uncanny," Freud reads E. T. A. Hoffmann's famous short story "The Sand-Man," and argues that this nightmarish eye-stealing creature touches on the universal anxiety (for Freud's presumed male audience) of castration.[23] For Freud, these anxieties are universal. And there is clearly evidence that a wide variety of cultures have anxieties with similar roots, as demonstrated in the common stock of monsters that appear in stories of various cultures from different geographical locations and time frames.[24] But this observation only tells half of the story; it is also true that each culture takes these stock characteristics of monsters (or even the same monster) and uses them to express specific manifestations of broadly shared anxieties, shaping each anxiety to the particular contours of the sociocultural context.[25] Monsters are metaphors, yes—but they are malleable metaphors, and their immense surplus of meaning allows them to be reinterpreted, given new life for a new cultural moment.[26]

Still a matter of scholarly debate is the degree to which cultural specificity determines a monster's interpretation.[27] Steven Jay Schneider, for example, has argued that while horror narrative monsters are "metaphorical embodiments" of universal psychological concepts, their "surface heterogeneity is historically and culturally contingent."[28] They are universal fears dressed up in local fashion. Other scholars, such as Robin Wood, have argued that the specific culture determines the anxieties of its individual members; as such, the monster will represent the particular anxieties of the culture that birthed it. My own understanding of monsters leans more towards Robin Wood's understanding of them as culturally determined, as is evidenced by the way in which the same monstrous figure can be given a wide range of interpretations in different narratives.[29] In this way, generations can continue to be frightened by the same figures: the vampire, the ghost, Frankenstein's monster. But these monsters are adapted, either by the text itself or by the reader's interpretation, to signify a different set of anxieties within a different cultural context. These aren't simple cosmetic adjustments to the monster, but reimaginings of their most essential functions and meanings. The monsters who have endured across time and space are the monsters who allow for a high degree of interpretive flexibility, who can be shaped by different cultural fears into generators of different meanings.

Kelly J. Murphy has explored the ways in the which the figure of the zombie has been adapted to different anxieties through the course of its introduction into popular culture in the twentieth century, its re-imagining by George A. Romero in *Night of the Living Dead*, and into the twenty-first century's newfound fascination with the figure.[30] Murphy traces the origin of the zombie in Haitian lore, in which the zombie was created by a sorcerer who exerted continued control over the zombie. This existence was understood as a punishment for "a person who had transgressed some social norm."[31] But when the zombie makes its way into the 1932 film *White Zombie*, they are seen as a figure of the racial Other; the terror explored by the film is the possibility that becoming a zombie could happen to white people as well as Haitians. The "fears of slavery and loss of power" that the zombie expressed in Haitian culture had been subverted to express "the fear that white American colonizers had of those who were different from them."[32]

If this were the only meaning to draw from the zombie, the monster would have had a rather short shelf life in American culture. But from being used as a troubling signifier of racial fears in *White Zombie*, Romero turns the figure of the zombie into one that forces us to question our understanding of race's role in contemporary American culture. *Night of the Living Dead* was released in 1968, at the height of the civil rights movement. This backdrop certainly plays into the spectator's experience of Ben, the film's African-American main character, who assumes the role of leadership of a small group of survivors barricaded inside of a farmhouse.[33] At the film's conclusion, Ben has survived the night, but a posse of zombie-killing white men (with unmistakable resonances to a lynch mob) mistake Ben for a zombie and shoot him, throwing his corpse on the fire with a pile of dead zombies. In this final scene, the lynch mob and the zombies are closely connected, asking us to reflect on how different the zombie hordes actually are from the population of contemporary America.[34]

And the zombie continued to be reinterpreted as metaphor into the twenty-first century, with the long-running TV series *The Walking Dead* being perhaps the most popular example. Here, the zombie becomes a means of reflecting on the despair many feel at the state of contemporary society, and how we might rebuild from what feels like our current apocalyptic situation.[35] With more and more of the population feeling like the country is on "the wrong track," zombies such as those found in *The Walking Dead* give us a chance to think through what it would look like to start over.[36] Contemporary questions of masculine authority, race relations, immigration, just to name a few, have been productively interrogated by recent zombie films and TV series.

The examples above demonstrate possible ways of "reading" horror, of connecting the fear on the screen to meanings within the world of the viewer.

While acknowledging that the psychological structure of humans maintains many points of connection regardless of culture, these reading methods emphasize the importance of locating a reading within a specific time and culture. In the next section, we will discuss two major approaches to exploring these connections between the horror narrative and culture.

PSYCHOLOGICAL AND SOCIAL APPROACHES

Many scholars agree on one of the key reasons that horror has endured as a genre: it provides a grammar for exploring uncomfortable thoughts and spaces, either within our social structure or within our own individual psychological makeup. A major point of difference among scholars is the degree to which a scholar interprets horror through a lens that is primarily psychoanalytic in nature, or one that is social/anthropological.

Unsurprisingly, Freud's approach is rooted in the psychological. For Freud, horror is primarily about bringing the viewer face-to-face with previous stages of development, which may not have been overcome as thoroughly as the viewer assumed. In Freud's reading of "The Sand-Man," the theft of the eyes stands in for a castration anxiety; this activates in the viewer's mind the latent Oedipal conflict, which still persists on an unconscious level. Horror offers the viewer the chance to continue working through these struggles and find symbolic resolution.[37]

Freud's approach laid the foundation for the theoretical work of Robin Wood, whose seminal articles on horror helped to establish horror films as a legitimate object of scholarly inquiry in the 1970s and whose influence continues today.[38] Wood argues that horror is a response to societal repression of the individual. Using the theories of Hebert Marcuse, Wood allows that some repression is necessary for society to function, but suggests that the root of psychic trauma lies in the repression inflicted by societies above and beyond that which is necessary ("surplus repression"). While all societies share a baseline level of repression, surplus repression varies from culture to culture.[39] This variance in the specific nature of surplus repression is what, for Wood, explains the differences in horror narratives among cultures. And it is this element of surplus repression on which horror is founded.

This allows Wood to divide horror movies into progressive and reactionary, depending on the degree to which the film attempts to critique or support the dominant cultural paradigms.[40] So while Wood's work is built on the theoretical foundations of Freud, he also perceives a high degree of interplay with the psychology of the individual and cultural conditions. For Wood, unique cultural conditions interact with the structures of the individual psyche, which are universal in nature. But for Wood, horror lies primarily in the realm of individual psychology, and the ways in which a given culture can either support or damage the psychology of its individual members.

Many scholars have built on the work of Wood, grounding their scholarship in psychoanalytic theories of the horror movie.[41] While psychoanalytic approaches to horror narratives have proliferated since Wood, they all share the foundational belief that monsters are, in some way, "projections of repressed infantile anxieties."[42] Particular films may be read as manifesting Oedipal fantasies, sexual aggression, or sadism, but the common thread is that horror films are understood as "the manifestation of psychic processes."[43]

Of course, not all horror scholars are satisfied with the psychological paradigm. The major competing model grounds itself instead in anthropology and sociology, viewing horror films as primarily a social product that must be analyzed through culture, rather than through the psychological makeup of individuals.[44] While Stephen Prince gestured towards this in his 1988 article,[45] this approach was given its most full expression by Noël Carroll in his 1990 monograph *The Philosophy of Horror, or, Paradoxes of the Heart*.[46] Focusing extensively on the construction of the monster, Carroll employs the anthropological theories of Mary Douglas to argue that horror films revolve around questions of social boundaries. While Carroll often roots his analysis in the emotions of the individual viewer, these emotions are engaged not by horror's connection to deep psychic structures, but by the employment of cultural taboos and the crossing of a variety of boundaries.[47]

Of course, neither of these paradigms have to be "either-or." Carroll, whose scholarly work has "expressed reservations about the application of psychoanalysis" to horror films, agrees that psychoanalysis "is certainly relevant, even apposite, to the analysis of many horror films."[48] In his earlier monograph, Carroll proposes a "deep structure" of horror fiction as a:

> three-part movement: 1) from normality (a state of affairs in which our ontologico-value schema rests intact); 2) to its disruption (a monster appears . . . shaking the very foundations of culture's cognitive map. . . ; 3) to the final confrontation and defeat of the abnormal, disruptive being (thereby restoring the culture's scheme of things by eliminating the anomaly and punishing its violations of the moral order).[49]

The same can be said of approaches that are primarily cultural in nature: some films are more heavily indebted to their culture, while others attempt to address more universal, psychological concerns. This looks remarkably similar to Wood's "basic formula" of horror narratives: "normality is threatened by the Monster."[50] In both Carroll and Wood's formation, a reading of the film, what Wood identifies as "the essential subject," lies in determining the film's construction of "normality" and what constitutes a threat to this normality. The major difference in the approaches of Carroll and Wood lies in whether they wish to pursue this "normality" on the level of psychology (as influenced by societal structures), or primarily through the lens of societal structures, with only a few nods to individual psychology.

The Hebrew Bible is full of narratives in which normality is disrupted by a monstrous presence; analyzing them through the lens of horror theory will help us to understand not only what the Hebrew Bible understands as "monstrous," but also what the text understands as "normality." In the next chapter, we'll use monster theory to interrogate some of these texts.

NOTES

1. Introductory texts on these newer methodologies are many, but they include Joel M. LeMon and Kent Harold Richards, eds., *Method Matters: Essays on the Interpretation of the Hebrew Bible in Honor of David L. Peterson* (Resources for Biblical Studies 56; Atlanta: SBL, 2009); Steven L. McKenzie and John Kaltner, eds., *New Meanings for Ancient Texts: Recent Approaches to Biblical Criticisms and Their Applications* (Atlanta: WJK, 2013).

2. Broadly speaking, these approaches all fall under what Eryl Davies terms "Reader-oriented approaches," in that they focus on reading the passage within a particular context, rather than assuming an overarching context that is valid for all readers. See Eryl Davies, "The Morally Dubious Passages of the Hebrew Bible: An Examination of Some Proposed Solutions," *CurBR* 3.2 (2005): 197–228.

3. Or in a more fundamentalist reading, assuming a high level of divine inspiration within scripture, the meaning intended by God. For insightful descriptions of fundamentalist hermeneutical procedures, as well as critiques, see Brian Malley, *How the Bible Works: An Anthropological Study of Evangelical Biblicism* (Lanham, MD: AltaMira Press, 2004); Christian Smith, *The Bible Made Impossible: Why Biblicism is Not a Truly Evangelical Reading of Scripture* (Grand Rapids, MI: Brazos, 2011).

4. The lectures collected in John J. Collins, *The Bible After Babel: Historical Criticism in a Postmodern Age* (Grand Rapids, MI: Eerdmans, 2005) do an excellent job of discussing the debates surrounding the relationship between historical criticism and newer methods in biblical studies; while Collins is an admitted proponent of more traditional historical-critical methods, he is open to the contributions that can be made by more postmodern approaches as well. A thought-provoking exploration of what it means to be a biblical scholar in the postmodern era can be found in Stephen D. Moore and Yvonne Sherwood, *The Invention of the Biblical Scholar: A Critical Manifesto* (Minneapolis, MN: Fortress, 2011).

5. An example of this "Bible in Film" approach is Catherine M. Barsotti and Robert K. Johnston, *Finding God in the Movies: 33 Films of Reel Faith* (Grand Rapids, MI: Baker, 2004). Matthew Rindge, for example, distinguishes between the more common "Bible *in* Film" approach, as opposed to a "Bible and Film" approach, in which the "rhetorical strategies" of both the Bible and film are analyzed to find points of commonality and disagreement. Rindge briefly discusses this, and then employs the method, in his essay "Lars von Trier's *Dogville* as a Cinematic Parable," in *T&T Clark Companion to the Bible and Film*, ed. Richard Walsh (London: T&T Clark, 2018), 260–269; quoting from 260 (italics original).

6. See the brief discussion of *The Exorcist* in the introduction. M. Night Shyamalan's *Signs* is also frequently cited as an example in this category; in this film, the alien invasion crisis serves as a backdrop for the most important conflict in the film, the faith crisis of Rev. Graham Hess (Mel Gibson, pre-*Passion of the Christ*) in the wake of his wife's death.

7. Larry J. Kreitzer, *Gospel Images in Fiction and Film* (Sheffield, UK: Sheffield Academic Press, 2002); George Aichele, "Film Theory and Biblical Studies," in *Close Encounters between Bible and Film: An Interdisciplinary Engagement*, eds. Laura Copier and Caroline Vander Stichele (SemSt 87; Atlanta: SBL Press, 2016), 11–26.

8. Aichele, "Film Theory and Biblical Studies," 17.

9. Ibid.

10. Ibid.

11. Laura Copier, *Preposterous Revelations: Visions of Apocalypse and Martyrdom in Hollywood Cinema 1980–2000* (Sheffield, UK: Sheffield Phoenix, 2012), 17–18.

12. As many scholars have noted, film is more than plot; cinematic techniques are also deeply embedded into the semiotic discourse of the medium. For an overview of how the discipline of film studies can be applied to biblical studies, see Gary Yamasaki, *Insights from Filmmaking for Analyzing Biblical Narrative* (Reading the Bible in the 21st Century: Insights; Minneapolis, MN: Fortress, 2016); other examples include Richard Walsh's comparison between D. W. Griffith's use of crosscutting in *Intolerance* and Gospel harmonies in "On the Harmony of the (Asocial) Gospel: *Intolerance*'s Crosscut Stories," in *Close Encounters Between Bible and Film: An Interdisciplinary Engagement*, eds. Laura Copier and Caroline Vander Stichele (SemSt 87; Atlanta: SBL Press), 43–77. I discuss the use of point of view in slasher films in conversation with the Phinehas narrative of Numbers 25 in my monograph *Reading Phinehas, Watching Slashers* (Lanham, MD: Lexington Books/Fortress Academic, 2018), 88–94.

13. For further discussions on the literature of horror theory, see the chapter "Horror in Theory" in my monograph *Reading Phinehas, Watching Slashers*, as well as my article "Text and Terror: Monster Theory and the Hebrew Bible," *CurBR* 16.1 (2017): 34–49. Another survey of horror-themed approaches to the Bible is found in Steve A. Wiggins, "Good Book Gone Bad: Reading Phinehas and Watching Horror," *HBT* 41.1 (2019): 93–103.

14. Carroll, *Philosophy of Horror*, 12–16. Carroll further distinguishes between horror and other genres that include monsters, such as myths, by the reactions of the characters to the monsters.

15. A frequent argument made against Carroll's definition is that it is too narrow and excludes obvious participants of the horror genre such as *Psycho* or *Silence of the Lambs*. But if we allow for human characters who are in some way monstrous, through extreme malevolence or other characteristics that mark them as somehow categorically different from the rest of humanity, this problem is solved. Of course, what exactly makes Norman Bates or Hannibal Lecter "monstrous" is a debate in and of itself.

16. One of the foundational discussions of this observation is found in Jeffrey Jerome Cohen, "Monster Culture: Seven Theses," in *Monster Theory: Reading Culture*, ed. Jeffrey Jerome Cohen (Minneapolis: University of Minnesota), 3–25.

17. Ibid., 4.

18. Matt Hills, "An Event-Based Definition of Art Horror," in *Dark Thoughts: Philosophic Reflections on Cinematic Horror*; eds. Steven Jay Schneider and Daniel Shaw (Lanham, MD: Scarecrow, 2003), 137–156. This idea is also discussed in Steven Jay Schneider, "Toward an Aesthetics of Cinematic Horror," in *The Horror Film*, ed. Stephen Prince, (New Brunswick, NJ: Rutgers University Press, 2004), 130–149.

19. Dawn Keetley, in an insightful post on the excellent *Horror Homeroom* blog, has argued for *127 Hours* as "geological horror." See Dawn Keetley, "127 Hours: Geological Horror," *Horror Homeroom*, Sept. 11, 2015. http://www.horrorhomeroom.com/geological-horror-of-rocks-and-danny-boyles-127-hours-2010/

20. The foundational works on the slasher films remain Vera Dika's *Games of Terror* (Madison, NJ: Farleigh Dickinson University Press, 1990) and Carol Clover's *Men, Women, and Chain Saws: Gender in the Modern Horror Film* (Princeton, NJ: Princeton University Press, 1992). See also my discussion on these films in *Reading Phinehas, Watching Slashers*, 88–94 and notes. Rhiannon Graybill has read Jael's murder of Sisera, told and retold in Judges 4–5, as a slasher narrative; see her article "'Day of the Woman': Judges 4–5 as Slasher and Rape-Revenge Narrative," *Journal of Religion and Popular Culture* 30.3 (2018): 193–205.

21. Always him, although often a male with a complicated relationship to gender. See Clover's discussion on the slasher and gender in *Men, Women, and Chain Saws*, 47–53. Perhaps the clearest example of the slasher's unstable gender can be found in the film *Sleepaway Camp*, which Clover overlooks in her argument.

22. And, indirectly, our own as well; see Noël Carroll's discussion in *The Philosophy of Horror*, esp. 12–27, on the ways in which the audience's emotions "mirror" those of the characters in horror films.

23. For a lengthier discussion on Freud's reading of "The Sand-Man," and his theory of the uncanny more generally, see the section on Freud in Grafius, *Reading Phinehas, Watching Slashers*, 78–80, and the sources included therein.

24. A good discussion of this phenomenon is found in David D. Gilmore, *Monsters: Evil Beings, Mythical Beasts, and All Manner of Imaginary Terrors* (Philadelphia: University of Pennsylvania Press, 2003), esp. 174–194. After surveying the monsters found in the stories of many different parts of the world, Gilmore notes that the focus on the monsters' "yawning, cavernous moths brimming with fearsome teeth, fangs, or other means of predation" (176), indicating a pervasive preoccupation with oral aggression.

25. Discussions are ongoing within many fields of humanities as to the degree to which capitalism as an international system has broken down culture differences, creating one monolithic culture throughout the more developed world. See, for example, Martha Nussbaum, *For Love of Country?* (Boston: Beacon Press, 1996), as well as the responding essays included in the volume; and the essays in Jean Comaroff and John L. Comaroff, eds., *Millennial Capitalism and the Culture of Neoliberalism* (Durham, NC: Duke University Press, 2001).

26. W. Scott Poole, *Monsters in America: Our Historical Obsession with the Hideous and the Haunting* (Waco, TX: Baylor University Press, 2011), provides an outstanding overview of how a variety of monsters have been interpreted and reinterpreted within contemporary American contexts. Jonathan Lake Crane, *Terror and Everyday Life: Singular Moments in the History of the Horror Film* (Thousand Oaks, CA: Sage, 1994), goes somewhat farther, arguing that monsters are so tied to their cultural moment as to be unable to speak beyond their particular situation without severe reinterpretation. Crane writes, "no matter how long we obsessively pore over obsolete celluloid, it is an exceptionally difficult task to find many moments from any horror film made before 1960 that can raise the least shudder from any audience" (47). For Crane, this is evidence enough to disregard the psychoanalytic view of horror, pursued by Freud, Julia Kristeva, Barbara Creed, and others, in favor of a critical model that places emphasis on social conditions over the individual ego.

27. This question is explored in-depth in the essays included in Glennis Byron, ed., *Globalgothic* (London: Manchester University Press, 2013). In the introduction, Byron notes: "in the late twentieth and early twenty-first centuries gothic was actually progressing far beyond being fixed in terms of any one geographically circumscribed mode." Instead, we see multiple strands of the gothic converging as the world experiences "the development of an increasingly integrated global economy" (1).

28. Steven Schneider, "Monsters as (Uncanny) Metaphors: Freud, Lakoff, and the Representation of Monstrosity in Cinematic Horror," in *The Horror Reader*, eds. Alain Silver and James Ursini (New York: Limelight Editions, 2000), 167–192, here 169.

29. A good introduction to this debate, using the film *The Cabin in the Woods* as the centerpiece of its discussion, is found in Michael J. Blouin's "'A Growing Global Darkness': Dialectives of Culture in Goddard's *The Cabin in the Woods*," *Horror Studies* 6.1 (2015): 83–99

30. Kelly J. Murphy, "The End Is (Still) All Around: The Zombie and Contemporary Apocalyptic Thought," in *Apocalypses in Context: Apocalyptic Currents Through History*, eds. Kelly J. Murphy and Justin Jeffcoat Schedtler (Minneapolis, MN: Fortress, 2015), 469–495.

31. Murphy, "The End Is (Still) All Around," 477.

32. Ibid., 485.

33. Along with Murphy's article, insightful readings of *Night of the Living Dead* can be found in Wood, "Normality and Monsters," in *Hollywood from Vietnam to Reagan . . . and Beyond* (New York: Columbia, 2003), 85–119; Crane, *Terror and Everyday Life*, 10–15; Linnie Blake, *The Wounds of Nations: Horror Cinema, Historical Trauma, and National Identity* (New York: Manchester University Press, 2008), 78–100. An early essay from R. H. W. Dillard's article "*Night of the Living Dead*: It's Not Just Like a Wind That's Passing Through," originally published in 1973, argues for the film's nihilism: "The film as a whole undercuts most of the cherished values of our whole civilization," including the rule of law, the value of the individual, and the inherent goodness of the family. Dillard's article is most easily found in *American Horrors: Essays on the Modern American Horror Film*, ed. Gregory A. Waller (Urbana, IL: University of Illinois Press, 1987), 14–29, quoting from 28. David J. Hogan, *Dark*

Romance: Sexuality in the Horror Film (London: McFarland, 1986), 242–245, downplays any possible political reading of the film, focusing instead on its historical role of introducing explicit gore into mainstream films as the film's primary innovation.

34. Romero himself has stated that he did not consider Duane Jones's race when casting him in the lead role; this raises questions as to whether the reading offered above linking *Night of the Living Dead* to American anxieties of race is a reading the film's author would have recognized. But as many contemporary theories of readings assert, the intention of the author is not a definitive reading of a given work. Romero would return to the figure of the zombie multiple times, using it to reflect on American consumerism (1978's *Dawn of the Dead*), militarism (1983's *Day of the Dead*), and society's class structure (2005's *Land of the Dead*), before making a series of less notable entries into his ongoing series. The literature on these films, while not as vast as that on *Night of the Living Dead*, is still quite large. Robin Wood was one of the early critics to take *Dawn of the Dead* seriously as a countercultural text worthy of study; see his section in "Normality and Monsters: The Films of George A. Romero and Larry Cohen," 104–107; Tony Williams, *Hearths of Darkness: The Family in the American Horror Film*, updated ed. (Jackson, MS: University of Mississippi Press, 2014), 149–155, discusses *Dawn* and *Day* as films that critique patriarchal structures; Williams provides a more full account of Romero's *Dead* films, as well as the rest of the director's fascinating oeuvre, in his monograph *The Cinema of George A. Romero: Knight of the Living Dead*, second ed. (New York: Columbia University Press, 2015). John Lutz, "Zombies of the World, Unite: Class Struggle and Alienation in *Land of the Dead*," in *The Philosophy of Horror*, ed. Thomas Fahy (Lexington: University Press of Kentucky, 2010), 121–136, argues that "the economic system depicted in *Land of the Dead* has a remarkable parallel with Marx's representation of a capitalist society" (121). See also the essays in *The Politics of Race, Gender, and Sexuality in The Walking Dead: Essays on the Television Series and Comics*, eds. Elizabeth Erwin and Dawn Keetley (London: McFarland, 2018).

35. While the scholarly work on *The Walking Dead* is still in its early stages, an essay from Stephen Olbrys Gencarella, "Thunder Without Rain: Fascist Masculinity in AMC's *The Walking Dead*," *Horror Studies* 7.1 (2016): 125–146, argues that *The Walking Dead* overturns the societal critique offered by Romero, instead presenting a world where patriarchal masculinity is our only hope of salvation. Questions of the role of masculinity for a functioning society are also present in many of the essays in Erwin and Keetley, *Politics of Race, Gender, and Sexuality*, cited in the note above.

36. Of course, this singular reading does not exhaust the metaphorical possibilities. For example, Pankaj Mishra, *The Age of Anger: A History of the Present* (New York: Farrar, Straus, and Giroux, 2017), 336, briefly remarks: "The current vogue for the zombie apocalypse in films seems to have been anticipated by the multitudes on city pavements around the world, lurching forward while starting blankly at screens." This reading strikes me as less encompassing than the dialectic of hope and despair described by Murphy, but also seems to capture some resonance, particularly with Romero's depiction of the zombies in *Dawn of the Dead* as mindless consumers, drawn reflexively back to the shopping mall in their undead afterlife.

37. This does raise the question as to what kind of "resolution" is found when the horror narrative ends with the triumph of the monstrous adversary, as is so often the case. I would suggest that even in these cases of "unhappy endings," the viewer is still afforded the pleasure of having their anxieties transformed into concrete fears, which at least have the possibility of being overcome.

38. Wood's work began as short articles in the journal *Film Comment*, and were gathered together into longer essays which made their way into his monograph *Hollywood From Vietnam to Reagan . . . and Beyond*. The most influential of these essays, "The American Nightmare: Horror in the 70s," has been reprinted in numerous volumes.

39. See Herbert Marcuse, *Eros and Civilization: A Philosophical Inquiry into Freud*, trans. Jeremy J. Shapiro (Boston: Beacon, 1966). The distinction between basic and surplus repression is further developed by Gad Horowitz in *Repression: Basic and Surplus Repression in Psychoanalytic Theory: Freud, Reich, Marcuse* (Toronto: University of Toronto Press, 1977).

40. Wood identifies the 1970s as ushering in a wave of progressive horror films, a period actually beginning with the release of *Night of the Living Dead* and *Rosemary's Baby* in 1968.

Subsequently, Wood reads *Halloween* and the films that followed its template as belonging to the reactionary strand of horror, serving as thinly disguised authoritarian arguments for a return to patriarchal societal and family structures.

41. Examples include Walter Evans, "Monster Movies: A Sexual Theory," *Journal of Popular Film* 2.4 (Fall 1973): 353–365; Steve Neal, "Halloween: Suspense, Aggression and the Look," in *Planks of Reason: Essays on the Horror Film*, ed. Barry Keith Grant (Lanham, MD: Scarecrow Press, 1984), 331–345; David J. Hogan, *Dark Romance: Sexuality in the Horror Film*; Barbara Creed, *The Monstrous-Feminine: Film, Feminism, Psychoanalysis* (New York: Routledge, 1993).

42. Steven Jay Schneider, "Introduction: Psychoanalysis in/and/of the Horror Film," in *Horror Film and Psychoanalysis: Freud's Worst Nightmare*, ed. Steven Jay Schneider (New York: Cambridge University Press, 2004), 1–15. As discussed above, scholars differ as to the degree to which they view these representations as being universal or culturally specific.

43. Stephen Prince, "Dread, Taboo, and *The Thing*: Toward A Social Theory of the Horror Film," *Wide Angle 10:3* (1988): 19–29, reprinted in *The Horror Film*, ed. and introduction by Stephen Prince (New Brunswick, NJ: Rutgers University Press, 2004), 118–130; subsequent references will be to pages from this edited volume.

44. Stephen Prince argues strongly against psychological models of horror interpretation in general, and Wood in particular. Discussing Wood's Marcusian distinction between basic and surplus repression, Prince argues that this distinction assumes "that society and culture are secondary derivations overlaying a more fundamental human reality." Prince continues: "However, as such disciplines as anthropology and sociology have long argued, there is no human reality outside of society. To be humans means to exist, already, within a social order." Prince, "Dread, Taboo, and *The Thing*," 119.

45. Prince, "Dread, Taboo, and *The Thing*."

46. Noël Carroll, *The Philosophy of Horror, or, Paradoxes of the Heart* (New York: Routledge, 1990).

47. Carroll's work will be discussed in greater detail in ch. 2.

48. Noël Carroll, "Afterword: Psychoanalysis and the Horror Film," in *Horror Film and Psychoanalysis: Freud's Worst Nightmare*, ed. Steven Jay Schneider (New York: Cambridge University Press, 2004), 257–270, here 257.

49. Carroll, *Philosophy of Horror*, 200.

50. Wood, *Hollywood from Vietnam to Reagan . . . and Beyond!*, 71.

Chapter Two

Monsters, Monster Theory, and Us

THE MONSTER IN THEORY

An expectant mother is spending Christmas Eve by herself, with her labor scheduled to be induced the next morning. Both her mother and her boss have offered to spend the evening with her. Sarah has declined, preferring to spend the evening alone. She falls asleep in her living room armchair but is awakened by a knock at the door. She nervously asks who it is through the closed door, deeply aware that she is a woman alone and vulnerable. From the other side comes a woman's voice, upset, saying that her car has broken down and she needs to use the phone. The frightened Sarah tells a lie: "No. Sorry, but, uh, my husband works. He's already gone to bed." The voice on the other side of the door calms down and chillingly says, "Your husband's not sleeping, Sarah. He's dead."

So begins the horror of the underappreciated French film *Inside* (2007), a tense and bloody roller-coaster ride of a movie. The nature of Sarah's assailant soon becomes apparent: this visitor (only given the name "The Woman") claims that Sarah's baby is actually hers, and that she plans to take it. It's the setup for a classic home invasion story, with two characters squaring off against each other in a life-or-death struggle made all the more intense by the vulnerability of the protagonist. But what gives it more depth is the strange dance the film plays with ideas of motherhood. From the beginning, the film provides scattered clues to indicate that Sarah doesn't really want this baby; the Woman, on the other hand, is a frighteningly devoted mother. At one point after Sarah has barricaded herself in the bathroom, the Woman whispers through the door, "You don't want this child. I'll take good care of him." The look that passes over Sarah's face tells us that she knows this might be true. The plot clearly tells us who is the protagonist (Sarah) and who is the monster (the Woman). But throughout the film, Sarah's ambivalence towards her impending role as a mother, and lack of interest in human relations in general, lends her more and more monstrous characteristics, while the single-minded devotion the unnamed woman expresses for the unborn child causes the viewer to rethink what are traditionally thought of as the traits that society admires in mothers.[1]

As viewers, we should know who is the heroine, and who is the monster. But sometimes, these clear boundaries are blurred, and we're left in a deeply unsettling space of uncertainty. The monstrous can represent the Other, the evil that is everything we are not. But the monstrous can also show us an uncomfortable part of ourselves, the part that we wish wasn't there.

Monsters have drawn scholars from a wide range of disciplines, all aiming to uncover the "meaning" of a particular monster, and of monsters in general.[2] After an orientation to monster theory, this chapter will examine some of the monsters of the Bible, most particularly the terrifying Leviathan. While Leviathan splashes through a number of biblical texts, its most conspicuous appearance is in the divine speech at the end of the book of Job. Through a careful examination of Leviathan's presence in this book, the chapter will argue that Leviathan and Job can be seen as mirror images of each other, each with an important role to play in the created order. Job and Leviathan, hero and monster, share a large number of traits with one another. Rather than excluding the monstrous from creation, the book of Job argues that the monstrous is an important part of it, and that creation can only be understood by taking the monstrous into account. The monstrous does not always come from outside of our community, or even outside of ourselves, but from within.

MONSTERS OUTSIDE, MONSTERS WITHIN

In the early history of cinema, many horror films depicted monsters as the threatening Other, often thinly coded as a racial or ethnic Other. Examples of this include the foreign Dracula from Bram Stoker's novel and Tod Browning's 1931 adaptation, Frankenstein's monster in the James Whale film (also from 1931), and even King Kong.[3] In this mode of horror, the monster is configured over/against the community. By its very nature, the monster's existence is outside the boundaries of what constitutes the human. Jeffrey Jerome Cohen cites *Beowulf* as an example of this, with the monster Grendel lurking in the swamps at the outside of the Anglo-Saxon camp, excluded from human society.[4] Grendel's exclusion from society goes back even further, as he is identified as a descendant of Cain.[5] The Hebrew Bible participates in this identification of the Other with the monstrous as well: examples include the spies' report of the inhabitants of the land in Numbers 13[6] and

Jeremiah's descriptions of the approaching armies of Babylon.[7] This process happens to individuals as well as to ethnic groups. In public discourse such as news media and popular entertainment, members of a community who transgress are frequently placed into the category of the monster as a way of excommunicating them.[8] The monster is everything that we wish to exclude from our communities, the "Not-Us" against who "Us" is defined.

But as we move into the modern era of horror, frequently considered to have started sometime in the late 1960s,[9] these boundaries become increasingly unstable. As a complex metaphor, the monster is not reducible to a simple Other.[10] Paradoxically, the monster also carries within itself some uncomfortable connections with the community. The monster often represents truths about ourselves that we are reluctant to admit, but which become more difficult to deny when reflected in the figure of the monster.[11] In *Night of the Living Dead*, the film's African-American protagonist Ben overcomes a blood-crazed horde of zombies, only to be shot by a group of white men who look an awful lot like a lynch mob, and behave an awful lot like the zombie horde. Romero makes the comparison between zombies and the mass of humanity even more explicit in the sequel, *Dawn of the Dead* (1978), in which a group of survivors attempt to hide out from the rampaging zombies in a shopping mall. Unfortunately, the zombies find themselves drawn back to the shopping mall, just as they were in life. Mindless consumers have become the mindless undead.[12]

A pair of monster movies from the 1980s reflect this dynamic in a most interesting way. In these two films, the blurring of boundaries becomes literal, as the monster is either to take on the appearance of the protagonists or incorporate its victims into one single, multi-visaged entity. John Carpenter's *The Thing* (1982), a loose remake of the 1951 film *The Thing From Another World*,[13] depicts a crew of scientists stationed at a remote arctic research station who are menaced by a monster with the power to replicate other life forms. The scientists gradually discover that this creature's powers of mimicry are so potent that the only way they can distinguish one of their fellow scientists from the monster is through blood testing. Much of the tension of the film evolves from this inability to separate the monstrous from the human. In a similar vein, the highly derivative but provocatively named film *Leviathan* (1989) follows a group of undersea explorers who find an abandoned laboratory that had been experimenting in genetic engineering.[14] As the monstrous beast claims its victims, it gradually incorporates their physical likeness into itself; when it is finally revealed at the film's climax, it is a shambling, chaotic mess of former crewmembers fused together into one horrific beast. The boundaries of these individuals have merged into one formless mass, and it is a terrifying spectacle.

In earlier horror film scholarship, the blurring of boundaries between monster and society, self and Other, was thought to be a feature unique to the modern horror film.[15] In this view, earlier horror films (pre-1970s) offer a "simple moral binary opposition," in which horror is "something strange, marginal, ex-centric, the mark of a force from elsewhere, the inhuman."[16] But more recently, scholars have recognized that this tendency towards viewing horror as emanating from within, rather than from without, has perhaps intensified in the modern period, but has been present throughout the history of horror. The Hebrew Bible offers a very early example of the blurred boundaries between the self and the monstrous, in the connections the book of Job makes between its protagonist and Leviathan. But who or what exactly is this monstrous Leviathan? How did it make its way into the pages of the Hebrew Bible?

Leviathan, King of the Sea

Swimming through the Hebrew Bible is the figure of Leviathan, the twisting serpent, king of the seas. In Psalm 74, Leviathan is the monster that YHWH defeated at the beginning of creation. The psalmist extolls, "You split the sea with your might, you broke the heads of the dragons in the waters. You crushed the heads of Leviathan, you gave him as food to the creatures of the desert" (Psalm 74:13–14). And in Isaiah 27, Leviathan is the chaos beast that will be defeated by YHWH at the end of time. "On that day YHWH will punish, with his hard and strong sword, Leviathan the fleeing serpent, Leviathan the twisting serpent; he will slay the dragon that is in the sea."[17]

YHWH's enemy might be Leviathan (Job 3:8, 41; Ps 74:14, 104:26), it might be Rahab[18] (Job 9:13, 26:12; Psalm 89:11; Isaiah 30:7), or a more generic term like "dragon"[19] (Job 7:12; Ezekiel 29:3, 32:2), or "serpent" (Job 26:13). Most likely, these various names all represent the same adversary. By whatever name it is called, this monster is the king of the ocean, the ruler of the watery chaos.

While he makes quite a splash in a handful of biblical passages, and seems to have morphed into the monstrous dragon of the book of Revelation,[20] the Hebrew Bible's waters aren't the only places Leviathan has swum; the cognate name *litanu* is attested in Ugaritic, describing a similarly terrifying sea monster.[21] And expanding out from creatures specifically named as Leviathan/Litanu, we see seven-headed sea monsters who seem to be the same monster given a different name in a wide range of myths and iconographic materials from cultures across the Ancient Near East.[22] The earliest texts depicting this great sea monster date from the second millenium BCE; the book of Revelation is generally dated to around 100 CE.[23] For thousands of years, these cultures understood the sea dragon as being an important part of creation, a character without whom the story of the world could not be told. For the religious traditions of these cultures, the world felt like a precarious place, one which could fall under attack from this dreaded enemy at any time.

To understand what Leviathan is doing in the book of Job, it's helpful to take a brief tour through the history of this dragon in both the Hebrew Bible and the earlier literature from which the Bible drew inspiration. A quick overview of some of these texts will help to explain how the book of Job presents a slightly different picture of the world. The next section will offer a summary of the work of Hermann Gunkel, who argued for a biblical creation story built around mythic combat between gods and monsters. This section will build off of Gunkel's work to demonstrate that the binary opposition between order and chaos that Gunkel saw is not always the case; frequently, the line between god and monster blurs. Furthermore, this section will engage with the work of more contemporary scholars who read the Hebrew Bible as reinterpreting these conflict stories to depict a world formed without a battle, but where evil is nonetheless a persistent presence.

Battles Between Order and Chaos

In the latter part of the nineteenth century, Hermann Gunkel developed a hypothesis concerning the monsters in the Hebrew Bible that would hold sway over biblical scholars for several generations to come. Gunkel noted similarities between many stories from the cultures surrounding Israel, most notably the Babylonian epic *Enuma Elish*, and the creation account in Genesis. Gunkel noted the frequency with which the gods of various Near Eastern traditions were forced to do battle with a monstrous embodiment of chaos, usually feminine, usually associated with the sea. In some cases, this monster was actually the sea personified: Yam, which also happens to be one of the Hebrew words for "ocean." Gunkel developed these connections into a story he referred to as the *Chaoskampf*, the battle against chaos.

Gunkel and many scholars since his work have seen this struggle as first arising in Genesis 1, as YHWH subdues the primal waters to create the world. In a key detail, Gunkel notes that YHWH "separates" (בדל, *badil*) these waters, just as Marduk "separates" Tiamat's body after he has defeated her, creating the heavens and the earth out of the two halves of her body. For Gunkel, this struggle between order and chaos looms just beneath the surface of Genesis 1 and shines through in the various references to embodied chaos mentioned above. YHWH is constantly at war with these forces of chaos, and creation only endures because YHWH is victorious. Gregory Mobley has referred to this continual conflict against chaos as one of the "backstories" of the Bible.[24]

In one form or another, this theory held sway for much of the twentieth century.[25] Scholars such as Bernard Batto[26] and Mary Wakeman[27] have found this theme to be prevalent throughout much of the biblical material.

John Day[28] sees the biblical accounts as primarily referring to Canaanite mythology, such as the Ba'al Cycle. Most recently, Robert Miller III has argued that the mythical underpinnings of the Hebrew Bible do not lie within any one myth, but in the constellation of myths found throughout the Ancient Near East.[29]

But an interesting phenomenon shows up repeatedly in these texts, one that also rears its head in contemporary horror films. While many of them seem to depict the forces of good struggling against the evil forces of chaos, the sharp division between "order" and "chaos" is not sustainable. As Karen Sonik has discussed, Tiamat only becomes a representative of chaos later on in her battle with Marduk; she is not always depicted as such.[30] In the description of Debra Scoggins Ballentine, "The enemies defeated by the victorious warrior deities across ancient West Asian conflict traditions are not agents of 'chaos' but rather agents of an alternative divine power structure."[31] Furthermore, the powers of these monstrous adversaries "lie within the realm of accepted institutions."[32] These monsters are not so much threats to the created order as they are simply the losers in the battle for institutional control. As such, they are portrayed as monstrous. And, as will be discussed in chapter 6, the gods (including YHWH) are not as clearly on the side of order as is frequently assumed.[33]

Perhaps the strongest critique of Gunkel's *Chaoskampf* theory is that Genesis 1 does not, in fact, depict any kind of *kampf*.[34] In Genesis 1, creation happens without any battle, without any bloodshed or violence. Gunkel found the remnant of this cosmic battle in Genesis 1:2's reference to the *tehom*, where he argued that the lack of an article on this noun indicated that it was to be read as more than simply the deep waters.[35] But Claus Westermann has thoroughly demonstrated that *tehom* frequently lacks the article in the Hebrew Bible, and is still clearly not personified.[36] However, the numerous connections between Genesis 1, the *Enuma Elish*, the Ba'al Cycle, and many other ANE myths pointed out by Batto and others are still evident. So why would the biblical authors leave out the combat to focus solely on creation?

Kenton Sparks and Mark Smith have each provided similar readings that answer many of these questions, in a reading that gets to the heart of how Genesis 1 conceives of the world.[37] In the views of these authors, the P creation account substitutes the divine combat of Marduk, Ba'al, and others for YHWH's power of speech. YHWH is supreme over all creation and, as such, has no need to wage war against YHWH's enemies. Instead, YHWH subdues them with a word, bounding the waters through a simple command.[38] Miller describes this as one of the strategies frequently employed by the biblical authors with their use of mythic material: "It takes what is the greatest mythological accomplishment of a foreign deity and makes it a task of no great difficulty for God."[39]

In this reading, Genesis 1 shares in common with the *Enuma Elish* the desire to place the deity (YHWH in Genesis; Marduk in *Enuma Elish*) in the position of supreme power. In the *Enuma Elish*, this power is achieved through the defeat of Tiamat in armed combat, whereas in Genesis this supremacy is assumed from the beginning of creation.[40] But, as Jon Levenson discusses, the authors of the Hebrew Bible also understood that YHWH's power did not indicate that evil had been banished from the world.[41] Leviathan endures as a part of creation, occasionally subdued by God, occasionally waiting for the right time to attack, and sometimes destined to be permanently defeated in a battle sometime in the future. Similarly, the *Enuma Elish* hints that Tiamat, somehow, endures after her dismemberment at the hands of Marduk and must be defeated again and again. The *Enuma Elish*, and other divine combat myths, understood that while there may be temporary ceasefires in the battle against chaos, the war has yet to end.

This monstrous sea creature—Leviathan, Rahab, the serpent, or the dragon—endures after YHWH has created the world, continuing as a part of creation that is kept in check by YHWH's power. As will be discussed below, the primordial waters, while not necessarily representative of evil, are still evidence of a piece of YHWH's creation that is not completely in accord with YHWH's will, and which could undo the order of creation (as envisioned by YHWH) at any moment, should the creator allow it.[42] Forces that threaten to undo YHWH's creation are an integral part of this creation. The monstrous is embedded as a deep part of creation.

As Jeffrey Jerome Cohen has noted, one of the key characteristics of the monster is that it always returns; the monster is never defeated completely.[43] Many horror narratives wrestle with this reality, depicting a struggle against evil that can never be won completely. In *The Exorcist*, the best that Father Damien can do is sacrifice his life to save young Regan, knowing that the demon that possessed her will still endure. In *The Night of the Living Dead*, the zombie hordes are too numerous to be stopped, a reality that becomes increasingly grim throughout director George Romero's sequels. And on a less existentially serious note, this characteristic of the monster has been manipulated by movie studios since the 1930s in the seemingly endless sequels to monster films.[44] The audience of these ancient myths understood Leviathan and the other monstrous opponents of their gods in the same way; in discussing the Ba'al cycle, Marjo Korpel and Johannes de Moor note that it concludes with a prayer for assistance in defeating Yam's monsters, who continue to endure even after their seemingly definitive defeat by Ba'al. They continue: "The struggle between the god of life, Ba'al, and his formidable opponents representing chaos and death, will never end."[45]

Interestingly enough, these insights connect perfectly with one of the key observations of contemporary monster theory. While monsters may seem like the threatening Other, they are an inextricable part of our world. Monsters are simultaneously, paradoxically, a representative of both the absolute Other and the deepest parts of the selves. The monster is the Other who marks the boundaries of our culture, the "not-us" who helps us to define ourselves. But the monster also reveals, uncomfortably, the parts of ourselves that we would like to deny.

ANCIENT MONSTERS, ANCIENT GODS

In recent decades, biblical scholars Timothy Beal and Safwat Marzouk have both used monster theory to explore the blurred boundaries between the ideas of order and chaos in the biblical world. Each of these scholars has posited a relationship between gods and monsters that is similar to what will be uncovered in the book of Job: the heroic god is frequently not quite as heroic as they first appear, and the monstrous antagonist is frequently less monstrous than they might seem.

In one of the earliest works using monster theory as a way to approach the biblical text, Timothy Beal reads the relationship between order and chaos in the Hebrew Bible as being fraught with overlapping connections between the two forces that, at first glance, appear to be solely oppositional.[46] In the early chapters of Genesis, water is both creation (Genesis 1) and destruction (Genesis 6–9), both order and chaos. And in the Divine Warrior myths, where chaos is embodied as a monster with which the gods must do battle, these monsters are also given a divine lineage and represented as part of the world.[47]

Safwat Marzouk argues that the monsters of *Enuma Elish*, the Ba'al Cycle, and Re and Apophis also contain a complicated relationship to the hero.[48] Marzouk suggests that traditional scholarship has viewed these texts through a binary, structuralist lens, with the good forces of order defeating the evil forces of chaos.[49] But a careful reading reveals "some aspects of common identity" between the "benevolent" and "monstrous" gods.[50] Marduk battles Tiamat, but before Tiamat was cast as a monster she was the mother of the gods. Tiamat then becomes the mother of us all, as the cosmos is formed out of her body. Furthermore, in descriptions of Marduk himself, Marzouk sees depictions of "horror and awe" gathering together into an "incomprehensible appearance," which makes Marduk participate in the monstrousness of his adversary.[51]

The interplay between Job and Leviathan exhibits a similar dynamic. While Job frequently proclaims his insignificance, Leviathan is described as the most fearsome and powerful of all of God's creation. But throughout the text, connections are made between Job and Leviathan. Before the theophanic speech, Job references Leviathan in his speeches on four separate occasions. Each of these times, the reference to Leviathan is connected, in some way, to Job himself. And throughout the theophanic speeches, descriptions of Leviathan recall descriptions of Job from earlier passages. This tension between these two major characters gets to the heart of this enigmatic book, providing a key insight into what the book of Job says about the world and humanity's relationship to it.

"Am I the Sea or the Dragon?"

In some ways, the book of Job is an outlier in the Hebrew Bible. Its main character is a non-Israelite, a man from the land of Uz (Job 1:1). The book begins with a short prose narrative, almost folktale-like in its simplicity, in which we are introduced to this "innocent and honest" (Job 1:1) man, who seems to be a wealthy landowner and a pillar of his community. But things go wrong pretty quickly. Unbeknownst to Job, a conversation is going on in the divine court between God and his servant the satan regarding the character of Job. At this point in the development of the tradition, the satan is not yet the figure of the Devil that we've come to know from the Gospels, the book of Revelation, and Milton's *Paradise Lost*; he doesn't even have a proper name yet, with Hebrew *satan* meaning "adversary."[52] He seems to serve the function of a prosecuting attorney, wandering the world and looking for places of weakness. The satan's question to YHWH is a provocative one. While YHWH praises Job for being "innocent and honest" (1:6), just like the narrator did a few verses earlier, the satan wonders why this might be. "Is it for nothing that Job fears God?" (1:9). Is Job a good person because of his relationship with God, or because God has given him so many material blessings that Job maintains his faithfulness? Peruvian theologian Gustavo Gutiérrez asks whether Job's faith is "disinterested," or if he is merely looking out for his own self-interest by maintaining fidelity to the God who gives him material benefits.[53] "Send out your hand now," the satan tells God, "and strike all that is his, and see if he will curse you to your face"[54] (Job 1:11). God agrees to this experiment, or "wager" as it is often called, and the next thing Job knows his life has fallen apart: his house is destroyed, his livestock killed or scattered, his children dead, and his body consumed by boils. Job sits down in misery on an ashheap on the outskirts of town, where three of his friends come to console him. Before too long, they are engaging in a spirited theological debate over the nature of God, the question of suffering, whether bad things can happen to good people (and vice versa), and where God is in all of this. Job's friends offer traditional words of comfort: perhaps Job has sinned, and he is being punished for it, so he must repent to have his blessings restored. Or perhaps he is being tested by God, and he will emerge stronger after the calamities have passed. Job refuses to accept these pat answers, and demands an accounting from God. Job needs to know the reason for the tragedies that have befallen him and his family, and how the principles of justice can still hold fast in the face of innocent suffering.

Through these discourses, the book of Job moves towards a seemingly inevitable conclusion: Job's confrontation with the divine presence. This confrontation itself culminates in YHWH's lengthy speech extolling the terror and the virtues of the great sea monster Leviathan, viewed as the pinnacle of God's creation and a counterpoint to Job's focus on his own suffering. Before the grand hymn to Leviathan, the monster's appearance is prefigured in several key passages throughout the book. When these passages are read in conjunction with the theophanic speech extolling Leviathan's virtues, linguistic cues link Job and Leviathan together.[55] Job and the monstrous Leviathan are obviously very different figures. But the book of Job provocatively asks the reader to consider the ways in which they might share some similarities. Furthermore, these similarities press us to consider what this says about the world as created by YHWH. Both Job and Leviathan have immense destructive powers—Leviathan through his overwhelming might, Job through his unwillingness to accept traditional understandings of the world. The text suggests that while both must be confined for the world to work according to YHWH's desires, both are integral parts of creation. Like Leviathan, Job is the chaos that endures at the heart of creation, bound by YHWH but always threatening.

Leviathan in the Poetic Dialogues

Traditionally, scholars have divided Job into several sections: a prose prologue (chs. 1–2), poetic dialogues (chs. 3–31), Elihu's speech (chs. 32–37), the theophany (chs. 38–42:6), and the prose epilogue (42:7–17).[56] While the bulk of the discourse on Leviathan is found in the culmination of YHWH's survey of creation, vv. 40:25–41:26 (ET ch. 41), there are four references to Leviathan scattered throughout the poetic dialogues.[57] Leviathan is referred to once as Leviathan (3:8), once as "the dragon" (7:12), and twice as "Rahab" (9:13; 26:12). Of these passages, the connection in 3:8 is by far the most convoluted. We will begin by examining the passages where the connections between Job and Leviathan are most explicit, before returning to 3:8.

Job's references to "Rahab" in 9:4 and 26:12 both serve a similar function: YHWH was powerful enough to defeat Rahab, so in comparison Job stands no chance against the divine might. In these two instances, Job uses Rahab as the Other against which he measures himself; Rahab is mighty, Job is weak. Rahab and Job are as far from each other as could be imagined. But as we know from monster theory, the Monster, even when configured as most radically Other, usually contains a trace of the self. With Job's invocation of "the dragon" in 7:12 and of "Leviathan" in 3:8, this sharp dichotomy begins to blur, and the trace of the monstrous within the self becomes readily apparent.

In 7:12, Job asks of God, "Am I the sea (*yamm*, יָם) or the dragon, that you put a watch over me?" This question is found near the end of Job's response to Eliphaz's speech of chs. 4–5; in Job's response, Job frequently expresses the feeling of being oppressed by YHWH.[58] In comparing himself to the mythological enemies of God, Job intends to make the point, through a rhetorical question, that he is far from these chaos monsters and not worthy of the attention he has found from God.[59] David A. Diewert argues that this verse should be understood in context with the similarly structured rhetorical question of 7:17: "What is a human being, that you raise him up, that you set your mind on him?"[60] Job expresses the wish that YHWH would view him as too insignificant to bother with so that he would be left alone. Through his rhetorical question, Job implies directly (albeit with ironic intent) that he is, in fact, like Leviathan.

This comparison becomes clearer when this rhetorical question is compared with two other passages in Job that describe God placing a guard or watch of some kind. The first instance of this trope occurs in the prose prologue.[61] In 1:9–10, the satan asks God if Job fears "God for nothing? Have you not put a fence (שׂכת, *sakat*, from the root שׂוך, *suk*) around him and his house and all that he has, on every side?"[62] The root שׂוך/סוך is rare in biblical Hebrew, used only four times in the Old Testament to mean "fence in;" three of these uses are in Job (1:10, 3:23, 38:8), and the fourth is in Hosea (2:8).[63] In Job 1:10, the verb describes a protective fencing in; Job is "fenced in" as a protection from the possible harm that forces in the world might do to him. But elsewhere, the context indicates restriction. In 3:23, Job laments that God gives light to "one who cannot see the way, whom God has fenced in," suggesting an oppressive confinement. This resembles Job's lament in 7:12 that he has had a guard placed over him; it also comes closest to the other Old Testament use of שׂוך/סוך in Hosea, when YHWH threatens the wayward Israel with having her way hedged up with thorns.

שׂוך/סוך is also used in the theophanic speech, when God is describing the boundaries he placed on the hostile, potentially threatening *yam* (38:8). This passage also suggests confinement, of a type very similar to Job's complaint in 7:12. In 38:8, שׂוך/סוך is used to describe God's "shutting in" the sea, to prevent it from covering the entire earth. While this "shutting in" is a restriction on the freedom of the sea, it is also a type of protective fencing in, as seen in Job 1:10. Rather than destroy the sea as a chaotic threat, God has simply bounded it. In this statement, we see one of the common motifs of the divine combat myth; in some iterations, the divine warrior destroys his opponent completely. We see the destruction of the monstrous enemy preserved in the biblical text in Isaiah 27:1, 51:9; Ezekiel 29:1–7, 32:1–10; Psalm 74:13 (74:14 ET), 89:11 (ET 89:10). But in other places, both in the biblical text and other ANE divine warrior myths, the divine warrior binds his adversary, but does not defeat it completely.

Not only does Job compare himself to Leviathan in this verse, Job also compares himself to Yam, another of the monstrous forces that opposes the heroic gods.[64] In this short passage, Job also answers one of his repeated concerns, expressed throughout the poetic dialogues, of whether YHWH will do violence to him. As we learn from the divine warrior myths, there are two ways in which the divine warrior can defeat the monster, both of which are preserved in the Hebrew Bible. The divine warrior can defeat the monster permanently through means of destructive violence. Or the divine warrior can bind the monster, circumscribing its reign, but nevertheless leaving it as an enduring part of creation. In Job's rhetorical question of 7:12, Job aligns himself with these forces who have fought against YHWH since the beginning of time. Implicitly, Job is also identifying himself with the monstrous.

In the poetic discourses, the most complex reference to Leviathan occurs in Job's opening lament. In Job's initial lament, he does not simply wish he had never been born; he wishes that his birthday would be wiped off the calendar, and imagines this day being plunged back into pre-creation chaos. This continues the lament begun in the first part of ch. 3, which Michael Fishbane describes as an "un-creation account."[65] In Fishbane's reading, this lament borrows the pattern of Genesis 1, but substitutes the creation of the world for a wish for its annihilation. In 3:3, Job wishes its destruction with a jussive form of אמד, "to destroy." Job 3:4–7 continues with Job's wish that the day would become darkness, that dark clouds would settle on it, that even the night of his birth would be seized by further thick darkness (אפל, *ophel*, one of several synonyms for night or darkness in this passage), that it not be counted among the other days of the year, and, finally, that it be barren, with "no joyful cry." Job wishes that the world could be returned to its state before creation.

As part of this diatribe, Job cries, "Let the day-cursers[66] curse it (the day), the ones skilled to stir up Leviathan."[67] The exact reference remains obscure; however, the poetic force of the language is clear.[68] Continuing with Job's wish for the destruction of the day of his birth in vv. 3–7, Job's lament looks to Leviathan as the ultimate power of destruction. While wishing for darkness to cover the day (vv. 4–5), and the night to be ejected from among the days of the year (v. 6), the evocation of Leviathan is the culmination of Job's wish for destruction. Finally, Job wishes for the removal of all light from this day in v. 9, concluding, "may it not see the eyelids of the dawn."[69]

Job also makes an interesting link between himself and Leviathan. Job calls upon the "day-cursers" to rouse Leviathan; throughout this pericope, Job himself has been cursing the day of his birth. Job has been proclaiming himself to be a day-curser, like these figures he is calling forth in v. 8. Even if Job is not ascribing to himself the power to rouse Leviathan, he is making an implicit analogy between himself and a magician who has such power; both Job and these magicians are "day-cursers." Again, Job is unwittingly aligning himself with Leviathan, even as he declares his innocence.

These brief references serve as foreshadowing for Leviathan's grand appearance in the divine speech, in which he[70] is the subject of YHWH's awe-filled praise. This speech will provide many more opportunities for comparisons between Leviathan and Job.

"I Will Not Keep Silent!": God's Effusive Praise of Leviathan

The book of Job culminates with YHWH's grand speech from the whirlwind, a theophany that takes up four chapters (38–41). It is commonly divided into two sections, with Job's brief interruption (40:3–5) serving as the dividing point. Throughout the speech, God presents Job with a lengthy catalogue of nature,[71] first describing natural beasts (chs. 38–39) before turning to the Behemoth and the Leviathan in chs 40–41.[72] The Leviathan speech is by far the longest, containing a significantly greater number of verses than God devotes to any other single animal in the divine speeches.

Job 40:25 (41:1 ET; further references in this passage will be to the verse numbers in the MT) begins with a series of rhetorical questions put to Job by YHWH, following the standard format for introducing a new creature in 38–41.[73] The Leviathan speech can be divided into two halves: 40:25–41:3 and 41:4–26, with the first half centering on the absurdity of capturing or confronting Leviathan, and the second turning to a description of Leviathan's awesome physical characteristics. Verse 40:25 begins a series of rhetorical questions aimed at Job, asking him whether he is the equal of Leviathan. Job is asked whether he can capture Leviathan, and whether it will plead with him once he has captured it (40:25–6). The implicit answer to these questions is that Job cannot, but YHWH can. This framework continues in 40:27, when YHWH asks Job if Leviathan will "make a covenant" with him to be his "servant forever." If we assume the pattern of implied answers is continued, this tells us that Job is not able to make a covenant with Leviathan, but that Leviathan has made a covenant with YHWH, and that Leviathan is YHWH's servant. Similarly to Job 7:12 (and Psalm 104:26), as well as the sea in Job 38:8, Leviathan is here depicted as a threat to be contained, not destroyed.

In 41:2a, God seems to reference Job's lament in 3:8: "No one is so fierce as to dare stir it up."[74] However, 41:2b has caused some difficulties for commentators, as the speech makes a sudden shift in subject matter. While 41:2b is often translated similarly to the NRSV's "Who can stand before it?" the pronominal suffix in the MT is in the first person, not third. The MT reads, "Who can stand before me?" As it stands in the MT, 41:3a reads literally "Whoever confronts me, I will repay."[75] YHWH asserts his dominion over all and confirms that YHWH reigns supreme even over Leviathan.

This leads into 41:3b, which is again frequently emended to a third-person ending and assumed to refer to Leviathan. But as the MT reads, it is a statement of God's dominion over all creatures: "All under the heavens are mine." Even though Leviathan is a fearsome beast, capable of unimaginable destruction, he is still under the dominion of God.

But while this beast is part of God's dominion, he is still an awesome creature in his own right. The second half of the Leviathan speech continues to lavish praise upon the beast. The translation of 41:4 is also disputed; the Hebrew could read either, "Did I not silence his boasting?" referencing the divine warrior myth, or "I will not keep silence concerning his limbs."[76] Two words cause this difficulty: בדין, *badayn*, which means either "limbs" as in Job 18:13, or "boasting," as in Job 11:3, and the hiphil form of חרש, which can mean either "keep silent" or "be silent."[77] Both are syntactically valid translations; the choice is an exegetical decision. I follow Kathryn Schiffendecker and others in preferring the second reading, "I will not keep silence concerning his limbs." If this passage is seen as a recurrence of the divine warrior myth, there is no transition to 41:5, which continues to extol the might of Leviathan. Understanding the verse as "I will not keep silence" also connects it with 41:2b–3, where God asserts dominion over all of creation, with Leviathan as one of the creatures whom God most admires. The implication of 40:25–41:3 is that YHWH has restrained Leviathan, not silenced him. Leviathan still reigns supreme in the sea, bound by the same borders with which YHWH as restrained the mighty Yam. But in spite of this, Leviathan is still worthy of God's greatest praise. Leviathan is less monstrous than he might at first appear.

There are several connections made in this speech between Leviathan and Job. Perhaps most evocative is the phrase עפעפי–שחר, *aphaphey-shakar*, "eyelids of the dawn," which appears only in Job 3:9 and Job 41:10 (ET 41:18), first in reference to the day of Job's birth, then in reference to the eyes of Leviathan. On some occasions, the dawn is used as an image of hope. In Isaiah 58:8, God's light is envisioned as "breaking like the dawn;" and in Hosea 6:3, YHWH's appearance is "as certain as the dawn." The corollary to this is that that the removal of dawn is an absence of hope. For example, in Isaiah 8:20, the prophet threatens those who seek to consult mediums instead of waiting for a word from YHWH: "Those who speak like this will have no dawn." The following verses contrast the dawn with the darkness these people will instead walk in.[78] The Song of Songs also contains a reference to dawn as an image of beauty in 6:10: "Who is this showing her face like the dawn?" Here, the image is of something beautiful emerging, as the sun emerges after the night.

An interesting use of "dawn" in a similar metaphorical construction is found in Psalm 139:9, in which the psalmist imagines riding "the wings of the dawn" (כנפי–שחר, *kanphey-shachar*). William Brown describes the image: "The psalmist envisions himself catching a ride on the sun as it is dawning (and thus accessible from ground level, as it were) and transported across the domed sky."[79] So this image also employs the idea of the dawn as signifying newness and hope.[80]

Job's use of the phrase "the eyelids of the dawn" employ several of these ideas at once. Job 3:9's closest parallel is Isaiah 8:20. The "eyelids of the dawn" of the final stiche are in parallel construction with the day's "hope for light." In this verse, the "eyelids of the dawn" indicate the beginning of morning, the sun opening its eyes after the night. In C. L. Seow's description of this phrase, "The point is that darkness should prevail through the triumph of the awakened chaos monster (v. 8), so much so that the slightest glimpse of first light will not be possible."[81] By denying the day the sight of the eyelids of the dawn, Job is pleading for an end to all hope.

At first glance, this makes this description as applied to Leviathan in 41:10 all the more baffling. David Clines, continuing his reading of Leviathan as a crocodile enhanced with mythical language, connects the image with the crocodile's "mictating membrane that sweeps across the eye as it opens."[82] Clines proceeds to note: "From the eyelids of the dawn comes rays of light . . . the eyelids . . . of the crocodile, on the other hand, emit nothing."[83] However, this reading would indicate that the text sees Leviathan's eyes as *unlike* the eyes of the dawn, not *like* them, as the text in fact claims. Norman Habel reads this image as referencing "the intensity of the heat" that comes from Leviathan's fiery breath, which causes Leviathan's eyes to "light up red like the dawn."[84] While this might serve as an appropriate physical description, it ignores the connotations of hope that "dawn" implies. Somehow, YHWH sees Leviathan as being associated with hope. Leviathan's eyes are like the rising sun. While Leviathan is usually associated with destruction, in this verse the monster is, paradoxically, associated with the hope of a new day. The text itself clearly understands Leviathan as a more complicated figure than a straightforward image of chaotic destruction.

This is not the only time that a description Job had used in his poetic speeches recurs in YHWH's description of Leviathan. In Job 6:12, Job laments, "Is my strength the strength of stones, or is my flesh bronze?" The strength of Leviathan's skin is a frequent object of description (40:31, 41:5, 7–9), and it is depicted as stronger than iron and bronze in 41:19. But the comparison between Job and Leviathan is even more clear in 41:16, where Leviathan's heart is also described as being "cast like stone."[85] Job's "strength" (כה, *koh*) and Leviathan's "heart" (לב, *lev*) are rhetorically cast as being of the same substance, and Leviathan shrugs off the same material of which Job's flesh is rhetorically made (נחוש, *nachosh*).

In the penultimate verse of the poem (41:25), God proclaims that Leviathan has no equal on the dust (עפר, *opher*). To translate this as "earth," as does the NRSV, misses the connection between Job and dust that runs throughout the book.[86] Initially, this phrase seems odd, as Leviathan is a beast of the water, not the dust. However, the strange phrase serves to sharpen the connection between Job and Leviathan. The dust is associated with Job's mourning (2:12; 30:19), and with his repentance in 42:6 (although the translation of this verse is contested). And frequently, Job associates his fate, or the fate that he fears YHWH is preparing him for, with the dust (10:9; 17:16; 20:11). Job poignantly declares in 10:9 to YHWH, "Please remember that you made me like clay, and you will return me to the dust." Job associates his ultimate fate with the dust, the realm within which Leviathan has no equal. By placing Leviathan with Job in the ashes, the divine speech once again makes the point of their kinship. Repeatedly, Job's status as protagonist and Leviathan's status as monster are blurred together.

Once this comparison has been entertained, the emphasis God gives to Leviathan's mouth and the power emanating from it becomes clear. Verses 41:11–13 are grand descriptions of the strength of Leviathan's breath, with flaming torches coming forth from his mouth, smoke coming from his nostrils, and his breath "kindling coals." John Gammie sees in this description of Leviathan a didactic tool that holds "up to Job a caricature of his verbal defenses and yet an affirmation of his very protests."[87] This helps to explain the two-sided nature of God's description of Leviathan: while Leviathan is a creature of terrifying, destructive potential, it is difficult not to read 40:25–41:26 as full of praise and admiration for Leviathan. Similarly, God praises Job in 42:7, telling Job's friends that Job was the only one of them who spoke rightly of God. Both Job and Leviathan carry the potential to destabilize the YHWH-ordered world, but both are admired by the creator for their strength. In both figures, YHWH recognizes the monstrous element of creation.

While Leviathan is a beast to be admired for his destructive power, God has also placed boundaries on him. His normal state is away from human reach, as no one is able to stir it up (41:2, cf. 3:8). Even before the divine speeches, Job understands that Leviathan has had a guard placed on him by God, like the Sea (7:12). And in the divine speech, God asks Job to imagine subduing Leviathan. Verses 40:25–6 describe Leviathan as a captive being led by the hook through his mouth, then pleading with his captor.[88] In 40:29, Leviathan has been turned into a children's plaything, confined and made (at least temporarily) harmless. In these images, Leviathan is tamed, his potential for destruction removed. Jon Levenson addresses this view of creation in his work *Creation and the Persistence of Evil*: ". . . the confinement of chaos rather than its elimination is the essence of creation."[89] But even this reads the evidence a little too strongly: these images of Leviathan tamed, captive, and bound are presented as rhetorical questions, the absurdity of which is apparent. While Levenson might imagine that YHWH answers yes to these rhetorical questions, as to the rhetorical questions that begin the divine speech, the description of Leviathan in 41:4–26 does not describe a tamed beast, but one awesome in its power. Instead of being enslaved, Leviathan remains as a part of creation, one of the beings under heaven who belong to God. While the speech begins with language referencing capture (40:25–32), by the time the divine speech comes to a close, God is lavishing praise upon Leviathan (41:4–26), causing a reevaluation of the initial images of captivity. In this passage, Leviathan is granted an amount of freedom rivaled only by Psalm 104:26. Leviathan is not captive; he merely has his proper place in creation.

Just as God holds Leviathan in deep admiration, God refers to Job as his "servant," a title usually reserved for Moses and David, and claims that Job "spoke what is right" (42:7).[90] While Job's claims that the universe is ruled by an unjust tyrant might be viewed as a threat to the divinely created order, there is something to be admired in the power and strength of the speaker. Throughout his poetic speeches, Job has revealed that the workings of the universe are not as comfortable as many strands of biblical tradition like to imagine. Instead, it is a world of threat, a world of mystery, and a world of sometimes inexplicable freedom. Like the monstrous Leviathan, these challenges to the created order are also a part of the fabric of God's creation.

While a complete reading of the book of Job lies outside the scope of this chapter, any attempt to provide an interpretive framework for the book as a whole must deal with Job's relation to YHWH and the world around him.[91] In this study, we have affirmed that Job is understood as participating in the same forces of chaos that oppose YHWH's ordering of the world. But just as Job is more monstrous than he might at first appear, Leviathan is less monstrous; instead of being portrayed as a destructive chaos monster (as in Job 3:8), Leviathan is one of the pinnacles of God's creation, a beast of awesome power and strength who holds an important place in creation. In this vision of the world, the monstrous is an integral part of God's creation, not an opposing force of destruction.

While Job and Leviathan might not be Carpenter's Thing, mashed into a gooey blob of a creature without any remaining sense of individuality, the boundaries between the two of them are permeable. Like *Inside*'s Sarah and her unnamed assailant, they share enough points of connection to be seen as two answers to the same question, two challenges to the same system. These connections help to identify Leviathan as the uncomfortable, frequently repressed part of Job; while life was good, Job was faithful and patient, but when his world started to fall apart, Job's inner chaos monster was unleashed. Like the most complicated horror films, Job and Leviathan are intertwined in consistently surprising ways.[92]

The book of Job also reveals connections to horror narratives in the vision of the world that it presents. As the book begins, Job's life is calm, predictable, and pleasant; he is fenced in by God's protection. But this world is revealed as incomplete, first through the calamities that puncture Job's hermetically sealed universe, and then in the mind-expanding tour of the cosmos on which YHWH takes Job. It's a cosmos that features lonely mountains, raging seas, and a great beast at the heart of the ocean, the terrifying Leviathan. This is the world as it truly is, riddled with danger and uncertainty, full of awe and wonder, but also with terror embedded within.

We'll be returning to Job and the God that this book depicts later on. But first, the next few chapters will take a detour into the haunted corners of the Bible before exploring the monstrous that's closest to home.

NOTES

1. For a more thorough discussion of this film, see my article "Ideas of Motherhood in *Inside*," *Horror Studies* 6.1 (2015): 57–68.

2. Introductions to monster theory can be found in Cohen, "Monster Theory," 3–25; Carroll, *Philosophy of Horror*, 42–52; Asma, *On Monsters*; Gilmore, *Monsters*. An early application of these theories to biblical studies is Timothy Beal, *Religion and Its Monsters* (New York: Routledge, 2002). For an overview of monster theory in biblical studies, see Brandon Grafius, "Text and Terror: Monster Theory and the Hebrew Bible," *CBR* 16.1 (2017): 1–16.

3. For example, Jules Zanger, "A Sympathetic Vibration: Dracula and the Jews," *English Literature in Transition, 1880–1920,* 34.1 (1991): 33–44, explores how anti-Semitic tropes helped to shape the public reception of not only Dracula, but also Jack the Ripper. For a reading of the 1933 film version of *King Kong* as manifesting "the threat of black male sexual predation," see Joshua David Bellin, *Framing Monsters: Fantasy Film and Social Alienation* (Carbondale, IL: Southern Illinois University Press, 2005), 21–47. Asma, *On Monsters*, 231–254; Cohen, "Monster Culture," 7–12, discuss the monster's natural habitat as being at the edge of the community.

4. The reason the poem gives for Grendel's hostilities to the Anglo-Saxons is that he cannot bear to hear the mirth emanating from their mead halls (lines 86–89a); see Ruth Waterhouse, "*Beowulf* as Palimpsest," *Monster Theory: Reading Culture*, ed. Jeffrey Jerome Cohen (Minneapolis: University of Minnesota, 1996), 26–36 (34).

5. David Williams, *Cain and Beowulf: A Study in Secular Allegory* (Toronto: University of Toronto Press, 1982).

6. Brian R. Doak, *The Last of the Rephaim: Conquest and Cataclysm in the Heroic Ages of Ancient Israel* (Boston: Ilex Foundation, 2013), 70–81; Cohen, "Monster Culture," 7.

7. Amy Kalmanofsky, *Terror All Around: The Rhetoric of Horror in the Book of Jeremiah* (LHBOTS 390; London: T&T Clark, 2008), 120–127.

8. Edward J. Ingebretsen has explored the rhetorical monstering of contemporary figures such as Susan Smith and O. J. Simpson in his *At Stake: Monsters and the Rhetoric of Fear in Public Culture* (Chicago: University of Chicago, 2001).

9. Often with either Alfred Hitchcock's *Psycho* (1960) or George Romero's *Night of the Living Dead* and Roman Polanski's *Rosemary's Baby*, both from 1968, as the films that marked the beginning of this new period in horror films.

10. Indeed, I find the monster to be a perfect example of Paul Ricouer's idea of symbols as containing a "surplus of meaning," never reducible to propositional statements. While this idea permeates much of Ricouer's work, it is discussed clearly in *Interpretation Theory: Discourse and the Surplus of Meaning* (Fort Worth: Texas Christian University Press, 1976).

11. Ehud Ben Zvi has explored how a similar phenomenon occurs throughout the Hebrew Bible, where an ethnic Other shares an "in-between area" with the Israelite community, what he refers to as the "mirror grammar" of Othering. Frequently, this is seen in the characters of non-ethnic Israelites who, nevertheless, become part of the community in one way or another. As examples, Ben Zvi cites Jethro, Job, and Ruth, among others. Ehud Ben Zvi, "Othering, Self-

ing, 'Boundarying' and 'Cross-Boundarying' as Interwoven with Socially Shared Memories: Some Observations." Ehud Ben Zvi and Diana V. Edelman, eds. *Imagining the Other and Constructing Israelite Identity in the Early Second Temple Period* (LHBOTS 456; New York: Bloomsbury T&T Clark, 2014), 20–40. The Midianites are a fascinating example of a group who is sometimes seen as part of Israel (Jethro, Moses's wife), and at other times wholly Other (Numbers 25, 31; Judges 6–8). See Grafius, *Reading Phinehas*, 48–61 and notes for a discussion of Midian's shifting depictions in the Hebrew Bible.

12. Wood, *Hollywood*, 101–107. Elsewhere, I have discussed the manner in which Wes Craven's *The Hills Have Eyes* (1978) juxtaposes the monstrous hill family with the supposedly "normal" suburban family, finding the same structures of violent domination present in both family systems. See my *Reading Phinehas, Watching Slashers: Numbers 25 and Horror Theory*, 86–87.

13. While the film was officially directed by Christian Nyby, most scholars agree that producer Howard Hawks was the primary director. John W. Campella Jr.'s 1938 novella *Who Goes There?* is credited as the source material for both films. A strong overview of the themes, cinematic techniques, production history, and reception of *The Thing* can be found in Jez Conolly, *The Thing* (Devil's Advocates; Leighton Buzzard, UK: Auteur, 2013).

14. To my knowledge, the only other mention of this film in the field of biblical studies appears in an essay by Reinier Sonneveld, "Incarnation of Death: Leviathan in the Movies," in *Playing with Leviathan: Interpretation and Reception of Monsters from the Biblical World*, eds. Koert van Bekkum, Jaap Dekker, Henk van de Kamp, and Eric Peels (Leiden: Brill, 2017), 280–296, in a brief (and dismissive) paragraph on 281. Sonneveld's Joseph Campbell-inspired essay finds Leviathan in many films that depict an overwhelming evil, including *Star Wars Episode IV: A New Hope* (the Death Star) and *The Shawshank Redemption* (the prison). This overly broad lens strikes me as being less helpful, as it removes the particularity of the Leviathan myth in biblical and ANE texts and replaces it with any powerful force of evil.

15. For example, Dana B. Polan, "Eros and Syphilization: The Contemporary Horror Film," in *Planks of Reason: Essays on the Horror Film*, ed. Barry Keith Grant (Landham, MD: Scarecrow, 1984): 201–214.

16. Ibid., 202.

17. Leviathan is also referred to as the "twisty serpent" in KTU 1.3 III 41. See discussion of this in Brendon C. Benz, "Yamm as the Personification of Chaos? A Linguistic and Literary Argument for a Case of Mistaken Identity," in *Creation and Chaos: A Reconsideration of Hermann Gunkel's* Chaoskampf *Hypothesis*, eds. JoAnn Scurlock and Richard H. Beal (Winona Lake, IN: Eisenbrauns, 2013), 127–145, esp. 134–136. Similarly, Miller finds a parallel in KTU 1.5 i. 1–4, calling Isaiah 27:1 "the closest thing to a direct quotation from the Ugaritic Ba'al Epic." *The Dragon, the Mountain, and the Nations*, 215. Leviathan has a long life in post-biblical texts as well, including the Apocrypha and rabbinic literature. For discussion of Leviathan's role in this literature, see K. William Whitney, *Two Strange Beasts: Leviathan and Behemoth in Second Temple and Early Rabbinic Judaism* (Winona Lake, IN: Eisenbrauns, 2006); a briefer overview is provided by Michael Mulder, "Leviathan on the Menu of the Messianic Meal: The Use of Various Images of Leviathan in Early Jewish Tradition," in *Playing with Leviathan*, 117–130.

18. Jaap Dekker notes that "Thus far the name Rahab (רַהַב) has not been found in extrabiblical texts" and suggests that this is most likely a specifically Hebrew name for the creatures which are elsewhere known as Tiamat or Yam. See Jaap Dekker, "God and the Dragons in the Book of Isaiah," in *Playing with Leviathan*, 21–39.

19. In the LXX, Heb "Leviathan" is translated as *drakon*, also used for the dragon who appears in Revelation.

20. Henk van de Kemp, "Leviathan and the Monsters in Revelation," in *Playing with Leviathan*, 167–175.

21. J. A. Emerton, "Leviathan and LTN: The Vocalization of the Ugaritic Word for the Dragon," *VT* 32.2 (1982): 328–331; also discussed by Marjo Korpel and Johannes de Moor, "The Leviathan in the Ancient Near East," in *Playing with Leviathan*, 3–20, esp. 7–9.

22. See the surveys in Korpel and de Moor, "The Leviathan in the Ancient Near East," 3–20; and Douglas Frayne, "The Fifth Day of Creation in Ancient Syrian and Neo-Hittite Art,"

in *Creation and Chaos*, 63–97. For a focus on similar motifs as represented in Proto-Indo-European sources, see Robert D. Miller, "Tracking the Dragon Across the Ancient Near East," *ArOr* 82.2 (2014): 225–245 and his monograph *The Dragon, the Mountain, and the Nations: An Old Testament Myth, Its Origins, and Its Afterlives*; EANEC 6 (University Park, PA: Eisenbrauns, 2018), 26–39. Miller argues that this Proto-Indo-European myth was the root of the ANE myths.

23. Miller, *The Dragon, the Mountain, and the Nations*, 67–80, identifies the Hittite myth as the oldest of the dragon-slaying myths. For the dating of the book of Revelation, see, for example, Brian K. Blount, *Revelation* (OTL; Atlanta: WJK, 2009), 8.

24. Gregory Mobley, *Return of the Chaos Monsters: And Other Backstories of the Bible* (Grand Rapids, MI: Eerdmans, 2012).

25. For scholars who accept most of this hypothesis, see, for example, Frank Moore Cross, *Canaanite Myth and Hebrew Epic: Essays in the History of Israelite Religion* (New York: Harvard University Press, 1973); and Bernhard W. Anderson, *Creation Versus Chaos: The Reinterpretation of Mythical Symbolism in the Bible* (New York: Association Press, 1967).

26. Bernard F. Batto, *Slaying the Dragon: Mythmaking in the Biblical Tradition* (Louisville, KY: WJK, 1992). He has offered some helpful qualifications in his more recent essay "The Combat Myth in Israelite Tradition Revisited," in *Creation and Chaos*, 217–236. Rebecca S. Watson, *Chaos Uncreated: A Reassessment of the Theme of "Chaos" in the Hebrew Bible* (BZAW 341; Berlin: de Gruyter, 2005); and David S. Tsumua, *Creation and Destruction: A Reappraisal of* Chaoskampf *Theory* (Winona Lake, IN: Eisenbranus, 2005) both argue that the *Chaoskampf* motif is not present in the Hebrew Bible.

27. Mary K. Wakeman, *God's Battle with the Monster: Study in Biblical Imagery* (Leiden, NL: Brill, 1973).

28. John Day, *God's Conflict with the Dragon and the Sea: Echoes of a Canaanite Myth in the Old Testament* (New York: Cambridge, 1985).

29. Miller, *The Dragon, the Mountain, and the Nations*, 145–156. Miller's work is a significant advancement on Gunkel's theories and should serve as a foundational text on this area for years to come.

30. Karen Sonik, "From Hesiod's *Abyss*," in *Creation and Chaos*, 1–25; esp. 12–18. Sonik distinguishes between "cosmogonic" chaos, which is pre-creation and stands against an ordered creation, and "kratogenic" chaos, which "is to be understood not as external or alien to the cosmos," but a "deeply embedded" element of the cosmos (18).

31. Debra Scoggins Ballentine, *The Conflict Myth and the Biblical Tradition* (New York: Oxford, 2015), 186.

32. Ibid., 187. However, I find the reading of C. L. Crouch, *War and Ethics in the Ancient Near East: Military Violence in Light of Cosmology and History* (BZAW 407; Berlin: de Gruyter, 2009) to be very compelling: enemies of the state are depicted as forces of chaos as a polemical argument in favor of royal power.

33. For example, Ballentine, arguing against applying the category of "chaos" in reference to Tiamat and other monsters, suggests, "While some would consider composite form itself to be indicative of 'chaos,' the biblical cherubim are an excellent counter example because their composite form is typically interpreted positively." *Conflict Myth*, 187. However, I will argue that there is no need to interpret these composite forms positively, just as there is no need to see YHWH as in all instances being on the side of "order" when the text portrays YHWH as unleashing destructive, creation-undoing floods.

34. See, for example, JoAnn Scurlock, *Chaoskampf* Lost—*Chaoskampf* Regained: The Gunkel Hypothesis Revisited," in *Creation and Chaos*, 258–268. Scurlock does not find the connections between the *Enuma Elish*, the Ba'al Cycle, and Genesis 1 to be compelling, noting many differences in the roles of the gods and their actions in the three myths. Most prominently, Scurlock notes that neither Ba'al or Marduk are portrayed as the supreme God, in stark contrast to YHWH's portrayal in Genesis 1. I think this underplays the creativity with which authors of Ancient Israel and the surrounding cultures were able to appropriate, reference, and adapt preexisting material into their own textual creations. The disconnect between Genesis 1 and *Enuma Elish* is argued much more forcefully by Watson (*Chaos Uncreated*) and Tsumura (*Creation and Destruction*, 1–140), but in my view both of them press the evidence far beyond

reasonable bounds. All of Gunkel's proposed similarities have not withstood the weight of several generations of scholarly scrutiny, but that does not mean that the Hebrew Bible betrays no influence of any of these myths whatsoever.

35. Hermann Gunkel, *Creation and Chaos in the Primeval Era and the Eschaton: A Religio-Historical Study of Genesis 1 and Revelation 12*, trans. K. William Whitney, Biblical Resource Series (Grand Rapids, MI: Eerdmans, 2006), 7.

36. Claus Westermann, *Genesis 1–11*, trans. John J. Scullion (Continental Commentaries; Minneapolis: Fortress, 1994) 104–105; see also Richard E. Averbeck, "The Three 'Daughters' of Baʾal and the Transformations of *Chaoskampf* in the Early Chapters of Genesis," in *Creation and Chaos*, 237–256, here 249. However, Averbeck also argues for an expanded presence of the *Chaoskampf* motif in Genesis 3, in which God's "battle" with the serpent in the garden of Eden is analogous to Marduk's battle with Tiamat. As much as I love monsters, I find this a stretch; the clear identification of the "serpent" of Genesis 3 with a land animal, especially one that will go on its belly and eat dust after losing the struggle with the deity (Genesis 3:14), indicates a starkly different character from the watery Tiamat. Apart from the generic terminology of *nahas*, "serpent" or "snake," I see little to connect these two figures, and this lexical similarity is not enough on its own.

37. Kenton L. Sparks, "Enuma Eliš and Priestly Mimesis: Elite Emulation in Nascent Judaism," *JBL* 126 (2007): 625–648, esp. 629–632; Mark S. Smith, *The Priestly Vision of Genesis 1* (Minneapolis, MN: Fortress, 2010): 41–85.

38. Scurlock points out that the Gods in the *Enuma Elish* also create by word, citing IV 19–26; see Scurlock, "Gunkel Hypothesis Revisited," 263. But Marduk's creation is predicated upon the defeat of opposing forces, forces which YHWH is not troubled by in Genesis 1.

39. Miller, *The Dragon, the Mountain, and the Nations*, 156.

40. Chaos in Genesis 1 and related priestly texts will be discussed further in ch. 6 below.

41. Jon L. Levenson, *Creation and the Persistence of Evil: The Jewish Drama of Divine Omnipotence* second ed. (Princeton, NJ: Princeton University Press, 1994).

42. Richard Averbeck notes that *tehom* and the *taninim* in Genesis 1 raise "no challenge to God or his creative work, in "The Three 'Daughters' of Baʿal," 249. As will be discussed in ch. 6 below, several passages in the P source do, in fact, depict this *tehom* as being set free from the bounds established by YHWH and threatening creation. The fact that this happens under YHWH's direction does not provide comfort.

43. Jeffrey Jerome Cohen, "Monster Culture: Seven Theses," *Monster Theory: Reading Culture*, ed. Jeffrey Jerome Cohen (Minneapolis: University of Minnesota, 1996), 3–25, esp. 4–6.

44. While most film buffs are thankful for the sequel *Bride of Frankenstein* (1935), the world could probably have done without *Abbott and Costello Meet Frankenstein* (1948)!

45. Marjo Korpel and Johannes de Moor, "The Leviathan in the Ancient Near East," *Playing with Leviathan*, 1–18, here 17. The authors further discuss incantation bowls, which contain incantations meant to ward off "The Sea, the Leviathan, the Tannin." The authors conclude, "This folk-religion apparently was a remnant of the ancient Canaanite belief that Yam and his monsters had never been defeated in a really conclusive way."

46. Beal, *Religion and Its Monsters*, 13–22. A similar reading can be found in Mobley, *Return of the Chaos Monsters*, 16–33.

47. Beal, *Religion and Its Monsters*, 15. In his article "Mimetic Monsters: The Genesis of Horror in *The Face of the Deep*," Beal has described Genesis as "critical of theological and cultural tendencies to demonize chaos and the monstrous." *Postscripts* 4.1 (2010): 85–93, here 86.

48. Safwat Marzouk, *Egypt as a Monster in the Book of Ezekiel* (FAT II/76; Tübingen, DE: Mohr Siebeck, 2015), 70–114.

49. Ibid., 78–83. This is certainly the reading the Gunkel pursues in his *Chaoskampf* hypothesis.

50. Marzouk, *Egypt as a Monster*, 84.

51. Ibid., 87. Other scholars have found slippage between the categories of self and Other in the Song of Songs (Fiona C. Black, "Beauty or the Beast? The Grotesque Body in The Song of Songs," *BI* 8.3: 302–323) and the Testament of Solomon (Thomas Scott Cason, "Creature

Features: Monstrosity and the Construction of Human Identity in the *Testament of Solomon*," *CBQ* 77.2 (2015): 263–279).

52. In Hebrew, (הַשָּׂטָן). See Pope, *Job*, 10–11, for a brief discussion; a more recent study arguing for the satan as YHWH's "executioner" is Ryan E. Stokes, "Satan, YHWH's Executioner," *JBL* 133.2 (2014): 251–270. C. L. Seow, *Job 1–21: Interpretation and Commentary* (Illuminations: Grand Rapids, MI, Eerdmans, 2013), 271–274, sees the satan as "Israelite monotheism's response to Persian dualism." Seow argues that the satan is the aspect of God's character that doubts humanity's good intentions. For a counterview that sees "the Satan" in Job and Zechariah as largely the same character as found in 1 Chronicles and the Pseudepigrapha (and, by extention, the New Testament), see Dominic Zappia, "Demythologizing the Satan Tradition of Historical-Criticism: A Reevaluation of the Old Testament Portrait of שָׂטָן in Light of Old Testament Pseudepigrapha," *SJOT* 29.1 (2015): 117–134. Zappia goes as far as to suggest that the satan's participation in the divine council is an invention of historical critical scholars. Robert S. Fyall also sees the satan in Job as the same character as is found in the New Testament, though he must read the New Testament backwards into Job in order to accomplish this. While most scholars acknowledge that the satan is not present in Job after the prose prologue, Fyall, attempting to resurrect an idea that was popular in the Middle Ages, finds him in the figure of Leviathan, "the prince of evil." See Robert S. Fyall, *"Now My Eyes Have Seen You": Images of Creation and Evil in the Book of Job* (NSBT 12; Downers Grove, IL: Intervarsity, 2002), 139–174. Zappia and Fyall's proposals have not found much support in the mainstream of biblical scholarship.

53. Gustavo Gutiérrez, *On Job: God-Talk and the Suffering of the Innocent*, trans. Matthew J. O'Connell (Maryknoll, NY: Orbis, 1987), 5–6.

54. The Hebrew is literally ברך, "bless," as in the remarks from Job's wife in 2:9. It is usually thought that this is a euphemism for "curse," as the authors of the Masoretic text were uncomfortable suggesting that God be cursed, even in the mouth of a character who is giving faulty advice. See Tod Linafelt, "The Undecidablity of ברך in the Prologue to Job and Beyond," *BibInt* 4.2 (1996): 154–172.

55. While the book of Job uses several names, I will refer to "Leviathan" in my own discussion for the sake of clarity. While "Rahab" and "the Sea" occur occasionally in Job, the beast of the climactic theophanic speech is referred to by YHWH as "Leviathan." However, as has been discussed above, these are epithets of the same creature.

56. There are some disagreements regarding subdivisions, but this broad structure is uncontroversial. See, for example, David Janzen, *Job* (Interpretation: A Bible Commentary for Teaching and Preaching; Louisville, KY: WJK, 1986), 3–4; David J. A. Clines, *Job 1–20* (WBC 18; Waco, TX: Word, 1988), xxxiv–xxxvii.

57. Fyall, building on the suggestion of Mowinckel, suggests a further reference in Job 28:8, as he argues for the translation of Hebrew שָׁחַל, *shakal*, not as the standard "lion," but instead as "serpent." This is part of Fyall's larger thesis of reading Leviathan as a figure for Satan. I do not find his argument convincing, as it relies on an ahistorical understanding of the concept of Satan as being present in the text of the Hebrew Bible, even if its authors were unaware of his presence.. See Fyall, *"Now My Eyes Have Seen You,"* 152–153.

58. Tiffany Houck-Loomis has explored Job's speech of chs. 6–7 from a psychoanalytic perspective, arguing that Job's anger and frustration is a response to "god-images that oppress and divide in times of crisis." Tiffany Houck-Loomis, "When Fast-Held God Images Fail to Meet Our Needs: A Psychoanalytic Reading of Job Chapters 6 and 7," *Pastoral Psychology* 64.2 (2015): 195–203.

59. David A. Diewert has surveyed the mythological allusions that commentators have found in this text, including *Enuma Elish* 4:1.39–140 and a number of Ugaritic texts. However, Diewert concludes that the most relevant texts for interpreting this passage are the immediate context of Job itself, particularly 7:17. David A. Diewert, "Job 7:12: *Yam, Tannim*, and the Surveillance of Job," *JBL* 106.2 (1987): 203–215. Diewert argues for understanding משמר as "watchtower," indicating a defensive posture rather than an aggressively hostile one. J. Gerald Janzen, in contrast, argues that the language of this passage is much more aggressive, and that the imagery is more closely in line with a siege than with a defensive tower. See J. Gerald Janzen, "Another Look at God's Watch Over Job (7:12)," *JBL* 108.1 (1989): 109–116. Mitchell

Dahood, "Mišmār 'Muzzle' in Job 7:12," *JBL* 80:3 (1961): 270–271, uses Ugaritic and Akkadian texts to argue for understanding this image as God "muzzling" Job. I am inclined to read this passage with shades of all three meanings—God's watch over Job is somewhere between defensive and aggressive, and it causes Job to feel the stifling "muzzling" described by Dahood.

60. Diewert, "Job 7:12," 210–215. And, of course, this question also seems strikingly similar to the Psalmist's question in Psalm 8:5 (ET 8:4), "What are human beings that you are mindful of them, mortals that you care for them?" (NRSV), though Job's feeling of divine persecution seems in direct opposition to the Psalmist's wonder at divine protection. For a reflection on this Psalm's view of humanity, see Gary A. Anderson, "What is Man That Thou Has Mentioned Him?: Psalm 8 and the Nature of the Human Person," *Logos: A Journal of Catholic Thought and Culture* 3.1 (2000): 80–92.

61. For an insightful discussion of the prose prologue's use in a final-form reading of Job, with close attention to differing genres and a strong argument for thematic connections between the prose and poetic sections, see Carol Newsom, *The Book of Job: A Contest of Moral Imaginations* (New York: Oxford University Press, 2003), 32–71. Paul Kang-Kul Cho summarizes perspectives on the relationship between the prose frame and poetic dialogue, and argues for an "older, outer frame" in 1 and 42:11–17, followed by the secondary addition of 2 and 42:7–10 in "The Integrity of Job 1 and 42:11–17," *CBQ* 76.2 (2014): 230–251.

62. Robert Moses, in his essay "'The Satan' in Light of the Creation Theology of the Book of Job," *HBT* 34.1 (2012): 19–34, reads the character of the satan as being an example of the freedom God gives to his creation; each creation has its role, but it also has a large degree of latitude within this role, and is even able to (at times) exceed its prescribed boundaries. As we will see below, this reading is very much in consort with this essay's understanding of the relationship between Job and Leviathan.

63. Kathryn Schiffendecker, *Out of the Whirlwind: Creation Theology in the Book of Job* (HTS 61; Cambridge, MA: Harvard University Press, 2008), 31, n. 22.

64. Of course, whether "Yam" is to be identified with Leviathan is a source of much scholarly debate. For Yam as at least sometimes referencing a mythic foe, see Koert van Bekkum, "'Is Your Rage Against the Rivers, Your Wrath Against the Sea?': Storm-God Imagery in Habakkuk 3," in *Playing with Leviathan*, 55–76; a counter-argument is offered by Benz, "Yamm as the Personification of Chaos?" 127–145, in which he argues that the association between Yam and Leviathan in KTU 1.3 is not as strong as is often supposed; see also Tsumura, *Creation and Destruction*, 49–53; and Watson. I find their arguments to be strong cautions against reading a mythological background for every appearance of *yam*, but I also find the language in Job 38:8–11 (and in other Hebrew Bible passages) to be a clear reference to YHWH's binding of the Sea.

65. Michael Fishbane, "Jeremiah IV 23–26 and Job III 3–13: A Rediscovered Use of the Creation Pattern," *VT* 21.1 (1971): 153–4.

66. The precise identity of these "day-cursers" is elusive. Marvin Pope hypothesizes that these were "magicians who can make a day good or bad by incantations," in *Job: A New Translation with Introduction and Commentary* (AB 18; New York: Doubleday, 1966), 30. David J. A. Clines suggests in *Job 1–20*, 86, that these might have been magicians who were able to cause eclipses, as evidenced by the references to the day being darkened in vv. 4–5.

67. The MT reads: יקבהו אדרי–יום העתידים ערר לויתן. Heb יוֹם (day) is frequently repointed to יָם, "sea." However, this misunderstands the parallel structure of the verse, and also lacks consistency. The 3ms suffix, rendered by the English pronoun "it," must refer to "the day" (or possibly "the night," from vv. 6–7), as "the day" is the subject of this entire lament. The "sea" has not been mentioned to this point, making it difficult to see how these cursers would be cursing a pronoun with no prior referent. Furthermore, the ones who rouse Leviathan are envisioned by Job as being on the side of this day's destruction: If they are rousing Leviathan, presumably they are on the side of the chaotic sea, not cursing it. As David Clines remarks, "Anyone who 'curses' the sea must be on the side of order and goodness, since the sea is a chaotic and evil power." See Clines, *Job 1–20*, 87. Leo Perdue repoints to יָם and understands the phrase as a "subjective genitive," reading "curses of [belonging to] Yam," which better fits the context but is still unnecessary. See Leo Perdue, "Job's Assault on Creation," *HAR* 10

(1986): 295–315, here 311, n. 24. Miller argues for reading "Yam," arguing that one need not understand "rousing Leviathan" as being "the opposite of binding him." *The Dragon, the Mountain, and the Nations*, 221.

68. Perdue, "Job's Assault on Creation," 312, n. 37, cites an Aramaic text from J. A. Montgomery, *Aramaic Incantation Texts from Nipur*, text 2, which offers a curse "with the spell of the sea and the spell of Leviathan the dragon." This seems a possible analogue for Job's "day-cursers."

69. ולא–יראה בעפעפי–שחר. Further discussion of this poetic and unusual phrase will occur below.

70. While Tiamat and Lotan are feminine in the cognate literature, Leviathan is gendered as male in the Hebrew Bible.

71. Gene M. Tucker, "Rain on a Land Where No One Lives," *JBL* 116.1 (1997): 3–17, contrasts this speech with Genesis 1–3, in which humanity is the pinnacle of creation. Instead, he argues that Job 38–41 presents a world in which humans are only one small part of creation. Many scholars have connected Job 38–41 with Psalm 104 as text that depicts the grandeur of creation and decenter humanity in the process. See, for example, William P. Brown, *Seeing the Psalms: A Theology of Metaphor* (Louisville, KY: WJK, 2002), 135–166; Walter Brueggemann, "The Creator Toys With Monster Chaos (Psalm 104)" in *From Whom No Secrets Are Hid: Introducing the Psalms*, ed. Brent A. Strawn (Louisville, KY: WJK, 2014), 56–79; Christian Frevel, "Telling the Secrets of Wisdom: The Use of Psalm 104 in the Book of Job," in *Reading Job Intertextually*, eds. Katherine J. Dell and Will Kynes (LHBOTS; New York: T&T Clark, 2012), 157–168; Ken Stone, *Reading the Hebrew Bible with Animals* (Stanford, CA: Stanford University Press, 2018), 140–163.

72. Scholars have been divided on whether Behemoth and Leviathan are mythical beasts or whether they represent the hippopotamus and the crocodile, respectively. For a thorough argument for the pair as natural beasts, see Samuel Rolles Driver and George Buchanan Gray, *A Critical and Exegetical Commentary on The Book of Job* (ICC; Edinburgh, T&T Clark, 1921), 351–71. For a review of the arguments in favor of them as mythical beasts, see John Day, *God's Conflict with the Dragon and the Sea: Echoes of a Canaanite Myth in the Old Testament* (UCOP 35; Cambridge, MA: Cambridge University Press, 1985), 62–72.

73. Schiffendecker, *Out of the Whirlwind*, 159 and n. 108, which notes the exception of 39:13–18.

74. In both verses, the Hebrew verb עור is used.

75. Many of the versions shift this to third person, causing Leviathan to be the subject. NRSV, for example, translates: "Who can confront it and be safe?" (41:11a, ET).

76. Newsom, *The Book of Job*, 251.

77. Schiffendecker, *Out of the Whirlwind*, 178–179.

78. Isaiah 8:22 employs three separate terms for darkness or gloom: מעוף, חשך, and אפל.

79. Brown, *Seeing the Psalms*, 210.

80. Also of potential interest is Isaiah 14:12, in which the king of Babylon is taunted as "Day Star, son of Dawn." Most likely, this is a mocking reference to the Babylon king's supposed divine status, which seems unsustainable in light of the defeat of Babylon by the Persian armies. Norman C. Habel, *Job: A Commentary* (OTL; Louisville, KY: WJK, 1985), 109, for example, writes that "The eyelids of the dawn . . . may conceal a mythological allusion to Shachar," citing Isaiah 14:12.

81. Seow, *Job 1–21*, 354. See also Seow's discussion of the precise meaning of the term "עפעפי," which he takes to refer specifically to "eyes in their sockets," noting that tears flow from the עפעפי in Jeremiah 9:17 (ET 9:18), 353. Clines also understands עפעפי to refer to eyes rather than eyelids.

82. David J. A. Clines, *Job 38–42* (WBC 18b; Grand Rapids, MI: Zondervan, 2015), 1196.

83. Ibid.

84. Habel, *Job*, 572.

85. Schiffendecker, *Out of the Whirlwind*, 181.

86. John G. Gammie, "Behemoth and Leviathan: On the Didactic and Theological Significance of Job 40:15–41:26," in *Israelite Wisdom: Theological and Literary Essays in Honor of*

Samuel Terrien, ed. John G. Gammie, Walter A. Brueggemann, W. Lee Humphreys, and James M. Ward (Missoula, MT: Scholars Press, 1978), 217–231, here 224.

87. Ibid. Similarly, Habel sees both Behemoth and Leviathan as points of comparison for Job, but argues that the text's purpose in making this comparison is to demonstrate that YHWH can control Behemoth, Leviathan, and Job. Writing of Behemoth, Habel says, "Behemoth, The Beast, is the symbol of those chaotic and threatening forces which God created at the beginning and which need to be kept subjugated. Perhaps Job should see himself as a similar threat." *Job*, 559. While I agree with Habel's observation that these passages make an implicit comparison, I suggest that Habel underestimates the freedom that YHWH continues to grant Leviathan, and by extension Job, and the admiration YHWH holds for both of them.

88. Pope, *Job*, 278–279.

89. Jon Levenson, *Creation and the Persistence of Evil*, 17.

90. In his commentary on Job, Tremper Longman III argues that this phrase refers only to Job's responses to YHWH, which Longman reads as submissive. In this way, Longman is able to read Job's theology as being much less in conflict with other strands of the Hebrew Bible. I find this to be a strained case of special pleading; there is no indication in the text that YHWH's praise is confined to two short statements of Job's. See Longman, *Job* (Baker Commentary on the Old Testament and Wisdom; Grand Rapids, MI: Baker, 2012), 458–460.

91. For such readings, see, for example, Schiffendecker, *Out of the Whirlwind*, 186–188; Janzen, *Job*, 225–269; Longman, *Job*, 451–456, 462; Michael V. Fox, "The Meanings of the Book of Job," *JBL* 137.1 (2018): 7–18.

92. Jordan Peele's provocative film *Us* was released just as I was revising this chapter, too late for inclusion. But it deserves serious discussion in regards to the questions of the boundary between the self and the monster.

Chapter Three

Hauntings of the Hebrew Bible

Young Simón tells his mother about a game he has been playing with his friends. They hide something, then leave a trail of clues for Simón to follow; each clue is an item out of place, leading Simón back to the item's original place, where he is presented with another out of place item. First, Simón's collection of coins has been replaced with his baby teeth. Simón and his mother open the drawer where the baby teeth had been kept, and find they have been replaced with sand from the garden. Eventually, this trail leads to the papers Simón's parents have kept hidden from him, which reveal both that he was adopted, and that he was born HIV positive. The "friends" who set up this game turn out to have been the ghosts of the children who inhabited this house several generations ago, when it was an orphanage.

The 2007 Spanish film *The Orphanage* chronicles the story of Simón, his mother, and these ghostly children. These children met a tragic fate many years ago, as they were poisoned by one of the orphanage workers. So they linger on in the place of their death as presences that are not malevolent but are longing for companionship and a mother. This narrative reveals several key elements of ghost stories, elements that repeat through the long tradition of ghosts. The ghosts are the bearers of uncomfortable truths, bringing knowledge from the past that the present would prefer to deny. And with this knowledge comes a demand for justice, a justice that was denied in the ghost's lifetime. These themes will recur both in the history of ghost stories, and in the haunted spaces of the Hebrew Bible.

THE PAST'S CLAIM FOR JUSTICE

The ghost story is, most likely, almost as old as stories themselves. While the popularity of ghost stories has ebbed and flowed over the course of time, they are attested across a vast spectrum of time, space, and cultures.[1] Like their spectral subjects, these stories keep returning. As P. G. Maxwell-Stuart notes, while the modern concept of life as "essentially materialistic" is a relatively recent development, the idea of ghosts may be the understanding of the connection between life and death "with the longest uninterrupted history of acceptance."[2] Maxwell-Stuart continues:

> Societies from very ancient times to modern have also had in common the notion that in some sense their dead form a community which is an extension of the living. They inhabit, as it were, a separate but connected country which the living may glimpse from time to time through the medium of individual and often familiar visitors: a mirror existence whose laws, customs, and modes of behavior are disturbingly like ours.[3]

While normally separate realms, humans have long been fascinated by the times when the barriers between these worlds become more porous, if only for a brief time. For in these times of rupture, we get a glimpse into what the world beyond our world might look like, what our deaths might hold, and how we might contextualize the meaning of our own lives.[4]

As cinema developed as an art form, the ghost story tagged along with it. *The Uninvited* (1944) is frequently considered to be the first film to take the idea of ghosts seriously, and it is often thought to stand at the head of a long line of films that explore paranormal hauntings.[5] In the latter part of the twentieth century, the form had been mostly dormant in popular cinema until the surprising success of *The Blair Witch Project* and *The Sixth Sense* (both 1999), two low-budget films that found enormous audiences and ushered in a resurgence in ghost films.[6]

Throughout the history of ghost films, consistent patterns have reoccurred with great enough frequency to allow us to speak of common themes, and to try to determine the nature of ghosts, at least as depicted in horror films. First, we note that the ghost is rooted in the past, and in an inability to move on from that past. As described by Colin Davis, "The dead return because their business on earth is not over."[7] In *The Sixth Sense*, each of the ghosts has something undone in their life that they need accomplished before they can be at rest; young Christopher, the boy who sees dead people, finds his peace in his ability to help these souls. In *The Others*, the ghostly family is unable to process the traumatic events that led to their deaths. Similarly, in *Mama*, the maternal ghost refuses to come to terms with the death of her infant. In Guillermo del Toro's powerful film *The Devil's Backbone*, in which the ghost story intertwines with a narrative concerning the Spanish Civil War, the narrator describes a ghost as "like an insect trapped in amber," stuck in the past.

Frequently, this relationship with the past causes the film's narrative to incorporate elements of the detective story in that the protagonist is required to uncover the buried secrets and unresolved traumas that have led to the ghost's persistent presence.[8] *Stir of Echoes* provides a perfect example of this formula, as does the American remake of *The Ring*.[9] The ghost serves as a persistent reminder of the past, which still lingers as an "echo" in the present.[10] In this way, the ghost simultaneously embodies both presence and absence. In recent decades, "haunting" has become a well-used metaphor in many disciplines for the ways in which the past influences the present, and the ways in which absence can still function as a lingering presence.[11]

In recent Hollywood films, the ghostly presence is frequently female.[12] In her discussion on female ghosts, using *The Woman in Black* as a test case, Robin Roberts notes several ways in which the female ghost can have different implications from her male counterpart.[13] Frequently, these narratives build the initial trauma around the experience of female disempowerment, in which the female ghost's past involves her unjust treatment at the hands of a patriarchal world. The ghost of *The Woman in Black* was an unwed mother who had her baby taken from her; a similar trauma lurks behind the ghost of *Mama*. In *Lights Out*, a young woman is diagnosed with mental illness and subjected to horrifying abuse in a psychiatric institution. But as ghosts, these mistreated women are able to reclaim their power, exerting control over the narratives' (frequently male) protagonists, as well as the narrative itself. Roberts' remarks on the Woman in Black serve to describe these other female ghosts as well: "The Woman in Black presents an alternative women's way of knowing, educates male characters into this subversive perspective, takes control of the narrative, and enacts justice on her own terms."[14] These female ghosts are destabilizing forces, offering a critique of patriarchal values and challenging the injustices of the past. Female ghosts bring a salient feature of hauntings to the foreground: in a wide variety of narratives, from a wide variety of origins, the ghost has a claim for justice on the present. The ghost represents a person (or idea) to whom justice was denied in the past; they are now making their claim for justice on the present. Like the children in *The Orphanage*, the Woman in Black was a vulnerable figure to whom justice was denied in life. But in the ghost story, justice delayed is not necessarily justice denied. The demand for justice endures, generation after generation.

It took Jacques Derrida to get philosophy and other disciplines in the humanities to take ghosts seriously. Derrida's *Specters of Marx* introduced the term *hauntology* into the scholarly discourse,[15] and, starting from the observation that the very first phrase of Karl Marx and Friedrich Engels's *The Communist Manifesto* offers a reference to the "specter of communism" that haunts Europe, unravels ideas of ghosts as a way to more deeply understand the historical relationship between communism and capitalism. Derrida explores the word *revenant*, literally meaning "one who returns," finding in this etymology the key to understanding the nature of the ghost.[16] But while the ghost continually returns, it is also continually and simultaneously present and absent, it remains "beyond the phenomenon or beyond being."[17] The specter is "visible-invisible," both seen and unseen, yet it is always the one who sees before it is seen; it's continual returning is "to pay us a visit," to see us.[18] In this continual returning, the ghosts stands in the place of broken time.[19] Martin Hagglund describes Derrida's project as being the creation of a "hauntology" as opposed to an "ontology;"[20] hauntology is a philosophy rooted not in existence and presence, but in absence. Mark Fisher unravels Derrida's conception of the ghost as traveling in "two directions:" "The first refers to that which is (in actuality is) *no longer*, but which is still effective as a virtuality. . . . The second refers to that which (in actuality) has *not yet* happened, but which is *already* effective in the virtual."[21] The ghost is simultaneously present and absent, simultaneously already past and not yet arrived. For the ghost, time is most severely out of joint; instead of being linear, time is circular and constantly overlapping.

Given Derrida's career-long exploration of the undecidable, unfinalizability, and repetition of all types, the ghost seems like an obvious figure for the philosopher to wrestle with.[22] In his concept of the trace,[23] Derrida describes the ways in which something—a being, a concept, a definition—makes itself present even in (or especially by) its absence. Building on the linguistic structuralism of Ferdinand de Saussure, Derrida starts from the proposition that words are meaningless in and of themselves; they only have meaning when interpreted within a system of signs. Derrida pushes this further: if meaning is entirely contextual, then a word (or sign) does not have meaning in itself; meaning is endlessly "deferred." (This is, to use Derrida's neologism, the concept of *différance*, a word which combines the French for "differ" and "defer.") For Derrida, this indicates that each concept contains its own negation, a trace of its opposite. This is not accidental, but the fundamental situation of language. The trace is the ghost that haunts language.

Perhaps the most Derridean of ghost films is the 2017 film *A Ghost Story*. Far from a horror story, and featuring hardly any narrative movement, the film serves as an extended meditation on ghosts, grief, and time. It is hauntology structured as (barely) narrative film. After the protagonist's death (Casey Affleck, referred to as "C" in the credits), he lingers as a ghost, first watching his partner's grief in the house they shared together, then observing as she moves out and a new family moves in. Soon, it becomes apparent that he is tied to this location,[24] but that his experience of time has been exploded. He witnesses the future, but then he is suddenly standing on the same spot of ground as settlers wander past in covered wagons, long before his house was built.[25] C. is primarily an observer, and is only able to interact with objects after experiencing further trauma; this seems to require a great deal of concentration and effort on his part. (We primarily see this in his dishes-shattering rage at the new family who has moved into the house he still regards as his.)

Eventually, C. observes himself when he was alive, and we realize that unexplained noises heard during the first part of the film, while C. was still alive, were actually caused by C.'s ghost. In the film's conclusion, C. finds a long-hidden note that his partner had left behind, reads it (the contents are never shared with the spectators), then disappears. Whatever was in the note was enough for the ghost to resolve his trauma. The unwillingness to share the note's contents with the spectator—giving us the knowledge that C.'s conflict has been resolved, but leaving unfinalized the means of resolution—is far from the only aspect of this film that is in concert with Derrida's discussions of ghosts and specters.

In this portrayal of C.'s ghost, we see an exploration of several elements of Derrida's discussions in *The Specters of Marx*. Most obviously, C.'s ghost experiences time in a nonlinear fashion; he is rooted in a singular place while time moves around. For C., time is most definitely out of joint, as his ghostly form even returns to the time when he was alive, standing over his own life as a silent observer. And this is the point in the film where Derrida's discussion of the ghost as observer becomes most poignant. Earlier in the film, before C's death, the couple hears a loud crash from their living room and notices the cover of their piano has been slammed down. It is not until this incident is replayed, from C.'s perspective as a ghost, that the audience perceives this act as an effort to communicate. The ghost interacts with the world in an attempt to communicate, but the living characters are unable to interpret these signs. Any impact he makes on the world comes at the cost of extreme effort and seems to take an inordinate amount of time. For example, R. brings home a new date, and C. wordlessly observes as they say goodnight to each other. Clearly upset at his partner's attempts to build a new relationship, C. focuses intensely, and lightbulbs start to shatter, then books fly off the shelves. However, as the books fall to the ground, the camera cuts to R. picking them up, dressed in different clothing, in full daylight. It is unclear how much time has elapsed between C.'s anger and the response, but it was at least overnight.[26]

In *A Ghost Story*, we see how the figure of the ghost becomes a vehicle for an exploration of the relationship between trauma, space, and time and engages with a discourse of spectatorship and presence. All of these elements will come into play as we read several figures of the Hebrew Bible with this understanding of ghosts: the character of Samuel, and the Other gods that Israel continually finds itself drawn back to.

THE GHOST OF SAMUEL (THE CHARACTER) AND THE GHOSTS OF SAMUEL (THE BOOK)

David Jobling has found *The Specters of Marx* to be a useful intertext for reading 1 Samuel.[27] This section of Jobling's wonderfully unusual commentary begins with a quote from Martin Buber: "Something has been attempted, but it has failed."[28] For Jobling, this sums up Derrida's view of Western culture's relationship to Marx: we were promised justice, but the project did not succeed. "This hoped-for future . . . is also perhaps a lost past," Jobling remarks.[29] This promise of justice is what continues to haunt our culture, long after the fall of the Soviet Union. Similarly, Jobling finds that 1 Samuel is haunted by the failure of the monarchy. Israel is haunted by "the egalitarian ideal," which should have come to fruit after Israel reached the promised land.[30] Jobling concludes: "The specter of Marx is the specter of Samuel, for Samuel stands for the very biblical past that produced Marx, and Derrida's reading of him." In Jobling's reading, 1 Samuel is haunted by the lost past, and by its uncertain future.

Building off Jobling's work, this section will look at both the metaphorical ghosts that haunt Samuel and the more literal ones. In addition, bringing Derrida into conversation with not only the biblical text but also with the tradition of ghost narratives will allow us to explore other avenues of haunting.

As JoAnn Scurlock has documented exhaustively, Israel's neighbors in Assyria and elsewhere in ancient Mesopotamia understood many of their experiences as hauntings. Inscriptions found in Nineveh describe rituals for cases where a person repeatedly sees the spirit of someone who met an unfortunate end, such as someone who was "killed with a weapon (and) abandoned in the steppe," burned to death, or drowned.[31] These ghosts might cause physical afflictions (mental illness, lockjaw, depression, headaches), or behave in ways that are more recognizable to a modern Western audience as a haunting.[32] Scurlock dates most of these texts to the late eighth to early seventh century BCE; certainly by this time, Assyria had a highly developed construction of ghosts and the various manners in which they could interact with the living.[33]

The Hebrew Bible itself demonstrates more than a passing knowledge of ghosts. As evidenced by the prohibitions against necromancy and mediums in Deuteronomy and the Deuteronomistic History (DtrH), the idea that the ancestors lingered in our world as spirit presences, who could impact humans for good or for ill, became a part of Israelite religion at some point.[34] While some scholars maintain that these influences are not native to Yahwistic traditions, and likely entered Judean culture during the postexilic era,[35] others have argued that necromancy and related practices were present in Judean religion from its onset, and only became the target of polemics in eighth century and later texts.[36] Esther Hamori reads the evidence as strongly suggesting that belief in the spirits of the dead is a native tradition of Israel, present in multiple layers of the biblical text. Hamori sees in these tendencies to ascribe a belief in ghosts to foreign influence the lingering "outdated theories of religion ... according to which 'magic' was defined negatively in contrast to 'religion'."[37] Instead, Hamori argues that we should understand these texts as attempting to shape normative Israelite religious practices according to the desires of their authors. Rather than describing the practices that currently existed within Israelite religion, these texts are polemical attempts to argue for a shift away from these practices.

The Hebrew word that most closely translates to "ghost" is אוב (*'ob*).[38] The root is usually understood to mean "a hollow sound" or a "chirping."[39] Scholars have also been tantalized by the possible connection between Hebrew אוב and Arabic *'wb*, meaning "come back,"[40] similar to the French conception of the *revenant*. The term is frequently found in parallelism with אוב is ידענים (*yada'nim*), "a knowing one," although the distinction in meaning between the terms is not immediately clear. Theodore Lewis and Ann Jeffers see the terms as roughly synonymous.[41] Hamori, however, makes an astute observation: "While we cannot be certain based on the data available, it is conceivable, for instance, that אוב refers to a spirit of the dead, and ידענים refers to a knowledgeable spirit, but not one of a dead person. People might inquire of אבות or ידענים, but a necromancer (בעלת–אוב, *ba'alat 'ob*) divines by an אוב (as Saul specifically requests)."[42]

In exploring why King Saul specifically sought a "female necromancer,"[43] Hamori notes that necromancy, and the accompanying belief in ghosts, was "as common a type of divination in Israel as it was among its neighbors."[44] However, Hamori cautions against reading too much into these texts concerning specific practices, as there is an inherent "difficulty of deriving historical evidence about diviners from these narratives,"[45] due to their setting in the distant past. It is difficult to say, for example, whether the author of Samuel is describing necromantic practices and belief in ghosts that were prevalent in his own times, imagining what might have been popular in Israel's past, or inventing this encounter with Samuel's ghost as a curious detail to enliven this historical narrative. But regardless of the historical reality of Israel's relationship with ghosts, Samuel exists as a haunting presence throughout the book that bears his name.

The ghost of Samuel haunts the book of 1 Samuel, literally when his ghost is contacted by Saul through a medium in 1 Sam 28, and figuratively through the rest of the book. While Samuel is only the main character of the narrative in 1 Sam 3, he hovers as a presence over the rest of the book, even (perhaps especially!) after his death. Even the names of these two books indicate Samuel's haunting, as Samuel dies in ch. 25, but the second book still bears his name. He continues to hover over this narrative in his absence.

Samuel appears most clearly as a ghost in 1 Samuel 28. Samuel's death is narrated as a brief note in the beginning of chapter 25.[46] At this stage in the narrative, Saul is increasingly losing his grip on both his kingship and his sanity.[47] Verse 28:3 repeats 25:1, with only a few differences in wording, reminding us of Samuel's death to introduce this new narrative, in which Saul becomes even more desperate. Here, the focus shifts from David to Saul, and we are introduced to the idea of ghosts with the narrator's brief note that "Saul had sent away the mediums and the spiritualists from the land."[48] But when the Philistine army starts massing in preparation for an assault on Israel, Saul gets nervous. His first response, in v. 6, is to ask YHWH for advice; however, YHWH does not answer, "by dreams, or by Urim,[49] or by prophets." Having already rejected Saul as king, YHWH now offers only silence in response to Saul's request. Saul's next response is to ask his servants to find a medium whom he may consult.

Saul is directed to a medium in Endor,[50] and he "disguises" himself with "other garments" to visit her. He takes only a small group of two men and visits her by night; everything about this visit indicates a covert action, one that Saul knows is not acceptable. But the desperate king persists regardless. Saul is so desperate for help that, in response to the medium's concerns for her safety, Saul swears an oath to YHWH that she will not be punished for providing assistance (28:10). When she finally agrees to help, Saul immediately asks for her to summon the ghost of Samuel.[51]

Through the course of this encounter, Samuel exhibits several characteristics that connect him with the ghosts we are familiar with from more contemporary horror narratives. He is a figure of fear; he can see Saul, but he cannot be seen; he is a marker of both presence and absence; and he is a bringer of knowledge. Most importantly, the knowledge that Samuel offers is a knowledge of the past, knowledge that Saul already knows but wishes were untrue.

Most obviously, Samuel inspires fear. It is an emotion that permeates this passage. Saul first becomes "afraid" (ירה, *yarah*), and his "heart trembles greatly" in 28:5, when he sees the Philistine army gathering.[52] When the medium recognizes Saul, she responds with a cry of fear (28:12–13). Upon first being made aware of Samuel's presence, Saul falls on the ground in a gesture of humility. But by the end of the encounter, Saul's mood has turned to terror (1 Samuel 28:20). Saul's fear is ostensibly because of the words of Samuel. But Samuel has delivered equally harsh words to Saul elsewhere in the text, and Saul's response is never described as one of fear. This suggests that Samuel's words alone are not the cause of Saul's fear.

Fear has played a part in earlier passages of 1 Samuel.[53] Earlier in the narrative, Samuel introduces Saul to the people, with instructions to serve the king and fear the Lord (12:14, 24). The Philistines have also been an object of fear in other places in 1 Samuel, as the people are described as being "afraid" of them in 7:7, and both Saul and the people are "afraid" of them in

17:11. The people's fear arises from the sight of the Philistine Goliath, specifically, in 17:24. But perhaps the most instructive comparison is with 18:12 and 29, in which Saul is "afraid" of David. In these passages, David has just defeated Goliath and has become the hero of the people for his exploits in battle. More importantly, Saul recognizes that "YHWH was with him [David] but had turned aside from Saul" (18:12), and that "YHWH was with David" (18:29). In both cases, Saul is not afraid of David himself, but afraid of the favor of YHWH that David had found. David does not do or say anything to instill fear in Saul; Saul is responding to the favor of YHWH, which has left Saul and fallen on David. Saul seems to recognize this in David's very presence, not in any actions or words of David. We see this most clearly in 18:13, when Saul responds to his fear of David by pushing David away from him. Saul makes David a commander of his army just to get him out of his courtroom. Saul is terrified by David's presence—or, more precisely, by what David represents: Saul's loss of YHWH's favor, and the predicted loss of his kingship.

Samuel's ghost does not tell Saul anything he has not heard before. Samuel has consistently given Saul the message that he has lost YHWH's favor due to his actions or inactions, including when Saul proceeds with an offering on his own rather than waiting for Samuel (13:8–14), and when Saul disobeys YHWH's instructions (given through Samuel) and does not execute king Agag after the Israelite's war with the Philistines (15:1–34). In both instances, Saul receives word from Samuel that YHWH has withdrawn YHWH's favor, and that Saul's kingship will come to a premature end. The narrative does not record Saul's response after Samuel's first accusation; after the second, Saul is grieved and attempts to repent. Twice, Saul asks for forgiveness and for Samuel to go with him, "so that I may worship YHWH" (15:25, 30). Samuel agrees to "turn back with Saul," and Saul worships YHWH as he had asked. Saul seems to believe (or at least hope) that this act of repentance was accepted; after worshipping with Samuel, the pericope ends with king and prophet each going their separate ways, Samuel to Ramah and Saul to Gilead. It is only in the end of this chapter, and the beginning of the next, that the omniscient narrator reveals to the reader, and eventually to Samuel, that YHWH "regretted" (נחם *naham*, in the *niphal*) that YHWH had made Saul king.[54] The next chapter narrates the account of YHWH and Samuel identifying David as the next king, a decision regarding which Saul is left out of. It is only after David has killed Goliath, and Saul understands that "YHWH was with David," not the king, that Saul is "afraid" of David. Saul's fear arises once he realizes that his repentance was not successful and that YHWH's verdict has not been reversed.

Similarly, when Saul is confronted with the ghost of Samuel, there is a hope that Samuel will offer a different word to him. Saul, facing the rising Philistine army, first inquires of YHWH (28:6), but receives no answer. So

Saul turns to the medium to raise Samuel. "I am in great distress, since the Philistines are fighting against me, and God has turned away from me (סר, *sur*) and will not answer me anymore" (28:15). Saul understands that YHWH has turned from him, but he hopes that he will receive a different word from Samuel, that the prophet will be able to bring a word from beyond the grave instead of the silence that Saul hears from YHWH. Samuel dashes Saul's hopes with the brutal honesty readers have come to expect from this prophet, stating directly that YHWH's turning away from Saul is not accidental, but is a direct result of YHWH's continued anger at the king. Samuel is incredulous that Saul has not already understood this message: "Why are you asking me?" Samuel says (28:16). Samuel repeats the phrase of Saul: "YHWH has turned (סר) from you." But then Samuel adds an additional piece of information: "and he is your enemy." The ghost of Samuel is able to state directly what Saul is afraid of but hopes will not be true. While Saul is still hoping there is another explanation for YHWH's silence, or a pathway for the king to escape from this silence, Samuel's ghost confirms Saul's greatest fear. YHWH's judgment has been rendered, and there is no turning away from it. YHWH is Saul's enemy. Saul has no words in response to this verdict. He is only able to fall on the ground in fear.

This fear is not a result of Samuel's ghostly presence directly, but of the confirmation of Saul's preexisting fear. The ghost itself is not the object of fear, but a messenger bringing a fearful verdict. Saul still held out hope that his acts of contrition were sufficient to change his fate, but the ghost of Samuel affirms Saul's greatest fear. For Saul, there is no end to his story other than tragedy. On some level, Saul understands that time is out of joint for Samuel, just as it was for C. in *A Ghost Story*. While Saul initially hopes that this out-of-jointedness could give him a different answer to his plight, perhaps allowing Samuel to see to a time when Saul has regained YHWH's favor, Samuel's response makes it clear to Saul that nothing will change, and that time is not the remedy Saul hoped for. After Saul's confrontation with the ghost of Samuel, Saul collapses into fear because he realizes that there is no remedy.

As the narrative of 1 Samuel has progressed, Saul is increasingly unable or unwilling to accept that the kingship has been taken from him by YHWH to be passed on to David as YHWH's new favored one. Saul becomes a ghost himself, lingering in this world and refusing to move on. Saul can only see himself as the hero of this story; he is only able to imagine himself as the story's subject. When he realizes he has been reduced to a supporting role in David's drama, he resists, gradually turning into a ghost of himself. But rather than being a ghostly presence like Samuel, Saul's presence is more like that of Malcom in *The Sixth Sense,* or Grace in *The Others*, unable to acknowledge the trauma of their own death. [55]

In his discussion of Derrida, Freud, and *The Sixth Sense*, Christopher Peterson attempts to unravel why Malcolm's status as a ghost is such a surprise to this character, and to the audience as well. When young Cole pronounces, "I see dead people," it does not occur to Malcolm, or to most spectators, that one of the dead people to whom he is referring is Malcolm himself. Because both we and Malcolm are spectators, Peterson suggests, we "witness the realm of the dead from a position of absolute safety and security." Peterson continues, "Spectatorship confirms our imagined self-presence in direct contrast to the mortality of others."[56] In this reading, because we are seeing, and we know we are seeing, we cannot be the ghost. However, we misunderstand the nature of the specter in assuming that the realm of the dead can be witnessed from a position of safety; as Derrida has explored, it is actually the dead who see everything, and the living whose perspective is most limited. Whether it is the lack of justice in their own lives, or the uncomfortable realities that characters in the present do not want to acknowledge, the dead are aware of truths that escape the living. Saul is finally forced to confront his own limited perspective as the Philistine army achieves their victory, routing the Israelite army and killing Saul's sons (31:1–2). Faced with the hopelessness of his situation, Saul opts to commit suicide, officially becoming one of the ghosts that will haunt the second book of Samuel.

GHOSTS OF THE OTHER GODS

While less direct than the ghost of Samuel, another ghostly presence haunts the landscape of the Hebrew Bible, and the religion of ancient Israel more generally. Even though indirect, this presence is more pervasive, spanning centuries, geographical locations, and textual traditions. Throughout the Hebrew Bible, the people are haunted by the ghosts of the other gods, non-Yahwistic forces who have a strange existence somewhere between reality and non-reality, who exist as shades and traces throughout the texts of the Hebrew Bible and as a part of YHWH.

Two of the main Hebrew terms for ghosts were discussed briefly above; however, another term, אלהים, (*elohim*) also appears on occasion to mean "spirits," as in 1 Samuel 28 and Isaiah 8:19.[57] This is the same word that means "gods" in general, and is sometimes used to refer to YHWH in particular.[58] Joseph Blenkinsopp explains: "This is not so surprising in view of the fact that in antiquity the boundary between the divine and human was for the most part fluid and permeable, and some texts give the impression that the dead formed a kind of buffer zone between the worlds of the human and the divine."[59] So conceptually for the ancient Israelites, the boundaries between gods and ghosts were thin indeed.

In one of Isaiah's polemics against necromancy, the prophet provides a list of whom the Egyptians will consult in vain: "They will consult their gods, and their shades, their ghosts and their wise spirits" (19:3). While the MT reads אלילים (*elihim*, idols) for the word I have translated as "gods," Theodore Lewis and Christopher Hays make a compelling case for an original *vorlage* of אלהים.[60] There are four nouns in this passage; three of them (אטים, אבנת, and ידענים) clearly refer to spirits of the dead. The first, אלהים, refers to the gods of Egypt. Grouping these nouns together in this way indicates that for Israel's conceptual worldview, the gods of the foreign nations and the ghosts of the dead were very similar concepts, seemingly with substantial overlap.

Karel van der Toorn discusses this boundary in relation to Old Babylonian religious practices. He notes that "the dead were conceived of as gods," as evidenced by the references to the "moment of death . . . as the point at which his or her gods would call on him or her to join them."[61] Continuing with a comparative reading of a Neo-Assyrian religious, which refers to the dead as "the gods that dwell in the underworld," Toorn remarks, "Hence the ghosts of one's parents can be referred to as the 'god of the father' and the 'goddess of the mother'."[62] When the ancestors die, they enter the realm of the gods. There is a large amount of overlap between conceptions of divine beings and spirits of the dead.

One passage in the Hebrew Bible specifically describes the *elohim* (here referring to gods) as being mortal, hence capable of dying. Psalm 82 presents a brief scene of God (referred to only as אלהים, elohim in vv. 1 and 8[63]) in the divine court, speaking to the lesser gods (confusingly, also referred to as אלהים; elohim in v. 6).[64] God tells the council members, "I say, you are heavenly beings (אלהים), all of you children of the most high; however, like mortals you will die, and like any prince you will fall" (vv. 6–7). According to this psalm, these "other gods," the אלהים, were living beings once, not mere idols made by human hands as claimed by other texts.[65] But like any other living being, they live, and they die.[66] However, their presence in the biblical text does not end with Psalm 82; they continue to follow the Israelites through the wilderness, through the monarchic period, and into the Babylonian exile. Throughout the Hebrew Bible, Israel is haunted by the ghosts of these other gods.

The text of Deuteronomy is consumed with fear that the people will follow other gods (אלהים אחרים, *elohim acherim*). While the decalogue begins with the prohibitions against following other gods, this is not enough; the fear of the people following other gods returns again and again throughout Moses's speech, a recurring nightmare from which the Deuteronomist cannot seem to wake up. Deuteronomy 6:14 warns the people not to "go after other gods, any of the gods of the people who surround you," and 11:16 provides the lurid admonition against being "seduced" (פתה, *patah*) into serving other gods.⁶⁷ In 13:7 (v. 6 ET), the threat is much closer to home, as the Mosaic speaker worries about the listener's brother, son, daughter, or even the "wife of your bosom" (אשת חיקך, *eshet heyqekah*) attempting to entice them into the worship of another god. This is not a discourse that exudes security about YHWH's status among the people.

And seemingly with good reason, as the people of Israel continually stumble into the worship of other gods. The book of Judges provides an excellent case study in this tendency; many of the stories follow the same pattern of the people of Israel worshipping another god, YHWH responding by giving them into the hands of an enemy nation, then sending a judge to deliver them after they cry out to YHWH. The cycle continues, however, as the people invariably forget YHWH and resume their idol worship.⁶⁸ Apparently, the only way they can be rescued from idol worship is by fighting against their neighbors.⁶⁹

Seldom is any reason given for Israel's addiction to the other gods, other than that they forget YHWH. Judges 2:11, for example, tells the reader laconically, "Then the sons of Israel did what was evil in the eyes of YHWH and worshipped the Ba'als."⁷⁰ If YHWH is "the God of their fathers" and the one "who brought them out of Egypt" (Judges 2:12⁷¹), the other gods don't seem to have anything to offer. Regardless, the Israelites continually return to worshipping them. And the other gods continually return to the people of Israel.

The book of Ezekiel offers a possible answer to this conundrum. While much of the biblical tradition views the Israelites' time in Egypt as a time of bondage, from which they were delivered by YHWH, Ezekiel offers a "revisionist history"⁷² of this time, particularly in chs. 20 and 23. This is most clear in chapter 23, the disturbing story of two sisters, Oholah and Oholibah, clearly meant to depict the Southern and Northern kingdoms of Israel.⁷³ YHWH narrates to Ezekiel a story of two sisters who "prostituted" (from זנה, *zonah*⁷⁴) themselves throughout their relationship with YHWH, first in Egypt (23:3). Egypt was not a time when the Israelites were victimized by an unjust power structure, but a time when they had turned away from YHWH to worship other gods.⁷⁵ According to Ezekiel's reading of Israelite history, there has never been a time when the people were faithful to YHWH. For Ezekiel, the glorified Exodus, when YHWH brought the people out of Egypt to worship him, did not exist, for the people were worshipping the gods of Egypt from the beginning.⁷⁶

And as they fled across the desert landscape, the ghosts of the other gods continued to haunt the people. They have barely escaped from the Egyptians when Aaron leads them into making golden calves, idols for new gods (Exodus 32).⁷⁷ They meet these foreign gods again in Numbers 25, when the Israelites are seduced into the worship of the Ba'al of Peor.⁷⁸ And the other gods come back with a vengeance in Deuteronomy, with passage after passage referring to the overwhelming anxiety that the people will return to worshipping these gods.

Much of the Hebrew Bible tries to depict exclusive worship of YHWH as the normative state of Israelite religion; worship of other gods is an apostasy that has, at times, taken the Israelite community away from this normative state. But the reality seems to have been far different. Instead of following YHWH after Moses's encounter with the burning bush in Midian (Exodus 3–4), the lived experience of Israel included worship of Ba'al, Asherah, and other gods, frequently in combination with worship of YHWH.[79] Indeed, as Mark Smith and others have documented, the conception seems to have developed through a process of borrowing the characteristics of other gods, gradually incorporating them into the figure of YHWH.[80] YHWH's very being is haunted by the ghosts of the other gods.

While the text tries to deny this, the reality keeps seeping through in the persistent reminders of the other gods. They hover over the text as a reminder that the people's history is more complicated than the straightforward narrative that the biblical text presents, and that the past continues to have an influence over the present. The other gods do not disappear, but continue to haunt the narratives through their unsuccessful repression.

Although YHWH imagines the death of the other gods in Psalm 82, they continue to come back, haunting the Israelite people throughout the wilderness landscape, during the monarchic periods, and beyond. This is not a ghost that leaves the people alone, but one that seems to be living in the very foundation of Israel's house. Wherever Israel is, the other gods move along with them and are waiting for them.

Derrida saw a world that was mourning the promise of justice, a reality which did not exist in the past, but which could nevertheless be felt as an absence in the present. We see this process of mourning recurring throughout ghost stories, mourning in which the past can never be reconciled because it continually imposes itself upon the present. Like C. in *A Ghost Story*, the biblical writers remember a past that never was and try to bring the present closer to this vision of a reality in which Israel is devoted to YHWH totally and completely. But through all of their efforts, they can only cause a small ripple in the present, a slamming down of the piano lid or a scattering of books.

Like the unburied past of ghost stories, the other gods are the dread that underlies so many of the biblical texts. The vision of an Israel who worshipped the one God, YHWH, was always accompanied by the fear that this was not Israel's past and not a true representation of its present. Israel tries to move into the promised future, but finds itself haunted by the ghosts of the other gods, gods who do not exist, but nevertheless continually make themselves known throughout the Hebrew Bible. The other gods bring with them the knowledge of a past that cannot be forgotten.

NOTES

1. An introduction to the study of ghost stories as folklore can be found in "Introduction: Old Spirits in New Bottles," in *Haunting Experiences: Ghosts in Contemporary Folklore*, eds. Diane E. Goldstein, Sylvia Ann Grider, and Jeannie Banks Thomas (Logan, UT: Utah State University Press, 2007), 1–22. In her survey of the ghost story traditions of the Hudson Valley, Judith Richardson notes the difficulty in determining their source: the responsibility for the stories and their underlying traditions might "fall heavily on the Dutch; they also land on Native and African Americans. Others single out Germans as primary sources of regional ghostlore. Still others have pointed at the invading New Englanders as the most prone to superstition, while similar credit or blame has fallen on later arriving immigrants." *Possessions: The History and Uses of Haunting in the Hudson Valley* (Cambridge, MA: Harvard, 2003), 31. As an example of non-Western traditions of ghosts and spirits, see the introduction to Japanese ghost stories in Komatsu Kazuhiko, *An Introduction to Yōkai Culture: Monsters, Ghosts, and Outsiders in Japanese History*, trans. Hiroko Yoda and Matt Alt (Tokyo: Japan Publishing Industry Foundation for Culture, 2017).
2. P. G. Maxwell-Stuart, *Ghosts: A History of Phantoms, Ghouls & Other Spirits of the Dead* (Gloucestershire, UK: Tempus Publishing Limited, 2006), 9.
3. Maxwell-Stuart, *Ghosts*, 11.
4. Leo Braudy in *Haunted* correlates the rise of belief in ghosts with the Reformation, which attempted to stamp out folk religions but had the effect of making the "Protestant individual . . . more vulnerable to the blandishments of the devil and his diabolic minions, at the same time that potentially benevolent presences like good witches and angels had also been banished," 48.
5. My own article, "*Mama* and Kristeva: Matricide in the Horror Film," *Post Script: Essays in Literature and Film* 36.1 (2017): 52–64, offers an overview of the ghost story in cinema, with a particular focus on ghostly mothers. Michael Walker, in *Modern Ghost Melodramas: What Lies Beneath* (Film Culture in Translation; Amsterdam: Amsterdam University Press, 2017), argues for the ghost story's generic connection with the melodrama, focusing on the family histories involved in ghost stories. Walker views *The Uninvited* as still participating in the comedic ghost stories of early Hollywood: "it ultimately mocks its scary ghost, as if uneasy about taking ghosts too seriously" (12). Instead, Walker suggests that *The Innocents* (1961) and *The Haunting* (1963) were "the first genuinely frightening English language ghost movies" (12). I would suggest that this distinction is too arbitrary; while *The Uninvited* does have a comedic strain, particularly in the climax when the ghost is finally dispelled by the protagonists' decision to laugh at it, there is still much of *The Uninvited* that is akin to more modern haunted house narratives. Walker's main distinction in identifying melodramatic ghost stories is that these are stories "where the ghost is not monstrous," but is instead an object of sympathy or identification (14), a distinction that can be useful in reading ghost stories if not pursued too rigidly. However, many movies complicate this dichotomy; I argue, for example, that the titular ghost of *Mama* is both monstrous and sympathetic at the same time.
6. Many critics also included the Japanese film *Ringu* in this group, particularly after its American remake *The Ring* (2002), but Daniel Martin convincingly argues that these efforts place *Ringu* within the mainstream of Western filmmaking. As a result, scholarly analysis that places this film in conversation with American ghost films have "little to do with its original Japanese context." Martin explores the critical reception of *Ringu* in the UK, arguing that critics and scholars tended to align it with *The Blair Witch Project* and *The Sixth Sense* as an example of restrained horror, in direct opposition to the more explicit gore of Wes Craven's *Scream* (1996). Martin argues that this focuses on a Western ideal of "art cinema" vs. popular cinema, but *Ringu* (and its sequels) are positioned differently within Japanese culture—in their Japanese context, the *Ringu* books and films are hugely popular, with the ghostly Sadako's image appearing on backpacks and lunch boxes. See Daniel Martin, *Extreme Asia: The Rise of Cult Cinema From the Far East* (Edinburgh: Edinburgh University Press, 2017), 22–40. Martin's essay does not attempt to place *Ringu* into dialogue with the long history of ghost stories in Japanese folklore and their appearances in film, particularly female ghosts, a filmic tradition that extends back at least as far as Masaki Kobayaski's 1964 *Kwaidan* and Kaneto Shindô's

1968 *Kuroneko* (*Black Cat*). (And while not a horror film, Kenji Mizoguchi's 1953 *Ugetsu Monogatari* employs the trope as well.) For an engagement with this history, see Elisabeth Scherer's article "Well-Travelled Female Avengers: The Transcultural Potential of Japanese Ghosts," in *Ghost Movies in Southeast Asia and Beyond: Narratives, Cultural Contexts, Audiences*, ed. Peter J. Bräunlein and Andrea Lauser (Leiden, NL: Brill, 2016), 61–82. See also Mitsuyo Wada-Marciano, "J-horror: New Media's Impact on Contemporary Japanese Horror Cinema," in *Horror to the Extreme: Changing Boundaries and Asian Cinema*, ed. Jinhee Choi and Mitsuyo-Wada Marciano (Aberdeen, UK: Hong Kong University Press, 2009), 15–38. David Kalat, *J-Horror: The Definitive Guide to* The Ring, The Grudge, *and Beyond* (New York: Vertical, 2007) is a knowledgeable introduction to the genre. Valerie Wee, *Japanese Horror Films and Their American Remakes: Translating Fear, Adapting Culture* (Routledge Advances in Film Series 27; New York: Routledge, 2014), reads the Japanese films together with their American counterparts as an interesting way of discussing how the ghost story traditions of the two cultures have developed and diverged. Blake, *Wounds of Nations*, 44–68, reads *Ringu* as being about "the spirit of subaltern vengeance," as Japanese culture wrestles with the traumatic legacy of World War II.

7. Colin Davis, "The Skeptical Ghost: Alejandro Amenábar's *The Others* and the Return of the Dead," in *Popular Ghosts: The Haunted Spaces of Everyday Culture*, ed. María del Pilar Blanco and Esther Peeren (New York: Continuum, 2010), 64–75, here 67.

8. In this, the ghost story is a particular example of what Noël Carroll refers to as the "complex discovery plot," in which horror movies are closely related to the detective story in their quest to uncover a buried mystery; Carroll, *Philosophy of Horror*, 99–118. Leo Braudy takes a slightly different approach, placing the rationality of the detective story (as epitomized by Arthur Conan Doyle's Sherlock Holmes stories) against the supernatural aspects of horror narratives in *Haunted*, 141–178. While Braudy's contrast of rational vs. supernatural is well-noted, I still find Caroll's description more helpful, as the horror narrative in general, and the ghost story in particular, frequently forces the protagonists to employ their reasoning skills in an attempt to understand nonrational events. Michael Cook's monograph *Detective Fiction and the Ghost Story* (London: Palgrave Macmillan, 2014) also makes this connection, though he uses Detective Fiction as his starting point. See also Allison Jack's essay "Tartan Noir and Sacred Scripture: The Bible as Artefact and Metanarrative in Peter May's *Lewis Trilogy*," in *The Bible in Crime Fiction and Drama: Murderous Texts*, ed. Caroline Blyth and Alison Jack (LHBOTS 678/STr 16; London: T&T Clark, 2018), 29–40. Jack describes these Irish detective novels as having "the Gospel narrative acting as a 'ghost story'" behind them (36).

9. In the Japanese film, little of the ghost's backstory is given in the first film, but is instead reserved for the sequel. Even in this sequel, the information regarding Sadako's past is presented in a much more streamlined, factual manner, without the detective narrative that is so prominent in the American remake.

10. One might think of William Faulkner's oft-quoted line from *Requiem for a Nun* (New York: Randon House, 1951), 73, viewing the past itself as a haunted, undead presence: "The past is never dead. It isn't even past."

11. Denise Kimber Buell opens her essay on Hauntology's potential for biblical studies by asking, "what doesn't sound sexier when described as 'haunting'?": "Hauntology Meets Posthumanism: Some Payoffs for Biblical Studies," in *The Bible and Posthumanism*, ed. Jennifer L. Koosed (Sem St. 74; Atlanta: SBL, 2014), 29–56, here 29; Martin O'Kane, "The Flight Into Egypt: Icon of Refuge for the H(a)unted," in *Borders, Boundaries, and the Bible*, ed. Martin O'Kane (JSOTSup 313; London: Sheffield Academic Press, 2002), 15–60, makes reference to the exiles as being haunted by the memories and love of their homeland (60), but is primarily concerned with the depiction of the Exodus event in visual art, making less of the idea of "haunting" than the title might lead the reader to believe. The metaphor of haunting has become particularly common in the field of sociology and education; see, for example, Avery F. Gordon, *Ghostly Matters: Haunting and the Sociological Imagination* (Minneapolis: University of Minnesota, 1997); Barbara Regenspan, *Haunting and the Educational Imagination* (Boston: Sense, 2014).

12. While examples abound, they include such films as *The Woman in Black*, *Mama*, *Crimson Peak*, and *Lights Out* (2016).

13. Robin Roberts, *Subversive Spirits: The Female Ghost in British and American Popular Culture* (Jackson: University of Mississippi Press, 2018), 41–62. Roberts's study analyzes the novel as well as the theatrical and filmic adaptations of *The Woman in Black*.

14. Ibid., 61–62.

15. Jacques Derrida, *Specters of Marx: The State of the Debt, the Work of Mourning, and the New International*, trans. Peggy Kamuf (New York: Routledge, 1994; French orig. 1993).

16. Derrida, *Specters*, 5, 10.

17. Ibid., 125.

18. Ibid.

19. Throughout *The Specters of Marx*, Derrida returns to a quotation from Hamlet: "Time is out of joint." It is in this "out of joint"-ness that the ghost lives. Ernesto Laclau's article, "Time Is Out of Joint," *Diacritics* 25.2 (1995): 85–96, views this phrase as a key to Derrida's conception of justice and politics.

20. Mark Hagglund, *Radical Atheism: Derrida and the Time of Life* (Redwood City, CA: Stanford University Press, 2008), 82. In the original French, "ontology" (the philosophy of existence) and "hauntology" (the philosophy of absence, perhaps?) would be virtual homonyms. Although in true Derridean style, this is less of an adversarial relationship, and more of an indication that the two concepts include one another. "Hauntology" contains more than a slight trace of "ontology," as the concept of "haunting" becomes, for Derrida, a way to think through what it means to exist. See also Mark Fisher's discussion of hauntology in *Ghosts of My Life: Writings on Depression, Hauntology and Lost Futures* (Winchester, UK: Zero Books, 2014).

21. Mark Fisher, "What Is Hauntology?" *Film Quarterly* 66.1 (2012): 16–24, here 19. Much of Fisher's article discusses the movement in postmodern electronic music known as hauntology, which has its roots in Derrida's theories of presence and absence; for more on connections between film, television, music, and hauntology, see Isabella van Elferen, *Gothic Music: The Sounds of the Uncanny* (Cardiff, UK: Wales University Press, 2012), 73–99; Jessica Balanzategui's article "Haunted Nostalgia and the Aesthetics of Technological Decay: Hauntology and Super 8 in *Sinister*," *Horror Studies* 7.2 (2016): 235–251, explores both the hauntology-inspired score of the film and makes aesthetic connections with the film's use of decayed, damaged, and broken Super 8 movies. All of the essays in this issue of *Horror Studies* explore the use of sound in horror films.

22. A decade before *The Specters of Marx*, Derrida discussed ghosts and the medium of film in an interview for Ken McMullen's 1983 film *Ghost Dance*. Further reflections on Derrida's connections between ghosts and cinema can be found in Antoine de Baecque and Thierry Jousse, "Cinema and Its Ghosts: An Interview with Jacques Derrida," *Discourse: Journal For Theoretical Studies in Media and Culture* 37.1/2 (2015): 22–39; in the same issue, see Timothy Holland, "Ses Fantômes: The Traces of Derrida's Cinema," 40–62.

23. While Derrida is notorious for refusing to offer a clear definition of his concepts, his early work, *Of Grammatology*, trans. Gayatri Chakravorty Spivak (Baltimore: John Hopkins University Press, 1976; French orig. 1967), is the starting point for much of his thinking see, for example, 61–65. See also the foundational work Jacques Derrida, *Writing and Difference*, trans. Alan Bass (Chicago: University of Chicago Press, 1978; French orig. 1968), 196–231.

24. Haunted places, though closely linked to the spirits that haunt them, will be the subject of the next chapter.

25. This "out-of-jointness" has been explored in somewhat more popularized fashion by Mike Flanagan in his recent Netflix series *The Haunting of Hill House*, particularly in the figure of the "bent-neck lady."

26. The film's explorations of time are frequently explored through cutting, or lack of cuts, where they might be expected. In a painful early scene, R. receives a pie from her sister; she begins to eat, then collapses on the kitchen floor, eating the entire pie through sobs. This scene lasts over four minutes without a cut, as C.'s ghostly figure observes her, motionless and speechless. Scenes such as this, in which cinematic time is elongated, serve as the counterpoint to scenes like the one described above in which a quick cut disguises a large and undetermined passage of time.

27. David Jobling, *1 Samuel* (Berit Olam; Collegeville, MN: Liturgical Press, 1998), 273–281.

28. Jobling, *1 Samuel*, 273; quoting Martin Buber, *Kingship of God*, trans. Richard Scheimann (New York: Harper & Row, 1967), 83.

29. Jobling, *1 Samuel*, 275.

30. Jobling, *1 Samuel*, 278.

31. Reference in JoAnn Scurlock, *Magico-Medical Means of Treating Ghost-Induced Illnesses in Ancient Mesopotamia* (Ancient Magic and Divination III; Leiden, NL: Brill, 2006), 5.

32. Scurlock's chapter on the symptoms of ghostly affliction provides an extremely helpful overview of these various types of hauntings in *Magico-Medical Means*, 5–20.

33. A further discussion on the conceptualization of ghosts in ancient Mesopotamia is found in Christopher B. Hays, *A Covenant with Death: Death in the Iron Age II and Its Rhetorical Uses in Proto-Isaiah* (Grand Rapids, MI: Eerdmans, 2015), 34–56.

34. Joseph Blenkinsopp argues that Deuteronomy demonstrates a polemic against the "cult of the dead." See "Deuteronomy and the Politics of Postmortem Existence," in *Treasures Old and New: Essays in the Theology of the Pentateuch* (Grand Rapids, MI: Eerdmans, 2004), 175–191. Blenkinsopp writes, "in a society like ancient Israel, organized according to kinship relations, the passage to statehood necessitates transferring allegiance from the kingship network to the state" (176). This seems at odds with the explanations discussed in the next footnote, which posit a later introduction through neighboring religions of conceptions of the spirit world.

35. Brian B. Schmidt, *Israel's Beneficent Dead: Ancestor Cult and Necromancy in Ancient Israelite Religion and Tradition* (Winona Lake, IN: Eisenbrauns, 1994). Schmidt summarizes his findings: "Belief in the dead's supernatural beneficence was nonexistent throughout most, if not all, of the pre-exilic religious histories of Israel and Judah" (275). He continues: "That belief was a late foreign introduction motivated in part by the combination of prolonged social crises, the failure of traditional religion, and intensive contact with other cultures." Elsewhere in this monograph (165–201), Schimdt argues, *contra* Blenkinsopp, that ancestor cults were not a particular concern of Deuteronomy. Using the DtrH as a further example, Schmidt argues that "ancestor worship or veneration" was not a very common feature of Israelite religion, as is often presumed by scholars. If so, "we would have expected them or their corresponding rituals to show up in the DtrH as the object of dtr polemic," instead of having only a handful of narratives (1 Samuel 28:3–25; 2 Kings 21:6; 23:24) that mention this as a problem. Schmidt's insistence on associating necromancy with foreignness is sometimes problematic, and, one suspects, seems to indicate an apologetic tendency on the part of the author; see, for example, Schmidt's claim that the medium of En-Dor is a Canaanite in his essay "The 'Witch' of En-Dor, 1 Samuel 28, and Ancient Near Eastern Necromancy," in *Magic and Ritual in the Ancient World*, eds. Paul Mirecki and Marvin Meyer (Religions in the Graeco-Roman World 129; Leiden, NL: Brill, 2015), 109–129.

36. Christopher B. Hays detects the influence of Assyrian religion in the text he terms "proto-Isaiah," though he views necromancy as an "indigenous Judean practice." See *A Covenant with Death*, especially 353–359 (quote from 357). Hays argues that these influences are pervasive enough, and the references treated as unremarkable enough, to indicate that Isaiah expected his audience to recognize these references, challenging whether they would have been viewed as "foreign."

37. Esther J. Hamori, "The Prophet and the Necromancer: Women's Divination for Kings," *JBL* 132.4 (2013): 827–843, here 827. In this outdated theory that Hamori describes, anything described as being "correct" religion by the biblical text is assumed to be normative for Israelite religion, whereas practices criticized by the text are considered to be both nonnormative practices of Israelite religion, and also as being representative of "magic" rather than "religion."

38. For example, Leviticus 19:31; 20:6; Deuteronomy 18:11; Isaiah 8:19; 19:3; 29:4. See Esther J. Hamori, *Women's Divination in Biblical Literature: Prophecy, Necromancy, and Other Arts of Knowledge* (AYBRL; New Haven, CT: Yale University Press, 2015), 107–108. Christopher B. Hays and Joel LeMon trace this word back to its Egyptian etymology in "The Dead and Their Images: An Egyptian Etymology for Hebrew ʾôb," *Journal of Ancient Egyptian Interconnection* 1 (2009): 1–4.

39. BDB, 15. Hamori, *Women's Divination*, 175–176, discusses several passages that connect the spirits of the dead to birds, frequently by using this idea of "chirping." For this motif in the broader context of Mesopotamian conceptions of the dead, see Hays, *Covenant with Death*, 46–47.

40. First proposed by William F. Albright, *Archaeology and the Religion of Israel* (Garden City, NY: Doubleday, 1969), 202, n. 32. Schmidt, *Israel's Beneficent Dead*, 151, prefers this connection, translating אוב as "the One-who-returns." Guillermo del Toro would approve.

41. Theodore J. Lewis, *Cults of the Dead in Ancient Israel and Ugarit* (HSM 39; Atlanta: Scholars Press, 1989), 114; Ann Jeffers, *Magic and Divination in Ancient Palestine and Syria* (Studies in the History and Culture of the Ancient Near East 8; Leiden, NL: Brill, 1996), 172.

42. Hamori, *Women's Divination*, 109–110.

43. A necromancer, בעלת אוב, "master of ghosts," not a "witch," מכשפה, as she is frequently called. See Hamori, *Women's Divination*, 105–107, as well as Hamori, "Prophet and Necromancer," 830–831.

44. Hamori, *Women's Divination*, 118. She surmises that the specific request for a "female necromancer" on the part of Saul is likely "a stereotype in the mind of a culturally distant author."

45. Hamori, *Women's Divination*, 117. She continues, parenthetically, "(For example, does the story indicate that necromancy was a common practice? Or that a later author thought it had been in Saul's time? Or that it happened but looked nothing like this? And so on.)" Furthermore, Hamori uses this lens to interrogate whether the necromancer's identity as female was based on historical connections between women and these kind of divinatory arts, suggesting that this connection is also tenuous. "The same issues hold for the matter of Saul's specific request for a female necromancer. Were necromancers more likely to be female? Or was the idea of a female medium out in the sticks a picture in the mind of an urban, scholarly author?" (117). Attempting to glean historical knowledge from this narrative seems similar to making conclusions regarding rural American folk practices of relating to the dead based on Lance Henrikson's visit to the mountain witch in *Pumpkinhead*, clearly the product of stereotypes of rural folklore rather than a depiction of actual folk practices.

46. The opening of 25:1 reads: "Then Samuel died, and all of Israel gathered and lamented for him. They buried him at his home in Ramah."

47. Many scholars have explored Saul as a tragic figure; for example, W. Lee Humphreys, *The Tragic Vision and the Hebrew Tradition* (OBT 18; Philadelphia: Fortress, 1985), 23–42; David Jobling, *1 Samuel* (Berit Olam; Collegeville, MN: Liturgical Press, 1998).

48. Divination involving contact with ghosts is prohibited in several texts, including Leviticus 19:31; 20:6, 27; Deuteronomy 18:10–11. Mordechai Cogan suggests that "The very fact that such practices could produce reliable results made them dangerous from the biblical point of view," in "The Road to En-Dor," in *Pomegranates and Golden Bels: Studies in Biblical, Jewish, and Near Eastern Ritual, Law, and Literature in Honor of Jacob Milgrom*, eds. David P. Wright, David Noel Freedman, and Avi Hurvitz (Winona Lake, IN: Eisenbrauns, 1995), 319–326.

49. On the Urim and Thummim, Suzanne Boorer, *Vision of the Priestly Narrative: Its Genre and Hermeneutics of Time* (AIL 27; Atlanta: SBL, 2016), 344, remarks: "Little is known about the Urim and Thummim beyond the fact that reference to them occurs in early texts such as Deut 33:8 (in relation to the Levites) and 1 Sam 14:41–42 (and see 1 Sam 28:6), where they are associated with discerning the divine decisions." Boorer sees the presence of these items on the priestly breastplate (Exodus 28:30) as indicating "that as high priests he mediates between the people and YHWH, indeed as clothed in this way he represents the place where the Israelites and YHWH meet" (353). See also Robert Kugler, "Urim and Thummim," *NIDB* 5:719–721.

50. While this study focuses on the ghostly figure of Samuel, several recent studies have emphasized the role of the unnamed female medium. April D. Westbrook views this as one of several "Woman Stories" in the books of Samuel, each occurring at a juncture where male power and the institution of the kingship is questioned; see *"And He Will Take Your Daughters . . .": Woman Story and the Ethical Evaluation of the Monarchy in the David Narrative* (LHBOTS 610; New York: Bloomsbury T&T Clark, 2015), 80–83. Esther J. Hamori sees her as the primary source of authority in this narrative: "In the En-Dor story, interpreters tend to

give divinatory credit disproportionately to Samuel. The text, however, does not," in "The Prophet and the Necromancer: Women's Divination for Kings," *JBL* 132.4 (2013): 827–843, here 832–33; on female divination more generally, see Hamori, *Women's Divination*. Similarly, the female medium has long been an important figure in horror narratives, most recently in the *Insidious* and *Conjuring* series. Maja Pandzic explores the power and agency of the female characters in *Insidious*, including medium Eloise, in "Female 'Madness' as the Driving Force in the *Insidious* Film Series," *Outskirts* 35 (2016): 1–20.

51. Samuel is described with the term *elohim*, which generally means "divine being," but is often used to refer to God or gods. See below for more discussion of this term in relation to ghosts.

52. The Hebrew contains a pun between Saul *seeing* (*vayarih*) the Philistines and *fearing* (*vayirah*) them. The roots ראה and ירה are homophonous in several forms.

53. This is not to imply that 1 Samuel is unique in this regard. Fear is a common trope in Hebrew Bible texts, usually fear of the enemy or fear of YHWH. See Zoltán Schwáb, "Is Fear of the Lord the Source of Wisdom, or Vice Versa?" *VT* 63 (2013): 652–662 for an exploration of the phrase "Fear of YHWH" in Wisdom literature, and an overview of the debate regarding whether knowledge is dependent upon the fear of YHWH, or vice versa. Daniel Castello, "The Fear of the Lord as Theological Method," *JTI* 2.1 (2008): 147–160, argues for the fear of YHWH was an underappreciated theological concept, threaded through all layers of the biblical tradition.

54. A fascinating recent article on YHWH's "regret" is by Rachelle Gilmour, "Saul's Rejection and the Obscene Underside of the Law," *Bible and Critical Theory* 15.1 (2019): 34–45. Gilmour makes use of Slavoj Žižek to argue that Saul's actual failing is in *not* living up to the description of the king in 1 Samuel 8. Whereas both Saul and David break the covenant, Saul also violates the law's "unspoken supplement."

55. Aviva Breifel, "What Some Ghosts Don't Know: Spectral Incognizance and the Horror Film," *Narrative* 17.1 (2009): 95–110 uses the phrase "spectral incognizance" to refer to the subgenre of ghost stories in which the ghosts refuse to acknowledge their deaths, including *The Sixth Sense* and *The Others*.

56. Christopher Peterson, "Derrida's Ouija Board," *Qui Parle* 17.2 (2009): 85–101, here 85–86. Susan Bruce explores the similar phenomenon of "misrepresentation" in *The Others*, though without the explicit use of Derrida in Susan Bruce, "Sympathy For the Dead: (G)hosts, Hostilities, and Mediums in Alejandro Amenábar's *The Others* and Postmortem Photography," *Discourse* 27.2/3 (2005): 21–40.

57. Numbers 25:2 is a likely addition to this list. The Moabites invite the Israelites to sacrifice to their אלהים; the parallel account in Psalm 106:28–31 describes the Israelites as eating sacrifices to the מתים, the dead.

58. Also relevant is Psalm 8:5, in which humanity is a "little lower than the אלהים," which is frequently translated as "angels" (KJV), "heavenly beings" (NET; compare LXX αγγελος), or "God" (NRSV).

59. Blenkinsopp, *Treasures*, 177.

60. Most compellingly, the LXX reads τοὺς θεούς, a phrase which the LXX never uses to translate אלהים. See Lewis, *Cults of the Dead*, 133; Hays, *Covenant with Death*, 281–282, n. 349.

61. Karel van der Toorn, *Family Religion in Babylonia, Ugarit, and Israel: Continuity and Change in the Forms of Religious Life* (Leiden, NL: Brill, 1996), 57.

62. Ibid., 58.

63. For an overview of Elohim within the psalter, see Terrance R. Wardlaw, Jr., *Elohim Within the Psalms: Petitioning the Creator to Order Chaos in Oral-Derived Literature* (LHBOTS 602; New York: Bloomsbury T&T Clark, 2015). The question of how the Elohistic psalter has contributed to the shaping of the book of Psalms is a vexing one, with a variety of proposals having been put forward over the years without finding widespread acceptance. See, for example, Laura Joffe, "The Answer to the Meaning of Life, the Universe, and the Elohistic Psalter," *JSOT* 27.2 (2002): 223–235; Joel S. Burnett, "Forty-Two Songs for Elohim: An Ancient Near Eastern Organizing Principle in the Shaping of the Elohistic Psalter," *JSOT* 31.1 (2006): 81–101.

64. The concept of a divine council is common in ANE literature and shows up occasionally in the Hebrew Bible, for example in Job 1–2. A classic introduction to the divine council is E. Theodore Mullen, *Assembly of the Gods: Divine Council in Canaanite and Early Hebrew Literature* (HSM 24; Chico, CA: Scholars Press, 1980); see also Patrick D. Miller, "Cosmology and World Order in the Old Testament: The Divine Council as Cosmic-Political Symbol," *HBT* 9.2 (1987): 53–78; Michael S. Heiser, "Co-regency in Ancient Israel's Divine Council as the Conceptual Backdrop to Ancient Jewish Binitarian Monotheism," *BBR* 26.2 (2016): 195–225.

65. See, for example, Deuteronomy 4:28; Isaiah 2:20, 31:7, 37:19; Jeremiah 10:5; Psalm 115:4, 135:15.

66. This point is explored in full by Peter Machinist, "How Gods Die, Biblical and Otherwise: A Problem of Cosmic Restructuring," in *Reconsidering the Concept of Revolutionary Monotheism*, ed. Beate Pongratz-Leisten (Winona Lake, IN: Eisenbrauns, 2011), 230. See also Mark S. Smith, *Where the Gods Are: Spatial Dimensions of Anthropomorphism in the Biblical World* (AYBRL; New Haven, CT: Yale University Press, 2016), 49.

67. This is the same root used in the legal texts describing the penalties for premarital sex, which may or may not constitute rape, in Exodus 22:16, or the sinners who seek to waylay the seeker of wisdom in Proverbs 1:10.

68. Among the many scholars who see the basic structure of much of Judges as being a structure of repetition, see Dennis Olson, "The Book of Judges," pages 721–888 in *The New Interpreter's Bible*, vol. 2 (Nashville: Abingdon, 1998).

69. Uriah Y. Kim, "Postcolonial Criticism: Who Is the Other in the Book of Judges?" in *Judges & Method: New Approaches in Biblical Studies*, second ed. (Minneapolis, MN: Fortress, 2007), 161–182.

70. A similar refrain of Israel "doing what was evil in the eyes of YHWH" recurs in Judges 3:7, 12 (here without specifically naming idolatry as "the evil"); 4:1, 6:1 (again without naming idolatry); 10:6, and 13:1 (without idolatry).

71. Of course, both of these descriptions of YHWH are common throughout the Hebrew Bible, which makes it all the more puzzling that the people are unable to remember these basic facts.

72. Marzouk, *Egypt as a Monster*, 125. Marzouk's full reading of these passages is found on 125–145.

73. This passage has been much discussed in recent decades, due largely to its misogynistic overtones and explicit depictions of sexual violence. Athayla Brenner, for example, has referred to this passage (along with Ezekiel 16 and several others) as "pornoprophetic" for the way it sexualizes violence against women. See Athalya Brenner, "On 'Jeremiah' and the Poetics of (Prophetic?) Pornography," in *On Gendering Texts: Female and Male Voices in the Hebrew Bible*, eds. Athalya Brenner and Fokkelien van Dijk-Hemmes (Leiden, NL: Brill, 1993), 177–93. A similar approach has been adopted by Renita Weems, *Battered Love: Marriage, Sex, and Violence in the Hebrew Prophets* (OBT; Minneapolis, MN: Fortress, 1995), 58–64; Weems argues, powerfully, that Ezekiel 16 and 23 collapse the voice of God and husband into a singular figure of authority, emphasizing the right of the male to use violence for control. Gail Yee agrees with these criitques and seeks to add a colonialist critique in *Poor Banished Children of Eve: Women as Evil in the Hebrew Bible* (Minneapolis, MN: Fortress, 2003), 111–134. For a thoughtful evangelical response to these critiques, see Andrew Sloane, "Aberrant Textuality? The Case of Ezekiel the (Porno) Prophet," *Tyndale Bulletin* 59.1 (2008): 53–76. Sharon Moughtin-Mumby, *Sexual and Marriage Metaphors in* Hosea, Jeremiah, Isaiah, *and* Ezekiel (Oxford Theological Monographs; New York: Oxford University Press, 2008), 156–205, also has an interesting discussion, which seeks to disentangle this passage from what she considers to be incorrect associations with the "marriage metaphor" described in texts such as Hosea, Isaiah, and Jeremiah 2:1–4. Amy Kalmanofsky reads Oholah and Oholibah as examples of "dangerous sisters," paired women with the power to disrupt the dominant narrative within the Hebrew Bible in *Dangerous Sisters of the Hebrew Bible* (Minneapolis, MN: Fortress, 2014), 53–68.

74. See the overview of this root in *TDOT* 4:99–104; *TLOT* 1:388–390 for brief discussions of its frequent use to connote idolatry, especially in passages of J, H, and prophetic texts.

75. Brad Kelle, *Ezekiel: A Commentary in the Wesleyan Tradition* (New Beacon Bible Commentary; Kansas City, MO: Beacon Hill Press, 2013), 232.

76. Jacqueline E. Lapsley, *Can These Bones Live?: The Problem of the Moral Self in the Book of Ezekiel* (BZAW 301; Berlin: de Gruyter, 2000), 126–129, makes the point that Israel's dynamic of remembering/forgetting operates on several levels in the book of Ezekiel. The people remember what they should have forgotten (how to live in sin) and forget what they should remember (how to live in relationship with YHWH).

77. See Mark S. Smith, who argues that this passage is a southern polemic against northern religious practices, taking Yahwistic worship of a different manner and portraying it as idolatry. The golden calves of Exodus 32 and the bull in I Kings 12:28–29 seem likely to have been part of Yahwistic worship, but in a non-Deuteronomistic approved fashion. See Smith, *Where the Gods Are*, 58–68.

78. This passage was the subject of my previous book; see Grafius, *Reading Phinehas, Watching Slashers*.

79. See Mark S. Smith, *The Early History of God: Yahweh and the Other Deities in Ancient Israel*, second ed. (Grand Rapids, MI: Eerdmans, 2002).

80. Mark S. Smith, *God in Translation: Deities in Cross-Cultural Discourse in the Biblical World*. (FAT 57; Tübingen, DE: Mohr Siebeck, 2008), 91–130.

Chapter Four

Haunted Spaces

HIDDEN TRAUMAS, REPETITIONS, AND THE WOUNDED PROTAGONIST

Shirley Jackson's 1959 novel *The Haunting of Hill House* provides one of the most enduringly chilling visions of a haunted house. To date, it has spawned two film adaptations (the 1963 classic directed by Robert Wise, and the less effective 1999 version directed by Jan de Bont, both entitled *The Haunting*), plus a loosely adapted Netflix series by Mike Flanagan, whose second season has just been announced for 2019.[1] In Shirley Jackson's vision, this house is not just a place where ghosts happen to have congregated; the house itself is malevolent. She famously describes it thusly:

> No live organism can continue for long to exist sanely under conditions of absolute reality; even larks and katydids are supposed, by some, to dream. Hill House, not sane, stood by itself against its hills, holding darkness within; it had stood so for eighty years and might stand for eighty more. Within, walls continued upright, bricks met neatly, floors were firm, and doors were sensibly shut; silence lay steadily against the wood and stone of Hill House, and whatever walked there, walked alone.[2]

In this chapter, we'll explore some unwell spaces of literary and cinematic history, as well as some of the unwell spaces of the Hebrew Bible: deserts, ruins, and the house of David.

As was touched upon in the previous chapter, ghosts don't tend to be free-floating entities, moving at will across the earth. They are deeply tied to a particular place. For ghosts, this is usually the haunted house, the space that was most closely associated with their earthly life and to which they are now tied after death. Frequently in ghost narratives, particularly modern ones, the association between the ghostly presence and the space they inhabit is so close that the space's architecture is infused with malevolence; the house itself is unwell. The house then becomes the center of the narrative of which the ghost is a part, serving as a link between the ghost, history, and the narrative's protagonist. The unwellness of the house extends beyond the mere presence of the ghost, and becomes embodied by the house's physical presence and the emotions it generates within the characters.

This characteristic of the haunted house is noted explicitly in many of the most famous examples of gothic literature, the fiction that laid the foundation for contemporary ghost films. An early example is Edgar Allen Poe's classic short story, "The Fall of the House of Usher." The narrator feels a distinct sense of "insufferable gloom" upon first seeing the house. While unable to articulate exactly what about the house is so unnerving, the narrator remarks, "I was forced to fall back upon the unsatisfactory conclusion that while, beyond doubt, there *are* combinations of very simple natural objects which have the power of thus affecting us, still the analysis of this power lies among considerations beyond our depths."[3] By the end of the narrative, a small imperceptible crack in the façade of the house has ruptured into a "fissure . . . the might walls rushing asunder," as a reflection of the repressed horror that has been unleashed.[4] In Shirley Jackson's imagination, the terrible Hill House is beyond the bounds of sanity in not only the emotions it invokes, but also in its angles, its construction, and its floor plan. She describes the house as "a manic juxtaposition" which seemed to have "formed itself, flying together into its own powerful pattern under the hands of its builders . . . without concession to humanity."[5] In both of these examples, the house isn't haunted simply by the presence of a ghost. The house's very architecture reflects its disturbing secrets and uncanny relationship to the present.[6]

Frequently, haunted house films will adopt a voice-over narration to describe this unnerving feature of the house, as in the narrative description of Hill House that opens the 1963 *The Haunting* (directed by Robert Wise), based on Shirley Jackson's novel.[7] But in addition to the voice-over narration, cinematic techniques contribute to the profound feeling of discomfort. In exterior shots, the house is frequently filmed from an extreme low angle so that it seems to be looming menacingly over the viewer. Furthermore, these shots are frequently off-center and slightly tilted, emphasizing the dissymmetry of the house. And the first interior shots of the house are filmed with the use of a "fisheye" lens, causing the frame to bend and warp slightly at the edges. These techniques have become standard methods of introducing haunted spaces.

It is a common tendency to personify a house, but this tendency is stretched to the extreme in haunted house narratives.[8] The house itself has a (malevolent) personality, demonstrated through subtle cues such as (in film) a shot of the characters first approaching the house, which can only be from the point of view of the house itself;[9] in literature, this is substituted by the narrator's voice, which describes the house as having "vacant eye-like windows,"[10] or a "face" that "seemed awake."[11] This trope is taken to its logical conclusion in the animated film *Monster House*, in which the haunted house literally comes to life, chasing the young protagonists through the neighborhood. What began as a metaphor here becomes literalized.

But even though the house may be malevolent, it still maintains its identity as house, the site of family life and history. The haunted house is the dangerous space where spirits return to trouble the living, but it still maintains many of the features of the family home. (Often, due to its grandeur, it is an extremely desirable family home, as evidenced by the excitement with which the new family is moving into the house at the narrative's beginning.) Noting the frequency in literature with which the narrator is unable to quite put a finger on what is wrong with the haunted house, Anthony Vidler returns to Freud's theory of the uncanny to describe the haunted house as both home and not-home, both familiar and strange.[12] And frequently, the narrative turns on the haunted house as being the site of tremendous danger, as well as the repository of family history. The house itself takes on this history.

In his exploration of haunted places in contemporary film, Barry Curtis notes that the haunted house is "a structure within which familiarity and extreme anxiety come together, where 'doubling' is brought to a crisis through reflections, encounters, and repetition, often a place where the passage of time is troubled."[13] In the haunted space, we see the house's often repressed traumatic past repeated and reflected through events in the present. The house has a history, and this history replays itself in the present. Often, revealing this history is enough to satisfy the requirements of the plot and put the ghosts to rest.

In many haunted house narratives, the narrative takes the form of a quest: the protagonists must uncover the house's traumatic past and make some gesture towards setting things right. *The Uninvited* is an early example of a film following this pattern.[14] The film follows Roderick and his sister as they purchase a new house in the British countryside, beautifully located on top of a cliff leading down to the ocean. The pair soon meets the former owner's granddaughter, Stella, who can't seem to part with the house. Stella is drawn both to the house and to the cliff outside, the site of her mother's untimely death. By the film's end, we have learned that one of the spirits inhabiting the house is of its former maid, who was Stella's true mother; once Stella learns this information, the ghost departs peacefully. Once the history of the house is uncovered, the occupants and the spirits can coexist peacefully.[15]

But in some cases, things are not so easy. In many haunted house stories, the protagonist is sucked into this cycle of traumatic repetition, becoming a living part of the house's echoes.[16] The house seems to find a kindred soul in the broken, damaged protagonist, and the traumatic past of the individual becomes merged with the traumatic history of the house. Because the protagonist is so deeply connected with the house, revealing the house's past is not enough to bring resolution; a protagonist who is unable to reconcile with their own past is incapable of reconciling the past of the house.

This is seen clearly in *The Shining*, in Stephen King's source novel but even more explicitly in Stanley Kubrick's 1980 film version.[17] In the film, Jack Nicholson plays Jack Torrance, a struggling writer who agrees to take a job as offseason caretaker for the Overlook Hotel; the job will entail him staying through the winter, when the mountain roads are impassable and the hotel is cut off from all outside contact. With his wife and young child in tow, Jack views this as an opportunity to work on his writing and get his life back in order. But the hotel has other ideas. Jack is soon pushed over the edge, either through isolation and paranoia or supernatural forces, and attempts to kill his family with an axe.

The Overlook Hotel has a haunted history, as is hinted at throughout the narrative. As the family is first traveling to the hotel, they remark that it is very near the location of the Donner party's terrible winter. And the hotel's manager Ullman tells Jack that the hotel was built on a Native American burial ground (a few years before *Poltergeist* would turn this into a horror movie cliché), and that the construction workers even had to fend off Apache attacks as they were building. But most chillingly, Ullman warns Jack that the winter maintenance man from a few years ago, Charles Grady, got some "cabin fever" and murdered his family. Danny, Jack's young son, is particularly in tune with the supernatural, and begins having visions of the hotel's violent past. The hotel's cook, Hollaran, tells him that he has "the Shining"—an ability the hotel also has. The hotel knows this connection and takes a special interest in Danny because of it.

As the film unfolds, the hotel's corridors take on a menacing quality, largely due to the film's unusual angles and long Steadicam shots.[18] And as Jack descends further into drink and madness, it is representatives from the hotel who come to claim him as one of their own, the butler, who identifies himself as Delbert Grady. The connection with the murderous Charles Grady seems uncanny—the shared last name leads Jack and the audience to suspect that this is, in fact, the caretaker, but the different first name gives us pause. And his appearance is further evidence of the out-of-jointness of time at the Overlook. When Jack asks him if he is the caretaker, Grady smirks and says, "Why no, you're the caretaker. You've always been the caretaker."

Dressed in a black tuxedo and speaking with a chilling calm, Grady convinces Jack that his problems are all the fault of his family and that he would be better off without them. The uncanny appearance of a man who is/ is not the former caretaker also serves as a reminder that the hotel has found a man whose trauma mirrors its own; in the film's beginning, we learn that Jack has a history of alcohol abuse, as well as at least one instance where he inflicted harm upon his child. Grady serves as a reminder of the hotel's traumatic past, but also a means through which this trauma will repeat itself through the character of Jack. By the film's end, it is clear that Jack was doomed from the beginning due to his past, a past which he will be unable to overcome. The monstrous hotel, however, welcomes him: in the film's final shot, the camera pans over the walls of the Overlook Hotel, resting on a portrait of the hotel's Fourth of July party from 1921. A smiling Jack Torrance has taken his place with the other staff members, forever a part of the hotel.

The idea that architecture can mirror the psychology of the individual, or the society as a whole, is obviously not unique to the horror film. Henri Lefebvre, for example, has written on space as a "social product," rather than a product of mere functionality.[19] Lefebvre's work attempts to describe the connections between the perceived space (physical space as it is lived in), the conceived space (as it is depicted metaphorically in forms such as language and maps), and experienced or lived space (as the space is used for everyday activities and experienced by those who live in it). Our buildings are more than physical presences, they are also embodiments of cultural values and anxieties.[20] Lefebvre writes:

> Any determinate and hence demarcated space necessarily embraces some things and excludes others; what it rejects may be relegated to nostalgia or it may be simply forbidden. Such a space asserts, negates, and denies. . . . Consider the great power of a façade, for example. A façade admits certain acts to the realm of what is visible, whether they occur on the façade itself (on balconies, window ledges, etc.) or are to be seen *from* the façade (processions in the street, for example). Many other acts, by contrast, it condemns to obscenity: these occur *behind* the façade. All of which already seems to suggest a 'psychoanalysis of space'.[21]

The way we create space, to a large degree, determines how we live in that space. Lefebvre remarks that our living spaces construct how we use our time: "The fact remains that a home-buyer buys a daily schedule, and that this constitutes part of the use value of the space acquired."[22] The space we live in, to a large extent, both reflects and determines how our time is organized. Public activities (dining, entertaining) are placed close to the front of the house, within rooms containing large windows that are open to the surrounding community. By contrast, private activities (eliminating waste, sleeping, sex) are confined to spaces in the back of the house, more hidden from public view. The organization of rooms reveal a significant amount about how the activity of each room is understood from the perspective of the contemporaneous culture.

Gaston Bachelard, in *The Poetics of Space*, observes a similar phenomenon in how our bodies acclimate themselves to our houses, particularly the houses in which we grew up. He describes how "gestures become commonplace" within a familiar house. "In short," Bachelard writes, "the house we were born in has engraved within us the hierarchy of the various functions of inhabiting. We are the diagram of the functions of inhabiting that particular house, and all the other houses are but variations on a fundamental theme."[23] He argues that "habit" is not nearly strong enough as a term to describe the connection between our bodies and the houses in which we grew up; these houses have inscribed their details, their floorplans, and all of their idiosyncrasies, into our bodies. The number of stairs leading up to our childhood bedrooms, for example, becomes an ingrained instinct.

Haunted house narratives understand the connection between space and mental geography deeply. The geography of the house reveals a deep tie between physical location and memory; as described by Barry Curtis, "The archetype of the haunted house is a place where the past is still alive and capable of making temporal connections that appear as spatial coordinates."[24] In *The Haunting*, key events happen in the library's spiral staircase, from which one of the house's maids hung herself, and at a tree on the house's grounds, where the first lady of the manor was killed in a carriage accident. These incidents will replay themselves (or attempt to) through the course of the film. And in both *The Haunting* and *The Woman in Black*, the nursery is deeply connected to the house's traumatic history; in both films, the door to this room is locked as the protagonist approaches, only to be mysteriously opened later on. The cellar is another recurring terrible place in haunted house narratives, hiding secrets that the houses' owners would like to keep hidden.[25] In all haunted houses, there are particular places that are more dangerous than others, and should be avoided at all costs.

A striking example of the connection between history and space is once again found in *The Shining*. Besides being located near the spot of the Donner party's grisly demise and a massacre of Native Americans, the Overlook Hotel presents a richly woven tapestry of rooms connected with specific traumatic memories, which replay themselves to the present inhabitants. Most noteworthy is Room 237, which Danny has been warned away from, but still finds himself inexplicably drawn towards. We learn that it was in this room that Delbert, the former caretaker, stored the bodies of his family and then killed himself. At first, the viewer is not allowed into the room with Danny; he enters alone, with the film only returning to him after he escapes an attack of some kind. When Jack goes to investigate the room, he finds a different kind of horror waiting for him. Time collapses in on itself in this room, as Jack is seduced by a young woman rising up from a bathtub (the former caretaker's wife, perhaps?), then sees himself reflected in the mirror, kissing an old woman. In the haunted house, time is fluid and unpredictable; space is the only constant.

HAUNTED HOUSES AND OTHER HAUNTED SPACES IN TRADITION

While the haunted house narrative is relatively new,[26] haunted spaces are present in a wide range of cultural traditions. Grendel's haunted marsh stands at the head of the Anglo-Saxon literary tradition. Terry Gunnell has documented Icelandic legends (the álagablettir) in which the locals know that a particular spot of ground is not to be plowed, with consequences ranging from the loss of livestock to the death of the person responsible for plowing.[27] John Lindow has explored the liminal space of the churchyard in Nordic folktales, finding them to frequently serve as a dangerous middle ground between the secular and sacred worlds.[28] And while it is difficult to sort out some of Japan's horrific traditions from Western influence,[29] the folktales that have been preserved depict ghosts who return to the site of long-past battles to hear tales of valor recounted, and the ghosts of an abandoned wife who continues to haunt her domicile as she waits for her husband's return. Even further back, Pliny the Younger wrote in the first century BCE of a house cursed by the spirits of the dead, and Plutarch described the ghost of a murder victim who was said to have haunted a local bathhouse.[30] In these traditions, and many others, the phenomenon of haunting is linked to a specific location, in which past events replay themselves through time.

The Hebrew Bible also features traditions of places that have become haunted. Frequently, YHWH threatens to turn the Israelites' towns into ruins; this threat is often connected with the experience of fear or terror, not necessarily at YHWH's destructive action but at the desolate landscape itself. In Jeremiah 4:7, YHWH declares to the people of Jerusalem, "[YHWH] has gone out from his place to put horror (שמה, *shamah*) on your land, your cities will fall to ruins (fem. plural of נצה, *natzah*) with no inhabitants." The threat of turning Jerusalem (or any city, for that matter) into a heap of ruins is often connected with turning it into an object of horror.[31]

In Job 15:20–35, the wicked are destined to live in "houses which are soon to become heaps," with "ruins" left as an unstated implication. In this passage, the wicked experience the emotions of despair and distress, but also terror (פחד, *pechad* in 15:21; בעת, *ba'at* in 15:24).[32] As the wicked will soon experience, a place that has been abandoned and made desolate is a place we experience the terror of absences and destruction.

Amy Kalmanofsky finds much in the book of Jeremiah to connect these ideas, arguing that the trauma of YHWH's destruction lingers in the destroyed place. "Although there are no haunted houses in the book of Jeremiah," Kalmanofsky writes, "there are haunted landscapes."[33] Discussing Jeremiah 4:23–26, Kalmanofsky obseves: "This passage does not describe the empty land as a placid void. Instead, the landscape, though empty of life, seethes in revolt." The landscape will become "formless and void" in Jeremiah 4:23, the תהו ובהו (*tohu vabohu*) of the world pre-creation in Genesis 1:1,[34] but Kalmanofsky looks at the earthquakes and moving hills and sees a landscape that "seethes in revolt."[35]

In Jeremiah 9:10 (9:11 ET), the city will not only become a "heap of ruins," but also a home for jackals who continue to haunt the ruined city after it has been abandoned. The people who used to inhabit this city have given way to the wild denizens. Several passages in Isaiah stand out for their extensive detail and the imaginative lengths they go to in describing these post-human inhabitants of ruined cities.[36] Isaiah 13:19–22 envisions Babylon fallen into ruin, a place abandoned by humans "for generations," which even nomadic peoples will avoid. A similar image is drawn for Edom in 34:8–15, in passage envisioning a land that will "lay waste for generations, and forever no one will pass through it" (34:10). In both passages, the ruined city has become home to a host of animals, including jackals, hyenas, and other nocturnal and shadowy creatures.[37] An even more evocative presence is the שָׂעִיר (*sa'ir*) of 13:21 and 34:14; while some scholars have viewed them as simple goats, most view them as a mythological satyr.[38] The humans have been forced out of their dwellings, and the creatures of the night (both natural and supernatural) have moved in.[39]

A final chilling example of ruined, haunted cities in the Hebrew Bible also comes from the book of Isaiah. In 29:1–4, Jerusalem's doom is described in striking language. Isaiah prophesizes to the city: "You will be brought lower than the earth and you will speak; from the dust your words will bow down. Your voice will come from the earth like a ghost, and from the earth your words will chirp."[40] The city will become a haunted, ghostly presence, trampled into the dust by her enemies and lingering only as a spirit. If any traveler were to enter it, they could only hear it speaking by pressing their ear close to the ground and listening to the dust. The picture becomes sunnier in the next passage, as YHWH rides to the rescue in 29:6, but the haunting image of the ghostly city remains.

Leviticus's Leprous House

In Shirley Jackson's *The Haunting of Hill House*, the psychic investigator Dr. Montague offers the suggestion that haunted spaces have been known across cultures and times.

> "You will recall," the doctor began, "the houses described in Leviticus as 'leprous,' *tsaraas*, or Homer's phrase for the underworld: *aidao domos*, the house of Hades; I need not remind you, I think, that the concept of certain houses as unclean or forbidden—perhaps sacred—is as old as the mind of man. Certainly there are spots which inevitably attach to themselves an atmosphere of holiness and goodness; it might not then be too fanciful to say that some houses are born bad."[41]

The doctor's connection between the haunted Hill House and the mold-infested houses of Leviticus is an interesting one. Leviticus 13 begins with detailed instructions of the procedure for an Israelite man who contracts a skin disease, traditionally translated as "leprosy."[42] Most of the prescriptions involve isolation; while the disease itself is not considered contagious, the impurity that stems from it is.[43] Saul Olyan views this disease as always having negative connotations within the Hebrew Bible, but other scholars see the moralistic and negative connotations with skin disease as being confined to the E source, whereas P presents these conditions as "an unfortunate fact of life much like other bodily conditions that render a person impure."[44] Whether a moral impurity or not, the consequences are severe: as long as the disease remains with the person, he shall repeatedly yell "Unclean! Unclean" to warn others away from him, and he will "live alone, outside of the camp" (13:45–46).

Leviticus 14 turns to the purification ritual for cleansing a man of leprosy. After a complicated procedure involving inspection, the sacrificing of birds and lambs, a grain offering, and many other details, the man can be declared clean.[45] For the purpose of this chapter, most interesting is the shift in 14:33, when the passage's attention turns away from the man with a skin disease, and to a house with a similar affliction (נגע צרעת בבית, *nega' tzar'at b'beyt*). We have explored above the frequency with which haunted houses are described as sentient, and the house comes to have its own body. The case is similar here, with the walls of the house being analogous to its skin. In this passage, the priest takes on the role of the psychic investigator, leading the home inspection and determining the situation of the house. The overriding question in this passage is whether the disease is "deeper than the wall" (שפל מן-הקיר, *shaphal min-haqir*; 14:34–37), and whether it will spread or go away on its own (14:37–39). After shutting up the house for seven days, the priest will return to see if it has continued to spread, and a poor inspection report will lead to a forced home renovation, involving replastering the walls and removing any "diseased stones" (האבנים אשר בהן הנגע, *ha'abanim asher bahen hanaga'*; 14:40–42) and dumping them outside of the city. If the disease still continues to spread after the stones have been replaced, the house needs to be torn down.

This leprous house comes to life in the Netflix series *The Haunting of Hill House*. In this series, the protagonists are a family who has moved into the house with the intention of renovating it and flipping it. While inspecting for damage after a recent storm, the family patriarch Hugh Crain notices something odd in the basement; as he peels away a patch of drywall to inspect, he discovers that the entire basement is covered with a thick, black mold. If there was any question as to whether the house was salvageable before, those questions are put to rest with this revelation.

While Hugh Crain refuses to believe that the house is beyond repair by natural means, Leviticus 14 understands immediately that a house of this nature cannot simply be repaired. The house's malady is a spiritual one, a sickness at the house's heart, which can only be cured through the divine intervention of a priest.

So Dr. Montague is not too far off when he connects the haunted Hill House with these "leprous houses" of Leviticus.[46] The leprous house is unclean, and all who enter it during the time it is under quarantine will likewise become unclean, as the house's impurity will spread to them. The sickness of this house is contagious in a most direct way; even entering into it causes people to be unclean until the evening (14:46). People who eat or sleep in the house during this period are specifically instructed to wash their clothes afterwards (14:47). While eating is frequently associated with questions of impurity, this is one of the only occasions on which sleeping enters into the legal code.[47] Perhaps the diseased houses of Leviticus were also more dangerous at night. Something has gone wrong with these houses, something which humans are limited in their ability to control. And like the climax of many haunted house pictures, when a house has become so deeply infected, the only possible solution is to destroy it.

However, Dr. Montague's comparison seems to be wrong on one account. In Leviticus 14:34, the leprosy is described as being put into the house by YHWH. For whatever reason, the deity has here decreed that this house should be leprous. For Hill House, the Overlook Hotel, and any number of more contemporary haunted places, there's no indication that God was involved in their haunting. On the contrary, these places exhibit a distinct absence of God.

While this leprous house is an oddly intriguing detail in Leviticus, it is far from the most prominent haunted house in the Hebrew Bible. One house casts an enormous shadow over the Deuteronomistic History in particular, and the Hebrew Bible as a whole more broadly: the house of David.

The Haunted House of David

While the בית דוד (*beyt david*; house of David) can literally refer to the palace, it is also frequently used as a metaphor for David's kin (1 Samuel 20:16; 2 Samuel 3:1, 6) and, even more commonly, for the institution of kingship in Israel that flows through David's bloodline. The earliest extra-biblical reference to David, found in the Tel Dan Stele (usually dated from the nineth to eighth century BCE) is to the "house of David," indicating that David's royal line was known outside of Israel.[48]

In the Hebrew Bible itself, the memory of David lingers for centuries after his death, and a longing for the return of the Davidic monarchy continues long after the Israelite monarchy is no more.[49] Throughout the books of

Kings, when Israel suffers through a parade of inept, inadequate, and idolatrous kings, David is continually held up as the model against which other kings are judged, and for whose righteousness the people hope will return in another king.[50] Especially after the people have been driven into exile by the Babylonian forces, David becomes a symbol of hope and the future. The "house of David" endures in Israel's memory long after it has been trampled into the dust by the armies of Babylon.

But the books that detail David's rise and reign, First and Second Samuel, also narrate a king who lets himself get wrapped up in his own power, bringing the judgment of YHWH on his household and setting in motion a chain of events that will have enormous effects on the nation.[51] It all starts with a king who has too much time on his hands, and who lets his desire get the better of him.

Only a few chapters after David had been promised that his "throne will be established forever" by YHWH (2 Samuel 7:16), David gets into trouble. While taking a nighttime walk on the palace roof, the king spies a beautiful woman bathing. The text already notes that this is "the time when kings go to war" (2 Samuel 11:1), seeming to imply that David is already shirking his duties.[52] Rather than leading his army into battle, he is wandering around aimlessly on his palace roof. On seeing this woman bathing, David enquires about her and has her sent (שלח) to the palace for his own pleasure.[53] After this encounter, Bathsheba "sends for David" (2 Samuel 11:5) and informs him that she is pregnant. Bathsheba, who was originally "sent for," now "sends" (שלח again) for David, as her pregnancy has temporarily reversed the power dynamics.[54]

This causes a tremendous problem for David, since Bathsheba is married to a soldier named Uriah, who is off fighting David's war. (The introductory statement regarding "the time when kings go to war" begins to seem even nastier at this point.) So David engages in a cover-up scheme to attempt to conceal his actions. His first step is to invite Uriah back from the front and try to encourage him to go home and sleep with his wife. But Uriah is too honorable for this; he knows that soldiers are supposed to abstain from intercourse with their wives immediately before battle (compare 1 Samuel 21:5). David tries to get him drunk, but rather than going home to his wife, Uriah falls asleep on one of the palace couches (2 Samuel 11:13). Since David can't convince Uriah to sleep with his wife, David sends Uriah back to the front with a note for Joab, instructing the commander to set Uriah in the front of the army, then have everyone else pull back during the fighting so that Uriah will be killed. The plan works just as David had hoped. David at least has the decency to wait until Bathsheba's time of mourning is over before having her brought to the palace.[55] We quickly learn that YHWH is less than happy with this behavior.

David's court prophet, Nathan, tells David a story about a rich man who steals an ewe from a poor man, a clear parable for David's "theft" of Uriah's wife. The specifics of this parable need not concern us here; most important for this discussion is David's acknowledgment of guilt, and the subsequent judgment delivered to him by Nathan.[56] Confronted with his own guilt, David says simply: "I have sinned against YHWH."[57] Even with this acknowledgment, David's actions will have severe ramifications for his family, the kingship, and the nation as a whole. This is the horrible event that turns the house of David into a haunted house, with trauma rhyming over generations.

In his role as prophet, Nathan delivers the word of YHWH to David.[58] Because David has repented, his life will be spared, but this doesn't offer any consolation for his (and Bathsheba's) newborn son, and for the future of his monarchic line. YHWH promises to "raise trouble" on David from his house by taking David's wives and giving them to David's neighbor. And finally, David's newborn son will die. "The sword will not turn aside from your house," YHWH promises. In this nine-verse proclamation, two of the promises directly reference David's "house," and the continued consequences upon this house.

It doesn't take long for these threats to come to life, as David's child immediately becomes ill. The death of a child is a common motif in haunted house films, a severe trauma with effects that frequently ripple out through generations.[59] David fasts and prostrates himself in an attempt to save the child's life, but to no avail.[60] The child dies after seven days, and David and Bathsheba conceive a new son, who will be named Solomon. But the other consequences promised by Nathan are soon to follow.

2 Samuel 11–12 presents a pair of spaces within David's palace, both of which will be important in subsequent events: the roof of David's palace, and the throne room. The narrative also introduces the themes of violence, particularly sexual violence, which will continue to recur in shifting patterns throughout the remainder of the DtrH. As David's house falls into disarray, we first note the prominence of repeated acts of sexual violence within David's family, and the return of the rooftop as a space of trauma.

While 2 Samuel 13 begins its narrative with "it was after this" (ויהי אחרי–כן; *vayhi acherey--ken*), indicating that some time passes between Nathan's pronouncement of judgment and the subsequent episodes, the narrative places the troubles that begin to plague David's house immediately after the episode between David and Nathan. In the narrative world of 2 Samuel, dire consequences continue to follow David's action in rapid succession. And as Nathan had promised, the trouble comes from within David's household, first arising from his son Amnon before spreading to another son, Absalom.

Amnon becomes smitten with his sister Tamar, and feigns illness in order to draw her into his bedroom and rape her.[61] This takes place in Absalom's house, rather than in David's, though Absalom's house can easily be read as a metaphorical extension of his father's house. While living in his own physical space, Absalom is still part of the "house of the father" (בית אב, *beyt 'av*).[62] With David unwilling or unable to act, the elder brother Absalom bides his time for two years, then orders Amnon killed in an act of revenge. This act leads to a struggle for power between David and Absalom, as Absalom leads a nearly successful revolt against his father before he too is killed. David's house collapses around him.[63]

In constructing the haunted house of David, we notice the repetitions that take place in this narrative, as well as the fulfillment of the curse delivered by Nathan. Nathan promised that trouble would arise from within David's house, as it did with the actions of both Amnon and Absalom. Furthermore, the text presents an echo between the sexual violence committed by Amnon against Tamar, and the sexual violence committed by David against Bathsheba. When Amnon is feigning his illness, David comes to check on him. Amnon tricks David, asking David to ask Tamar to come to him. So, like he did for Bathsheba, David "sends" (שׁלח, *shalach*) for Tamar, unaware that he is sending her to be assaulted by her brother. In his ignorance of the situation, David is here a closer match for Uriah, unaware that the note that has been "sent by the hand of Uriah" is his own death sentence.[64]

The theme of sexual violence continues into Absalom's rebellion, with a further stunning echo of the initial traumatic event. David flees the palace in fear of Absalom, but leaves a group of his concubines behind. David's former counselor, Ahithophel, advises Absalom that the best way to assert his power over David would be for Absalom to rape these concubines so that "all Israel will hear" of this deed and know that Absalom has shamed David.[65] As Nathan promised, David's wives shall be taken from him and given away "in the eyes of this sun" (2 Samuel 12:11). The promised curse has, again, come true. But even more striking is the location of this act, with Absalom and his advisors pitching a tent for him on the palace roof (2 Samuel 16:22), the same spot from which David first spied Bathsheba. The roof has become one of the "terrible places" of the house, gathering to itself a history of awful events. Like *The Shining*'s Room 237, the palace roof becomes a site where traumatic events are transformed, then repeated.

The roof is not the only location of trauma within the house of David. Throughout David's reign, the throne room serves as the focus of many of the house's traumatic experiences. Dr. Montague describes the nursery as the "heart of Hill house," a function which shifts to the "red room" in the Netflix series. In *The Woman in Black*, the house's heart is also a nursery; in *Ouija*, it is the basement, site of the former occupant's horrifying medical experiments. Every haunted house has a heart, a space which is most closely associated with the house's traumatic history, and where the house's malevolent power is at its strongest. In David's story, this function is filled by the throne room. In haunted house narratives, the characters who are more attuned to the malevolence of the house quickly ascertain which spaces they should stay away from. In the Deuteronomistic History, the throne room is one such place.

Prior to David's reign, Saul's throne room becomes a place of evil and torment for the soon-to-be-replaced king.[66] King Saul is portrayed in his throne room in four scenes, all of which involve an evil spirit and a violent outburst from Saul. In 1 Samuel 16:14–23, 18:10–11, and 19:9–10, Saul is haunted by an "evil spirit from God/YHWH" (רוח אלהים/יהוה רעה, *ruach elohim/Yahweh ra'ah*). In the first episode, Saul is so tormented that his servants recognize his distress, and they seek out a lyre player to soothe him. This is how David and Saul first meet, although the soothing that David's harp can provide the mad king is only temporary. When an evil spirit from God rushes on Saul again, he tries to kill David with his spear. ("But David avoided him two times," the narrator laconically tells us.) 1 Samuel 19:9–10 again depicts Saul overtaken by an evil spirit and attempting to kill David; this time, the future king is smart enough to run away. In the final episode, David is absent, so Saul attempts to spear his son Jonathan instead.[67] With minor variations, this scene is repeated four times: Saul is visited by an evil spirit, attempts are made to soothe him, and if these attempts are unsuccessful, he attempts to kill either David or David's stand-in. We see the haunted pattern of not only the evil spirits, but the connection with the location of the throne room and the repetition of a traumatic scene. It is as if time loops back upon itself whenever Saul steps into the throne room. Saul is the damaged character whose trauma finds an echo in the house. Like Hill House and the doomed Eleanor, Saul and his house seem to have a mutually self-destructive relationship.

David's first palace is in Hebron (2 Samuel 2:1–11), but his palace in Jerusalem is finally constructed in 2 Samuel 5:11–13, with the help of King Hiram of Tyre.[68] After David's house is built, he must immediately leave to make war against the Philistines. He finally "dwelled in his house" (ישב, *yashav*) in 2 Samuel 7. His first experience in his new house is immediately positive, as he receives word from his prophet Nathan that his kingdom has been established by YHWH for eternity. But associations with the palace soon turn darker.

In this new palace, the throne room is quickly established as a similar space to the room Saul inhabited. It is the heart of David's haunted house. Instead of being named directly, the setting is implied, left unstated like a lacuna in the narrative. But it is clear that when David is receiving messengers or discussing matters with his court prophet Nathan, that the setting is David's throne room; this would have been, after all, where David received his audience. The fact that this room is never named only adds to its haunted presence. Like one of Derrida's specters, it is present and absent, always leaving a trace even when it remains unnamed.

The episode with Bathsheba and Uriah occurs in a variety of locations, including the palace roof and the banquet halls. After Uriah refuses David's request, the scene shifts to David's throne room, with the king sending and receiving notice of Uriah's death. This is the first trauma of the throne room; while Uriah dies on a battlefield, his death is assured in David's throne room. When Nathan comes to visit David in his throne room, the prophet also brings death with him. The throne room now becomes the site of judgment, the space where David's promised kingdom falls apart and his first child is lost to him and Bathsheba.

The throne room returns to a place of prominence in another story, this one the story of Bathsheba's revenge of sorts. As the book of 1 Kings begins, David has grown old, but has not made his succession plans clear. His eldest son Adonijah is ready to claim the throne for himself, but Nathan and Bathsheba work together to crown Bathsheba's son Solomon in his place. Their plan involves taking advantage of an aging monarch by convincing him that he has promised to name Solomon as his successor, although the text gives no indication that the king has actually made such a promise.[69] Here, the location is described as "the room of the king" (המלך החדרה, *hamelek hachadrach*; 1 Kings 1:15), a phrase that seems most likely to refer to the throne room. (This is the closest the text comes to naming the throne room directly). Through this deception, Bathsheba is able to secure her position as Queen Mother, both enhancing her power and avoiding any negative consequences she might suffer from having another heir placed on the throne. Whereas once the throne room was the site of Bathsheba's mistreatment at the hands of the king, here it becomes the site of her empowerment.

As Solomon becomes king, he builds a new house for himself, one more glorious than David's (1 Kings 6–7), also using the aid of Hiram of Tyre, along with forced Israelite labor. But he might as well have built his house on the foundations of David's haunted house, like the now-cliched burial grounds that underlie the haunted houses of *The Shining* and *Poltergeist*. Even though it is a new structure, Solomon's house is still the haunted house of David. Like his father, Solomon is undone by his desire for women; rather than lasciviously spying on Bathsheba from his roof, Solomon amasses a great harem of women from many different nations, leading him into idolatry in his old age (1 Kings 11:1–8). It is this idolatry that will lead to a further curse on the house of David, causing it to turn into a cracked House of Usher for Solomon's son Rehoboam, split into the Northern and Southern kingdoms.

The shadow of this house looms over the books of 1 and 2 Kings, with a series of kings who fail to live up to YHWH's expectations, meet tragic downfalls, and lead their people astray. The books of Kings become an endless cycle of trauma and repetition, with the same events (idolatry, social injustice) leading to the same outcomes (judgment from YHWH). Finally, the house is torn down by the Babylonian invasion of 586, although the house of David still casts a lengthy shadow over the hopes of Israel. As David Jobling has noted, Israel is haunted throughout the book of Samuel; in the exilic and postexilic biblical texts, this haunting takes the form of the remembered house of David.

One other common feature of haunted houses remains to be explored: the repression of the initial trauma. As we have discussed above, the trauma that sets events in motion is frequently hidden or intentionally ignored. We see this clearly with the attempt to covertly restructure the family lineage by raising another child as the family's own in narratives such as *The Uninvited* or *The Changeling*. In the Hebrew Bible, we see this repression of trauma in another way: through the book of Chronicles, which attempts to erase Uriah and Bathsheba from David's story.

As is widely known, the books of Chronicles largely retell the books of Samuel and Kings, frequently repeating the same language verbatim.[70] While most of David's exploits are repeated in the same order and with the same details in the book of Chronicles, the story of Bathsheba is left out entirely. I side with the many scholars who view this as an intentional erasure, an attempt to write David's sins out of his story to make him truly seem like the ideal king (and man) of God. But as Freud first noted, and as haunted house movies have shown us again and again, what is repressed always comes back. Bathsheba gets her revenge in 1 Kings by orchestrating her son Solomon's rise to the throne, but it is not an easy reign for Solomon or for any of his successors. Trouble always arises from within their own houses, and the sword never departs.

NOTES

1. A forthcoming volume of essays on the Flanagan series is *The Streaming of Hill House: Essays on the Haunting Netflix Adaptaion*, ed. Kevin J. Wetmore, Jr. (Jefferson, NC: McFarland, 2020).

2. Shirley Jackson, *The Haunting of Hill House* (New York: Penguin, 1984).

3. Edgar Allan Poe, "The Fall of the House of Usher," in *Complete Stories and Poems of Edgar Allan Poe* (New York: Doubleday, 1966), 177–191, here, 177. Italics original. Anthony Vidler views this as the "paradigmatic haunted house." *The Architectural Uncanny: Essays in the Modern Unhomely* (Cambridge, MA: MIT Press, 1992), 17–19.

4. Poe, "House of Usher," 191. For comparison, note the many cinematic versions of this short story, including the 1928 French version by Jean Epstein and the 1960 version by Roger Corman (titled *The House of Usher*), starring Vincent Price.

5. Jackson, *The Haunting of Hill House*, 34–35.

6. Ilse M. Bussing, "Complicit Bodies: Excessive Sensibilities and Haunted Space," *Horror Studies* 7.1 (2016): 41–59, suggests that the architecture of the haunted house not only reflects the house's past, but also the damaged psyche of the characters in the narrative present. She uses as examples Edgar Allen Poe's "The Fall of the House of Usher" (1839) and Algernon Blackwood's "The Empty House" (1906), but, as will be explored further, this paradigm holds for a number of more contemporary narratives as well. Suzette Mayr has also written an

interesting study on the connection between the house and the emotional state of the narrative's protagonists in Andrew Pyper's recent novel *The Guardians* (2011). "'House of Mirrors': The Sentinel House as Homosocial Space in Andrew Pyper's *The Guardians*," *Horror Studies* 8.1 (2017): 97–114.

7. This film is widely regarded as one of the first haunted house films that still maintains its power to unsettle, based largely on its remarkable restraint and ability to suggest rather than show directly. See, for example, Pam Keesey, "*The Haunting* and the Power of Suggestion: Why Robert Wise's Film Continues to 'Deliver the Goods' to Modern Audiences," in *Horror Film Reader*, eds. Alain Silver and James Ursini (New York: Limelight Editions, 2000), 305–316. Contemporary haunted house films owe a tremendous debt to the style of *The Haunting*.

8. Gaston Bachelard, *The Poetics of Space*, trans. Maria Jolas (Penguin Classics edition. New York: Penguin, 2014), 38–50, describes the "psychology" of the house, with the "rational" attic contrasted with the superstitions of the cellar, a geography that will play out in many haunted house narratives. Goldstein, Grider, and Thomas, *Haunting Experiences*, 143–144, briefly discuss some of the ways in which haunted houses are personified.

9. This has become so common in cinema as to almost rise to the level of cliché. Among the numerous examples are films such as *The Amityville Horror* (1979), *The Woman in Black* (2012), and even the Disney-produced Eddie Murphy vehicle *The Haunted Mansion* (2003).

10. Poe, "House of Usher," 177.

11. Jackson, *Hill House*, 34. This is echoed by Robert Wise's 1963 film, in which a shot from the window of the supposedly unoccupied house observes the protagonists arriving to the house by car.

12. Vidler, *Architectural Uncanny*, 17–44.

13. Barry Curtis, *Dark Places: The Haunted House in Film* (Locations; London: Reaktion Books, 2008), 12.

14. Prior "haunted house" films, perhaps most notably *The Cat and the Canary* (1927), used gothic motifs of trap doors and secret passageways to instill feelings of dread, but the stories were resolved by unmasking a mere mortal (usually a greedy relative) as being behind the supposed hauntings. In this regards, they were similar to the classic gothic fiction of authors such as Ann Radcliffe and Horatio Waldpole. Wheeler Winston Dixon, *A History of Horror* (New Brunswick, NJ: Rutgers University Press, 2010), 19, puts the film into the context of other silent horror films; Ian Conrich, "Before Sound: Universal, Silent Cinema, and the Last of the Horror Spectaculars," in *The Horror Film*, ed. Stephen Prince (New Brunswick, NJ: Rutgers University Press, 2004), 40–57, provides a more thorough overview of the film's place in the sound era. W. Scott Poole, *Wasteland: The Great War and the Origins of Modern Horror* (Berkeley: Counterpoint, 2018), 210–213, pushes back on the general perception of *The Cat and the Canary* as relying more heavily on comedy than horror.

15. Walker, *Modern Ghost Melodramas*, 37, suggests that *The Changeling* (1980) was the first film to adopt this "quest" approach to the haunted house, comparing it with *The Haunting*. He writes of *The Changeling*'s relationship to the earlier film: "First, it provides the house with a backstory that resonates in the present. The ghost here strives to communicate because it wants something. Second, this communication results in an investigation into a past injustice. In *The Haunting*, the haunted house is deadly, but there is nothing that can be done about this, and Eleanor is killed by its power. *The Changeling* has a different dynamic: here the haunting generates a quest, and this is the pattern in most of the subsequent ghost melodramas." I would suggest that this quest pattern is also followed in *The Uninvited*, even if the film's climax is (disappointingly) comedic in the ways Walker suggests. Walker also seems to overlook *The Legend of Hell House* (1973), which only merits a few brief mentions in his book (centered entirely around a surprisingly sexualized ghost), but follows this pattern several years before *The Changeling*.

16. In his reading of many ghost stories as melodramas, Walker, *Modern Ghost Melodramas*, reads *The Haunting* (1963) in such a manner: "the history of the house includes an incident that parallels Eleanor's own recent behavior—and attendant guilt—concerning the death of her mother. This is an early example of a character entering a haunted house after a

bereavement: it is as though the house 'knows' Eleanor, and eventually she succumbs to its power—in effect, surrendering to the death drive" (24).

17. Stanley Kubrick's version is widely regarded as one of the greatest horror films of all time, and the scholarly literature on it is appropriately vast. An overview can be found in Laura Mee, *The Shining* (Devil's Advocates; Leighton Buzzard, UK: Auteur Publishing, 2017); see also Greg Smith, "'Real Horrorshow': The Juxtaposition of Subtext, Satire, and Audience Implication in Stanley Kubrick's *The Shining*," *Literature/Film Quarterly* 25.4 (1997): 300–306; Dixon, *A History of Horror*, 158–160; John Lutz, "From Domestic Nightmares to the Nightmare of History: Uncanny Eruptions of Violence in King's and Kubrick's Versions of *The Shining*," in *The Philosophy of Horror*, ed. Thomas Fahy (Lexington: The University Press of Kentucky, 2010), 161–178; Tony Williams, *Hearths of Darkness*, 240–252. For a reading of the film employing Kristeva's theory of abjection, see Robert Kilker, "All Roads Lead to the Abject: The Monstrous Feminine and Gender Boundaries in Stanley Kubrick's *The Shining*," *Literature/Film Quarterly* 34.1 (2006): 54–63. Kilker argues that the film is more patriarchal than is usually understood, demonstrating a fear of all power that is coded feminine. For an insightful podcast discussion of the film, see Andrea Subissati and Alexandra West, "All Work and No Play: Stanley Kubrick's *The Shining* (1980)," *Faculty of Horror*; Podcast Audio, Dec. 21, 2015.

18. Amy Nolan has explored how the "labrynthine" nature of the hotel's halls serve as a means for Kubrick to explore power dynamics, inner psychology, and even the repressed in American history in *The Shining*, in "Seeing Is Digesting: Labyrinths of Historical Ruin in Stanley Kubrick's *The Shining*." *Cultural Critique*, 77 (2011): 180–204. Much has been made of how Kubrick's use of the Steadicam to explore the hotel's halls serves as a major contributor to the film's sense of dread; see, for example, Paul Sunderland, "The Autonomous Camera in Stanley Kubrick's *The Shining*," *Sydney Studies in English*, 39 (2013): 58–85. Alain Resnais's film *Last Year at Marienbad* (1961) seems to have been a strong influence; while not a horror film per se, the tracking shots of the hotel's hallways (among other elements) give the film a persistent atmosphere of dread. The technique of the "wandering camera" as a means of creating dread in *The Shining*, *Last Year at Marienbad*, and many other films, is explored in Kenneth Johnson, "The Point of View of the Wandering Camera," *Cinema Studies* 32.2 (1993): 49–56. Another recent article, looking at the gothic tradition more broadly, is Roger Luckhurst, "Corridor Gothic," *Gothic Studies* 20:1–2 (2018): 295–310.

19. Henri Lefebvre, *The Production of Space*, trans. D. Nicholson-Smith (Malden, MA: Blackwell, 1991), 26.

20. Christl M. Maier, *Daughter Zion, Mother Zion: Gender, Space, and the Sacred in Ancient Israel* (Minneapolis, MN: Fortress, 2008), uses Lefebvre's theories to explore the conceptualization of Zion in the Hebrew Bible, focusing in particular on how Zion as conceived by the prophets produces a picture of the idealized city. See also Maier's essay "Zion's Body as a Site of God's Motherhood in Isaiah 66:7–14," in *Daughter Zion: Her Portrait, Her Response*, eds. Mark J. Boda, Carol J. Dempsey, and LeAnn Snow Flesher (Ancient Israel and Its Literature 13; Atlanta: SBL 2012), 225–242.

21. Lefebvre, *The Production of Space*, 99; italics original.

22. Lefebvre, *Philosophy of Space*, 339.

23. Bachelard, *Poetics of Space*, 36.

24. Curtis, *Dark Places*, 40.

25. *The Innkeepers* (2011), *Ouija* (2014), and *Crimson Peak* (2015), among many other films, feature a cellar that served as a hiding place for corpses and has subsequently become a focal point for the houses' angry spirits. Bachelard, *Poetics of Space*, 43, describes the house's cellar as where "secrets are pondered."

26. Though some cultures demonstrate folktales that are similar to modern Western ideas of a haunted house; see, for example, Ülo Valk, "Ghostly Possession and Real Estate: The Dead in Contemporary Estonian Folklore," *Journal of Folklore Research* 43.1 (2006): 31–51, for traditional haunted house stories from Baltic islands.

27. Terry Gunnell, "The Power in the Place: Icelandic *Álagablettir* Legends in a Comparative Context," in *Storied and Supernatural Places: Studies in Spatial and Social Dimensions of*

Folklore and Sagas, eds. Ülo Valk and Daniel Sävborg (Studia Fennica Folkloristica 23; Helsinki: Finnish Literature Society, 2018), 27–41.

28. John Lindow, "Nordic Legends of the Churchyard," in Valk and Sävborg, *Storied and Supernatural Places*, 42–53. See also Kaarina Koski's essay, "The Sacred and the Supernatural: Lutheran Church Buildings in Christian Practice and Finnish Folk Belief Tradition," 54–79 in the same volume.

29. This is problematic due to the work of Lafcadio Hearn (or Koizumi Yakumo), a Western immigrant to Japan who "documented" Japanese folktales in his 1904 book *Kwaidan: Stories and Studies of Strange Things* (Clarendon, VT: Tuttle, 2015). These tales are clearly filtered through a Western lens, making it difficult to determine how much of the original Japanese tale remains. Masaki Kobayashi used several of these stories as source material for his important 1964 film *Kwaidan*.

30. Stuart, *Ghosts*, 24–27; Curtis, *Dark Places*, 33–34. Stuart also discusses a ghost story told by Cicero.

31. In addition to Jeremiah 4:7, see also 2 Kings 19:25–26, which connects the ruins with the emotional response of "חתת," which Kalmanofsky identifies as describing "a fear that is intimately linked to a self-perception of weakness and vulnerability." *Terror All Around*, 15–20 (quoting p. 20). Kalmonfsky discusses the ruined city as an object of horror as an example of "indirect horror," a pervasive trope within horror narratives in which people are horrified by victims as well as by monsters. See *Terror All Around*, 31–41.

32. For פחד and בעת as terror or fear, see BDB and *HALOT*. פחד is quite commonly used to refer to terror or strong anxiety. See, for example, Genesis 31:42, 53; Exodus 15:16 (in hendiadys with אים); Deuteronomy 2:25; 11:25; 28:66; 1 Samuel 11:17; and numerous times throughout the prophetic literature and the psalms, particularly in Isaiah and Jeremiah. בעת is used frequently in Job (3:5; 7:14; 9:34; 13:11, 21; 18:11; 33:7), and also in 1 Samuel 16:14; 2 Samuel 22:5; Isaiah 21:4; Psalm 18:5; Esther 7:6; Daniel 8:17; and 1 Chronicles 21:30.

33. Kalmanofsky, *Terror All Around*, 102.

34. Many have noted this connection; Michael Fishbane has famously read Jeremiah 4:23–26 (and Job 3:3–13) as an "uncreation" narrative, reversing YHWH's creation of Genesis 1:1; see Michael Fishbane, "Jeremiah 4:23–26 and Job 3:3–13a: A Recovered Use of the Creation Pattern," *VT* 21.1 (1971): 151–167.

35. Kalmanofsky, *Terror All Around*, 102.

36. Joseph Blenkinsopp calls these doomed cities "Chaos Town," citing the Hebrew קרית-תהו in 24:10. He suggests that the picture of the "doomed city" in this passage indicates that "ecological disaster is inseparable from the moral corruption of society." "Cityscape to Landscape: The 'Back to Nature' Theme in Isaiah 1–35," in *"Every City Shall Be Forsaken": Urbanism and Prophecy in Ancient Israel and the Near East*, eds. Lester L. Grabbe and Robert D. Haak (JSOTS 330; Sheffield, UK: Sheffield Academic Press, 2001), 35–44; here 43.

37. Blenkinsopp briefly discusses some of the difficulties involved with identifying the precise creatures depicted by the Hebrew; the picture is similar, regardless of how one translates the details; "Cityscape to Landscape," 40–41, n. 12. Ken Stone also provides a helpful overview in *Reading the Hebrew Bible with Animal Studies* (Stanford, CA: Stanford University Press, 2018), 125–129.

38. Blenkinsopp notes, "dancing, while in order for satyrs, would be unusual activity for goats." See "Cityscape to Landscape," 41 n. 12. Esther J. Hamori compares this with the hyenas "singing" (ענה) in 13:22 and reads both images as metaphorical; however, it seems to me that describing hyenas as singing is in a different category than describing goats as dancing; Hamori, *Women's Divination*, 67. Stone summarizes: "Though the nature of these creatures . . . is obscure, something other than simple goats seems to be in view," *Animal Studies*, 206, n. 26. Even if the image is only of natural goats, this can still be menacing, as evidenced by the recent film *The Witch* (2015).

39. Isaiah 34:14 mentions another possible supernatural overture with the introduction of "Lilith" (לילית) resting in the ruins, the only appearance of this demoness (known mostly from Mesopotamian literature and Talmudic writings) in the Hebrew Bible. A brief history of Lilith is found in John D. W. Watts, *Isaiah 34–66* (WBC 25; Waco, TX: Word Books, 1987), 13–14;

Thomas Römer, "Lilith. I. Ancient Near East and Hebrew Bible/Old Testament," in *Encyclopedia of the Bible and Its Reception*, vol. 16 (Berlin: de Gruyter, 2018), cols. 661–663.

40. ושפלת מארץ תדברי ומעפר תשח אמרתך והיה כאוב מארץ קולך ומעפר אמרתך תצפצף. Hays, *Covenant with Death*, 46–47, 51–53; and Hamori, *Women's Divination*, 167–176, discuss the motif of the spirits "chirping" in biblical and other ANE literature. Sometimes, ANE literature conceives of birds as being emissaries of the dead sent to bother the living.

41. This speech is also preserved in the 1963 film adaptation, but is absent from the 2018 miniseries.

42. The text is masculine; see the next chapter for further discussion. While often translated as "leprous," it's unclear as to what type of skin condition the root צרע actually refers to. An early investigation into this is John Dyneley Prince, "Notes on Leprosy in the Old Testament," *JBL* 38.1 (1919): 30–34; a more recent article is Joel S. Baden and Candida R. Moss, "The Origin and Interpretation of ṣāraʿat in Leviticus 13–14," *JBL* 130.4 (2011): 643–662. Milgrom, *Leviticus 1–16*, 816–820, provides a thorough overview of the ritual. For an argument that this ritual carries a strong influence of Persian culture, see Kazen, "Purity and Persia," in *Current Issues in Priestly and Related Literature: The Legacy of Jacob Milgrom and Beyond*, eds. Roy E. Gane and Ada Taggar-Cohen (RBS 82; Atlanta: SBL, 2015), 435–462, esp. 449–451.

43. Elizabeth W.Goldstein, *Impurity and Gender in the Hebrew Bible* (Lanham, MD: Lexington Books, 2015), 32–33.

44. Quoting Goldstein, *Impurity and Gender*, 33. See Saul M. Olyan, *Disability in the Hebrew Bible: Interpreting Mental and Physical Differences* (Cambridge, MA: Cambridge University Press, 2008), 56.

45. A recent overview of this passage, with comparison to Assyro-Babylonian rituals, is provided by Isabel Cranz, *Atonement and Purification: Priestly and Assyro-Babylonian Perspectives on Sin and Its Consequences* (FAT II/92; Tübingen, DE: Mohr Siebeck, 2017), 126–142.

46. While not directly referencing Leviticus, as noted above, the Hill House of the 2018 Netflix series behaves in ways very similar to these Levitical houses, with unexplained flooding in the walls leading to mold outbreaks that seem to spread faster than the family can clean them up.

47. The closest parallel is Deuteronomy 24:12–13, which prohibits sleeping in a garment given to one as a pledge, but commands returning it to its rightful owner before nightfall.

48. There has been much written on this stele since its discovery in 1993. Although most scholars view it as conclusive evidence that David's dynasty was known outside of Israel, a minority of scholars offer alternative readings. William G. Dever, *Beyond the Texts: An Archaeological Portrait of Ancient Israel and Judah* (Atlanta: SBL, 2017), 348–349, provides a concise overview of this find, along with a typically pugilistic argument against the archaeological "minimalists" who do not read this text as evidence of a historical Davidic dynasty.

49. Brueggemann refers to this aspect of the Davidic tales as the "Hopeful Truth of the Assembly," when David becomes an idealized figure of the past, and the hopes of the people turn to the "*anticipated* David who will restore well-being to the historical process," *David's Truth in Israel's Imagination*, second ed. (Minneapolis, MN: Fortress, 2002), 86–112, quote from 89 (itals. orig.). Allison Joseph has explored the ways in which the DtrH uses David as a "prototype" against which the other kings are compared in "Who Is Like David? Was David Like David?: Good Kings and the Book of Kings," *CBQ* 77.1 (2015): 20–41, and in further depth in her monograph *Portrait of the Kings: The Davidic Prototype in Deuteronomistic Poetics* (Minneapolis, MN: Fortress, 2015).

50. But of course, the books of Kings have been shaped for the theological purposes of the Dtr, which often involves evaluating the kings on principles other than the economic and political success of the nation during their reign. Megan Bishop Moore and Brad Kelle, *Biblical History and Israel's Past: The Changing Study of the Bible and History* (Grand Rapids, MI: Eerdmans, 2011), 145–332, offer a fascinating, if quite skeptical, evaluation of the biblical text and what we know about the history of the monarchical period from other sources. A more specific example is Ernst Axel Knauf's essay, "The Glorious Days of Manasseh," in *Good Kings and Bad Kings*, ed. Lester L. Grabbe (LHB/OTS 393; London: T&T Clark, 2005), 164–188, in which Knauf argues that the archaeological records indicate that King Manasseh,

in spite of his terrible treatment in the 2 Kings, was actually one of the most successful kings of Judah.

51. The question of why David's failures were preserved by the Dtr is a fascinating one. Steven L. McKenzie, *King David: A Biography* (New York: Oxford, 2000), argues that the David narrative is, in essence, a work of royal propaganda, in spite of some of the less flattering details. McKenzie reads the Bathsheba incident, in particular, as being "a later addition to 2 Samuel. It was added in its present place in order to produce a scheme of 'sin and punishment' or 'cause and effect' with respect to Absalom's revolt" (155). In essence, he argues that even the failings of David in regards to Bathsheba and Uriah have the effect of explaining why his household would fall apart after his rise to the throne, and to put him in the sympathetic position of the repentant sinner. This point is explored further, with a more detailed argument for 2 Samuel 11–12 as a post-Dtr addition, in McKenzie's article "The So-Called Succession Narrative in the Deuteronomistic History," in *Die sogenannte Thronfolgegeschichte Davids*, ed. A. de Pury and Thomas Römer (OBO 176; Freiburg, DE: Universitätsverlag, 2000), 123–135. John van Seters offers a counterargument, seeing the later additions to David's story as instead being driven by a different "royal ideology" than is reflected in the earlier DtrH. See his discussion in *The Biblical Saga of King David* (Winona Lake, IN: Eisenbrauns, 2009), 34–39. Taking a purely literary-critical perspective, Robert B. Chisholm, Jr., "Cracks in the Foundation: Ominous Signs in the David Narrative," *Biblio* 172 (2015): 154–176, argues that hints of the character traits that will lead to David's downfall are scattered throughout the earlier narratives of Samuel. Unfortunately, Chisholm does not develop the article title's metaphor of a "foundation."

52. While "war" is not stated directly in this passage, the Hebrew root יצא often refers to battle, as in Genesis 14:8; Numbers 1:3, 20; Deuteronomy 20:1, 23:10; 1 Samuel 8:20, 18:30; 2 Samuel 18:2–4, 6. See the entry יצא in *TLOT* 2:561–566. Meir Sternberg, *The Poetics of Biblical Narrative: Ideological Literature and the Drama of Reading* (Bloomington: Indiana University Press, 1985), 194–195, makes this point very well.

53. While a long history of tradition views Bathsheba as a temptress, there is no indication of this in the text. The question has shifted in recent times as to whether David's actions can be reasonably construed as rape. I would argue that this is clearly the case, since Bathsheba is given no agency in this narrative and would not have been in a position to turn down David's request. For a counterargument, suggesting that this imposes modern ideas of rape onto a biblical text, see Alexander Izuchukwu Abasili, "Was It Rape?: The David and Bathsheba Pericope Re-Examined," *VT* 61.1 (2011): 1–15. As a response, we might consider whether rape is, in fact, a cultural construct, or a reality that can be understood more or less adequately by constructions and norms imposed by various cultures. Caryn Tamber-Ross, using Laura Mulvey's theory of the male gaze, makes a compelling argument that neither Bathsheba nor Susanna, another bathing woman, should be "blamed for being looked at," but she also suggests that the text of Judith does portray a woman who intentionally uses her beauty to her advantage. See "Biblical Bathing Beauties and the Manipulation of the Male Gaze: What Judith Can Tell Us About Bathsheba and Susanna," *JFSR* 33.1 (2017): 55–72.

54. For further exposition of this point, see Sternberg, *Poetics of Biblical Narrative*, 196–201. A very insightful reading of this passage with a focus on the power dynamics at play is found in Ken Stone, *Sex, Honor, and Power in the Deuteronomistic History* (JSOTSup 234; Sheffield, UK: Sheffield Academic Press, 1996), 93–106.

55. An excellent extended discussion of this passage is found in Sternberg, *Poetics of Biblical Narrative*, 186–229. Sternberg uses this narrative as an example of the highly "gapped" nature of biblical narrative, in which key pieces of information are withheld from the reader, and the reader is forced to fill in these gaps on her own. Is Uriah completely unaware of David's plan, or does he have an idea of what is going on, in which case his actions are an intentional refusal to participate?

56. For more details on this parable see, in addition to the commentaries, the helpful article by David Janzen, "The Condemnation of David's 'Taking' in 2 Samuel 12:1–14," *JBL* 131.2 (2012): 209–220. Janzen surveys the work of many scholars who have noted the disconnect between the parable Nathan tells and David's actions; in particular, David committed murder and adultery, whereas the rich man in Nathan's parable is only guilty of theft. Janzen reads this

as indicating that it is primarily David's "taking" of Bathsheba that angers YHWH. Tod Linafelt provides an excellent essay on the taking of women as a source of male power in the books of Samuel; see "Taking Women in Samuel: Readers/Responses/Responsibility," in *Reading Between Texts: Intertextuality and the Hebrew Bible*, ed. Danna Nolan Fewell (Literary Currents in Biblical Interpretation; Louisville, KY: WJK, 1992), 99–113.

57. The two words of Hebrew, הטאתי ליהוה, produce an even more stark and understated effect.

58. April Westbrook's careful reading and focus on the ways in which David has abused his power provides an excellent overview of the prophetic judgment against David. See Westbrook, *"And He Will Take Your Daughters,"* 132–141.

59. Examples include *The Changeling* (1979), *The Woman in Black* (2012), and *Mama* (2013).

60. Several studies have recently examined David's processes of mourning. For 2 Samuel 12 specifically, see David A. Bosworth, "Faith and Resilience: King David's Reaction to the Death of Bathsheba's Firstborn," *CBQ* 73.4 (2011): 691–707. On David's mourning more generally, see Yisca Zimran, "'Look! The King is Weeping and Mourning': Expressions of Mourning in the David Narratives and Their Interpretive Contribution," *JSOT* 42.4 (2018): 491–517.

61. Stone's reading of this passage, along the same lines as his reading of the David and Bathsheba story, is also highly illuminating. See *Sex, Honor, and Power*, 106–119. See L. Juliana M. Claassens, *Claiming Her Dignity: Female Resistance in the Old Testament* (Collegeville, MN: Liturgical Press, 2016), 38–50, for a detailed reading of ways in which Tamar attempts to resist her brother's violence using the means available to her.

62. Alternately, one could read this as a haunted house that functions as the house in the Japanese *Ju-On (The Grudge)* series; while the initial trauma is located within a single house, anyone who enters that house becomes consumed by its grip. Leaving the house is not enough to escape from the malevolent ghosts. Once a person has come into contact with the house, the ghosts are able to follow him or her anywhere.

63. An insightful overview of this rebellion, with a focus on the political machinations of David, Absalom, and their various supporters, is found in Moshe Halbertal and Stephen Holmes, *The Beginning of Politics: Power in the Biblical Book of Samuel* (Princeton, NJ: Princeton University Press, 2017), 100–143.

64. Sternberg, *Poetics of Biblical Narrative*, 201–209, thinks that the text leaves open the possibility of Uriah being aware of David's machinations and goes along anyway out of a sense of duty. If this is true, then David's ignorance in sending for Tamar does not compare favorably to Uriah's knowingly sending his own letter.

65. Halbertal and Holmes, *Beginning of Politics*, 131–132, summarize succinctly: "Possessing David's concubines in public had the effect of reassuring Absalom's supporters and forcing undecided bystanders, who were naturally waiting to see how events transpired, to choose sides." The connections this passage makes between sexual control of women and honor will be discussed further in the next chapter.

66. Much has been written on the tragic downfall of King Saul; classic studies include David M. Gunn, *The Fate of King Saul: An Interpretation of a Biblical Story* (JSOTSup 14; Sheffield, UK: JSOT Press, 1980); W. Lee Humphreys, "From Tragic Hero to Villain: A Study of the Figure of King Saul and the Development of 1 Samuel," *JSOT* 7.1 (1982): 95–117; and W. Lee Humphreys, *The Tragic Vision and the Hebrew Tradition* (OBT 18; Philadelphia: Fortress, 1985), 23–66.

67. One might think of any number of haunted house narratives in which the house convinces a parental figure to attempt to harm their children: *The Shining*, for example, or the Netflix series of *Haunting of Hill House*.

68. King Hiram will also be an important player in the reign of King Solomon; see Michael S. Moore, "Big Dreams and Broken Promises: Solomon's Treaty With Hiram in Its International Context," *BBR* 14.2 (2004): 205–221.

69. This is the standard reading of this passage, followed by commentaries such as John Gray, *I & II Kings: A Commentary* (OTL; Philadelphia: Westminster, 1963), and Marvin A. Sweeney, *I & II Kings* (OTL; Louisville, KY: WJK, 2008), 56; also argued for in articles such

as Harry Hagan, "Deception as Motif and Theme in 2 Sm 9–20; 1 Kgs 1–2," *Bib* 60.3 (1979): 301–326; David Marcus, "David the Deceiver and David the Dupe," *Prooftexts* 6 (1986): 163–171; and Michael S. Moore, "Bathsheba's Silence (1 Kings 1:11–31)," in *Inspired Speech: Prophecy in the Ancient Near East*, ed. John Kaltner and Louis Stulman (JSOTSup 378; London: T&T Clark, 2004), 336–346; see also John Van Seters, *Biblical Saga of King David*, 331–334. A counterargument is provided by Matthew Newkirk, who argues that the text depicts Solomon's rise to the throne as the fulfillment of God's plan in "Reconsidering the Role of Deception in Solomon's Ascent to the Throne," *JETS* 57.4 (2014): 703–713.

70. See the standard commentaries for summaries and information on this. A recent exploration of Bathsheba's absence from Chronicles, attributing it to the Chronicler's glorification of David and the developing messianic ideals of the Persian period, is provided by Yossi Leshem, "'And David Was Sitting in Jerusalem': The Accounts in Samuel and Chronicles," *HUCA* 87 (2016): 49–60. A focus on generic differences as explaining the discrepancies is provided by Ron Bruner, "Harmony and Historiography: Genre as a Tool For Understanding the Differences Between Samuel-Kings and Chronicles," *Restoration Quarterly* 42.2 (2004): 79–93. A. Graeme Auld differs in seeing both Samuel-Kings and Chronicles as sharing a common source material, which he terms the Book of Two Houses; see his *I & II Samuel: A Commentary* (OTL; Louisville, KY: WJK, 2011), 9–17. Few scholars have accepted this theory, finding that "Occam's Razor" supports the theory of a Chronicler who used Samuel-Kings as his primary source and adapted it for his own theological purposes.

Chapter Five

"The Calls Are Coming from Inside the House!"

The Monstrous Within the Community

The setting is a small Canadian town in the early 1970s. Over Christmas break, the sisters of Phi Kappa Sigma receive a slew of anonymous phone calls that start off as merely obscene, but soon turn violent. In the midst of this, one of the sisters goes missing, and a local high school girl is found murdered in the nearby park. The sisters begin to wonder if all of these events are related and enlist the aid of the police. A security detail is stationed outside their house, and groups of concerned citizens are combing the town for hints of the killer. But as the police trace the source of the latest call, they make a horrifying discovery: "The calls are coming from inside the house!" The suspect is killed after a dramatic confrontation, and normalcy seems to be restored. But in the concluding scene, we learn that, in their haste to comb the park and the rest of the town, no one thought to check the attic, where the real killer has been hiding all along.

Borrowing from the urban legend of "The Babysitter and the Man Upstairs,"[1] the 1974 Canadian film *Black Christmas* is often thought of as setting the template for the slasher film that *Halloween* would perfect several years later. (But in *Black Christmas*, the Final Girl is most definitely not a virgin, and is even considering having an abortion. It's not until *Halloween* that the characters are punished for sexuality.) It's the first time this urban legend has been used in horror films; it would subsequently be reused in *When a Stranger Calls* (1979). It also served as a red herring in the film *Urban Legend* (1998), when a character thinks his caller ID has helped him identify the source of the call. He begins to climb the stairs in search of the killer, only to be told by the voice on the other end of the phone, "Wrong legend." This simple plot twist reveals a common assumption: horror comes from outside. While this assumption holds sometimes, it is frequently proven wrong. As we saw in chapter 2, the monstrous can be found within the self. In this chapter, we'll explore the ways the monstrous can come from within the community, as well as the ways that parts of the community can be transformed into a monstrous Other as an expression of power and domination.

ANXIETY AND AMBIGUITY

Clearly, threats can come from outside of the community. But perhaps even more common is the practice of scapegoating outsiders in the face of a (real or perceived) threat. Whether it's the Ammonites, Moabites, or numerous other tribes who served as the enemy of Israel (historical or rhetorical) in the Hebrew Bible, the Islamic world in the wake of the terrorist attacks of 9/11, or Mexican immigrants in the age of Trump, we have seen the consistency with which foreigners are blamed for a community's problems, and turned into monsters as a result.

There are also elements within a community that are deemed monstrous, that must be included within the community (at least partially) but which are, nevertheless, experienced as threatening. In cases like this, the monstrous comes from within the community, from within the house, even from within the family. In the Hebrew Bible, this "monster within" the community is most frequently figured as women.

Amy Kalmanofsky has explored the "dangerous sisters" of the Hebrew Bible, arguing that these sisters are frequently portrayed in narratives as "destabilizing figures who assert an independent agency that challenges patriarchal authority and threatens the stability of the natal household."[2] These female characters emerge at times of crises within the family or the community at large, and frequently serve as an indicator of male anxiety. They are the elements within society that must be controlled, but which are, nevertheless, necessary for the society's continuation.[3]

But Woman as a category in the Hebrew Bible, particularly in the priestly literature (and most dramatically within the Holiness Code), brings another important insight from monster theory to the surface. As Noël Carroll has observed, monsters are not merely threatening. They are also disgusting.[4] The titular monster from the *Alien* series features multiple sets of terrifying jaws, but when she[5] menaces Ripley in the film's climactic confrontation, the string of drool stringing from the monster's mouth is emphasized as much as the deadly teeth.[6] Numerous examples could be offered of different ways in which the disgusting elements of the monster are emphasized throughout various horror films. And frequently, bodily fluids such as saliva and vomit serve as the markers of the female monster.

The Hebrew Bible takes a similar view of women, both Israelite and foreign. For women in the Hebrew Bible, the defining bodily fluid is most frequently blood, a fascination the book shares with horror films. Erin Harrington discusses the frequency with which the onset of menses serves as the grounds for narratives of horror: "Menarche is framed as an immensely significant event, and one that is traumatic both in terms of the horror that engenders and the abrupt shift in the capacities and affects of the reproductive body."[7] Horror's view of menstruation is perhaps best summed up by the puppet-wearing Mr. Garrison in the *South Park* movie: "I don't trust anything that bleeds for five days and doesn't die."[8] As Barbara Creed has documented, the "monstrous-feminine" in contemporary horror movies is frequently linked with both childbirth and uncontrollable bodily fluids. As figured in horror films, female monsters are terrifying in large part because they are disgusting, and this disgust is frequently linked to sexuality and reproduction.

In a shockingly memorably scene from *Alien* (1979), an unfortunate crewmember experiences the reproductive power of the maternal alien firsthand, as a newly birthed alien bursts through his stomach in a barrage of gore. (Unbeknownst to him, the creature had been gesticulating inside of him.) Here, the reproductive process is fatal to the male crewmember. In the alien's adult stage, the female alien is marked by its acidic drool. And it doesn't take a committed Freudian to view the alien's multilayered, mouth-within-a-mouth as a terrifying embodiment of the *vagina dentata*.[9]

David Cronenberg's *The Brood*, released the same year, offers another striking example of the monstrous-feminine as an expression of female reproduction. The deaths that seem to follow the family of Frank and Nola turn out to be murders committed by the monstrous children of Nola, created as embodiments of her anger. After this brood of murderous offspring has grown out of control, Frank tracks his wife back to her nest to find her having mutated into a monstrous mother, a distended birthing sack hanging outside of her body. These children may be expressions of Nola's rage against the patriarchy,[10] but the film's focus remains on the male protagonist's horror at the possibilities of his wife's body.

And as Carol Clover has documented, even victimized women are made monstrous within the confines of the horror movie.[11] Possessed Regan, from *The Exorcist*, is a classic example: she terrifies us not only by spinning her head around and yelling obscenities at the priest, but also by spewing vomit and masturbating violently with a crucifix. In these actions, the disgusting capacity of her body is foregrounded and linked with young Regan's budding sexuality. *Carrie* also serves as an excellent example of a film in which the female's sexuality is deemed monstrous and serves as an object of horror.

We first see Carrie in the high school showers, casually exploring her body, until she is shocked to see blood streaming from between her legs. Unaware of processes of menstruation, she stumbles out of the shower, holding out her bloody hands and pleading for help. The other girls respond by throwing tampons at her and chanting "Plug it up!" The image of blood returns in the film's climactic scene, when Carrie is humiliated at her senior prom by having a bucket of pig's blood dumped on her. It is this humiliation that finally solidifies her transition from monstrous victim to monstrous aggressor, using the psychic powers that seem to have arrived with the onset of puberty. (Indeed, horror films often link the monstrous-feminine with the onset of puberty; *Ginger Snaps* and *Teeth* both critique this linkage.) Carrie is a living embodiment of male fears of female sexuality—her sexuality gives her enormous powers.[12]

In the Hebrew Bible, and in many other traditions, this is the power that must be tamed. Frequently, texts in the Hebrew Bible serve the purpose of describing how the community may control the sexuality of the females among it. But even in the midst of this control, these texts exhibit a deep anxiety. Women's sexuality is a dangerous and powerful force; while numerous attempts are made to control this force throughout the Hebrew Bible, the text remains deeply anxious about whether the control is complete. Like the slasher from an 80s horror film, this anxiety never quite dies. Complete control is never assured.

And this anxiety is linked to a deep ambivalence within the text, centered around an undecidability regarding the status of women within the community. As a whole, the Hebrew Bible understands women to occupy a subservient place to the men in the community, but a position higher than that of property. This leads to an unanswered question: what, exactly, is woman? If she is a human being, why is she not granted full equality with men? But if she is not fully equal, then what is she?

Nicole Ruane has noted the "ambiguous status" of women within the Pentateuchal texts. "Women in a family have no descendants, but they are parents," she writes. "They are not part of the family line, but they are part of the family. They do not possess their offspring, but they do have authority over them. . . . Because women do not fit neatly into the system of lineage and inheritance, that system must constantly adjust to accommodate them. . . ."[13] Ruane's observation regarding the multiple shifts and contradictions within the legal code invite some provocative questions. This chapter will explore these ambiguities further, suggesting that the text is unable to determine whether women occupy a position within the community as subject or object. As such, women become a threatening, monstrous abject.

Women and Bodily Fluids

As is well known, priestly literature has a great concern with questions of purity. But the priestly literature often defines the concept of purity in ways that are distinct from modern conceptions; as such, contemporary readers need to be cautious when wading into these texts. At its most basic meaning, purity is that which allows one to associate with the realm of the holy; in contrast, the holy and the impure, in the words of Jacob Milgrom, "are mutually antagonistic."[14] Milgrom continues to describe the relationship between purity/impurity and common/holy by noting that the boundaries are not fixed, but are under constant negotiation. The responsibility of the people of Israel, guided by their priests, is to manage these boundary negotiations, keep their distance from God when they are in a state of impurity, and utilize the proper rituals to return themselves to a state of purity.[15]

In modern Western culture, we tend to think of purity and impurity as moral states; purity is the absence of sin. Once the state of impurity has set in, purity can only be returned to through miraculous acts of divine forgiveness. This is very different from how P conceives of purity and impurity. Baruch J. Schwartz notes that the "holy" is that which is "separated," "belonging to," or "designated for," not that which is intrinsically superior.[16] In the same article, Schwartz continues his description of the root qds (holy):

> Another pitfall is that 'sacred' and 'holy' as used in Western languages, no matter how they are defined or derived, in the final analysis always express value. The holy is always in some sense superior, intrinsically good. Generally it is thought as pertaining to that which is of the highest ethical or moral order or possessing supreme religious importance. In particular, holy persons are distinguished by the greatest possible piety or ethical standards. As used in the Hebrew Bible, on the other hand, the root $qd\hat{s}$ does not convey any value judgment at all.[17]

The holy is associated with the realm of God, while the impure is that which must be kept away from this realm. But as we will see below, P assumes that all people will frequently fall into states of impurity, often simply through the daily activities of life. This is not a flaw, it is simply a state that must be rectified through ritual.[18] For P, impurity is frequently a ritual state, not a moral one (although the two sometimes overlap).

Most interestingly for the purposes of this chapter, questions and anxieties regarding states of purity seem to cluster around areas where life and death meet, such as birth, death itself, sexuality, and eating. As Marcel Poorthuis and Joshua Schwartz remark, "Purity rules also seem to reflect man's grappling with the numinous and ambiguous elements of life and death."[19] Questions of boundaries are fraught with anxiety and insecurity, both in the Hebrew Bible and in a wide variety of other cultures.

Anthropologist Mary Douglas, in her seminal work *Purity and Danger*, reads the Hebrew Bible's food laws as participating in the same questions of boundaries that almost all cultures wrestle with. [20] For Douglas, each culture constructs a worldview based on categories and classifications; whatever does not fit comfortably within a single category is threatening. Douglas famously describes dirt as "matter out of place,"[21] suggesting that categories are determined by a culturally constructed worldview, not by their inherent qualities. Nicole Ruane describes Douglas's thesis thusly: "Douglas emphasizes that impurity systems are constructs; they are ways of understanding the natural world through a subjective lens that characterizes and values objective phenomena."[22] Societies construct categories to make sense out of the world, but matter, animals, or people that do not fit neatly within one category threaten the integrity of the system. For Noël Carroll, this is why monsters frequently blur categorial boundaries. Carroll divides the monstrous into the categories of "fusion," in which two categories are crammed together: "inside/outside, living/dead, insect/human, flesh/machine, and so on."[23] In contrast, Carroll describes "fission" monsters, in which "the contradictory elements are . . . distributed over *different*, though physically related, identifies," such as "*doppelgangers*, alter-egos, and werewolves."[24] In both cases, the boundaries the monster violates are the source of horror.

The boundary between life and death, often ambiguous and permeable, is a particular source of anxiety. Areas of sexuality are highly fraught, as they frequently involve boundaries of the body (including elements of bodily penetration, and fluids that emerge from within the body) and boundaries of life and death, as the reproductive function is tied so closely to birth.

Questions of sexuality and bodily discharges figure prominently in several places in the P text of Leviticus. Recently, many scholars have argued convincingly that P is concerned with the bodily discharges of both men and women, and that these discharges are discussed and treated in a relatively equal manner.[25] In Leviticus 15, for example, the chapter is divided into two equal panels: the first discussing male discharges (vv. 2b–18), and the second discussing female (vv. 19–30). While sexual intercourse involving male discharge only makes the participants impure until the evening (vv. 16–18), menstruation makes a woman unclean for seven days (vv. 19), and a man having sexual intercourse with her is also unclean for this same period. As Philips notes, this correlates with the different length of the discharges: "Menstruation lasts approximately seven days, which is also the duration of its impurity for a menstruating woman (v. 19)," whereas the brief discharge of an ejaculation causes the man and his sexual partner to be unclean until the evening, "the shortest possible time span" for an impurity to last.[26] Philips notes, however, that blood is not usually inherently impure in P, and the text gives no reason for the impurity of menstrual blood.[27] This lacuna has given a space into which the H author has stepped into, offering a different interpretation of menstrual blood.

Whereas scholars have made highly plausible arguments regarding the equal treatment given to male and female bodies by P, this argument becomes much more difficult to make as the text moves into the H source.[28] As Goldstein has very ably chronicled, H exhibits a hostility towards women that is largely absent from P.[29] This first becomes apparent when comparing the two sources' views on sexual intercourse during menstruation. As noted above, P allows for this on the condition that both partners become unclean for one week after intercourse (Leviticus 15:19). H, however, flatly prohibits sexual contact while the female is menstruating in two places, Leviticus 18:19 and 20:18. Both passages are part of lengthy lists of who the male Israelites are not allowed to have sexual intercourse with: their family members, who by virtue of being kin are no longer considered possible sexual partners; animals (18:23 and 20:15–16); and other men (18:22 and 20:13). In 20:15–16, men are prohibited from having sex with animals, and men are directed to punish women who have sex with animals, but women are not addressed as a subject. This is similar to the prohibitions against homosexuality in 18:22 and 20:13—the subject addressed is male homosexuality, with same-sex female relations seeming not to have crossed the mind of the H author.

In contrast to P's refusal to offer a rational for the impurity of female menstruation, H recoils in disgust at the idea of a menstruating woman. While sex with a menstruating woman is a source of impurity for both partners in P, which requires particular rituals to regain a state of purity, H instead views this act as forbidden.[30] Sex with a menstruant is described in Leviticus 18:28 as "defiling" the land (טמא, *tama'*, in the *piel*), which Goldstein declares "indicates that we are dealing with moral impurity."[31] This verdict is confirmed by Leviticus 20:18, which commands that the man and woman who have sexual intercourse while she is menstruating "shall be cut off from their people." What was a purely ritualistic impurity in Leviticus 15 has been transformed into a moral impurity, with no means of reconciling the individual to YHWH or community.

What began in P as a concern for the emissions of both genders that occur as a result of reproductive functions has shifted in H to an attack on the female body. The female body itself has been made monstrous.[32] And this monstrosity is a threat to the male partner and the community as a whole, a threat so severe that once the man has become exposed to it, both he and his female partner have no avenue to return themselves to a state of purity. They must be expelled.

While this particular view of the monstrous-feminine, rooted in male fears of women's biological functions, is an innovation of H, female sexuality is conceived of as dangerous at many layers of the biblical text. This danger has been expanded upon in the texts' afterlives. Below, we explore a few cases of the Hebrew Bible's portrayal of dangerous female sexuality, with a focus on how the patriarchal community seeks to control this power.

Woman and Dangerous Sexuality

Patriarchal structures frequently view women's sexuality as a dangerous force. While it is necessary for the continuation of the community, it is a power that lies just outside of the patriarch's ability to entirely control and is thus a constant source of anxiety. In twenty-first-century America, feminist scholars, political scientists, and sociologists have documented the lengths to which reactionary forces will go in an attempt to control the sexuality of women. This same dynamic is at play within a large number of horror films and the Hebrew Bible.

The introductory section above briefly touches on a few horror films where woman's sexuality marks the female as monstrous, particularly for the male spectator. In *The Exorcist*, a young woman's body becomes the source of disgust; this parallels with the view of women found in H, discussed above. But frequently, females in horror narratives are terrifying not only because they are disgusting, but also because of their potential for violence.[33] In *Carrie*, female sexuality is directly linked to aggressive power. And in *Alien*, the monstrous mother kills her prey both through her bodily fluids and the violence of her procreative method. In a few recent films, the threat that women's sexuality and maternal functions present to men are made even more explicit.

The French film *Inside* was touched upon briefly in chapter 2. The plot is structured as a standard home-invasion film, following pregnant Sarah, trapped inside her home, as she fights for her life against a woman who wants to claim Sarah's baby as her own. The Woman believes she can be a better mother than the maternally ambivalent Sarah. When Sarah's boss arrives, unaware that Sarah is in danger, The Woman dispatches him with a pair of knitting scissors to the crotch. With one blow, she has asserted that she is the master of the domestic realm (with her weapon of knitting scissors), and that there is no place in this realm for a male presence. Anything that gets between The Woman and this child is in danger of meeting a violent end. In this film, maternity is depicted as being a sphere that has no room for adult men.

More recently, the British film *Prevenge* (2016) follows a pregnant woman, Ruth, who hears the voice of her unborn child encouraging her to kill the people she holds responsible for her husband's death.[34] The film is clearly sympathetic towards Ruth, as many of her victims are portrayed as contributing to oppressive societal structures. Among her victims are a man who is interested in Ruth until he finds out she is pregnant, then suddenly treats her as devoid of value; and a corporate woman who declines to offer Ruth a job, seemingly because of Ruth's impending motherhood. Many of her attacks specifically target the sexuality of her male oppressors, including a bloody castration scene. The film presents Ruth as a monstrous killer, but forces the viewer to consider whether the social constructs surrounding Ruth's motherhood should be accepted as the state of normalcy to which the film longs to return.

In both of these films, the woman is monstrous because of her intense desire to inflict violence on the men surrounding her; furthermore, these violent impulses are directly linked to maternal instinct.[35] And both films provide the means of reading them as a critique of the social structures within which the women find themselves embedded. But as I have argued in a previous monograph, the horror genre that shares more in common with the Hebrew Bible's relationship to women is the slasher film, in which the slasher serves as the patroller of boundaries who punishes transgressive women.[36] While the story of Phinehas is the Hebrew Bible's clearest depiction of such a close relationship between an unsanctioned expression of female sexuality and violent death, there is much that indicates female sexuality is a constant source of anxiety for the (male) authors of the biblical text.

Frequently, the source of the anxiety is the worry that a woman has had sexual intercourse with another man. Interestingly, this is simply assumed to be a problem by the biblical writers—the rational for this anxiety is not made explicit.[37] The expectation is that a woman's husband, master, or father will have control over her sexuality; loss of this control, as evidenced by her having intercourse with another man, is a source of shame. In narratives, one might think, for example, of the outrage of Dinah's brothers after she has been raped. Gen 34:2 describes Shechem's action towards Dinah with three verbs: לקח (*laqach*; to take, one of the standard biblical verbs for sexual intercourse), שכב (*shakav*; to lie down, another verb often used to indicate sex), and, most clearly, ענה (*'anah*; to oppress or humiliate, clearly indicating that this is an act of rape). But when Dinah's brothers (described as Jacob's sons, not as Dinah's brothers, seeming to imply that their actions are on behalf of their father, not their sister) hear of this in 34:7, they refer to it only as נבל (*naval*), "a foolish thing," and refer to the act itself using the verb שכב. They are concerned with the act of sexual intercourse itself, not with whether Dinah has been raped. Dinah's experience is irrelevant to their own feelings of shame.[38]

Similarly, in 2 Samuel 12, Nathan the prophet has called David to account for his rape of Bathsheba and murder of Uriah. As part of YHWH's judgment, YHWH will "take your women before your eyes, and give them to your friend, and he shall lie with your women in the eyes of this sun" (2 Samuel 12:11). Again, rape is under discussion, but what the male participants in the conversation refer to is simply sexual intercourse, using the verb

שכב. This comes to pass in 2 Samuel 16:20–23, during Absalom's rebellion. On Ahitophel's advice, a tent is pitched on the roof of the palace so that Absalom can "go into" (בוא, *bo'*, also a common verb used to indicate sexual intercourse) all of David's concubines.[39] While Ahitophel's statement is not entirely clear in its particulars,[40] the overall meaning comes through loudly: David's inability to control the sexuality of the women in his charge will be seen as a source of shame for him, and a source of power for Absalom.[41] Ken Stone describes the effect of this action:

> By having sexual relations with the ten concubines of David, Absalom has demonstrated David's inability to fulfill a crucial part of a culturally inscribed view of masculinity. As all Israel can see, David has been unable to maintain control over sexual access to the women of his house, and so has failed with regard to what is, in many cultures, a critical criterion for the assessment of manhood.[42]

What is at issue in this passage is David's "performance" of the role of man.[43] In Stone's summary, Absalom's rape of David's concubines is seen by the text as "an attempt to attack David's gender-based prestige, rather than as a simple declaration that David is no longer king."[44] To dethrone the king, Absalom must humiliate him sexually, and the concubines are simply collateral damage in this power struggle between the two men. The text does not consider the experience of the concubines themselves, only that their sexuality can be used as a source of power in a conflict between two rival men.

In many ways, the two texts referenced above are all about men—women are objects, incidental players in a game of masculine pride. Their only role is that of ignored victim. But somehow, the ability of women to provoke such high stakes in the realm of the male ego transforms them, in the eyes of some legal texts, into a monstrous figure, whose power must be brought under control by the community.

Perhaps the clearest example of this is found in Numbers 5:11–31, often referred to as the trial of bitter waters.[45] The trial is frequently referred to as the *sotah*, after the term used in the Mishnah to refer to a woman suspected of adultery.[46] This trial depicts such a woman, but no witnesses can be presented to confirm her act; while the crime of adultery is punishable by death for both parties (Leviticus 20:10; Deuteronomy 22:22–27), other laws also demand that at least two or three witnesses be available to confirm the crime in a case involving capital punishment (Deuteronomy 17:6, 19:15; Numbers 35:30).[47] Because no witnesses are available, the woman is put through a ritualistic ordeal, with YHWH serving as judge.[48]

The literature on this passage is quite lengthy. Along with the theological and ethical challenges presented, the passage raises two main exegetical conundrums: 1) Its literary unity (or lack thereof); and 2) The exact nature of the consequences described. Briefly, the repetitions and inclusion of what appear to be three separate rituals "intertwined,"⁴⁹ including a meal offering, a drink offering, and an oath or curse, have led some scholars to posit multiple sources underlying the final form of the text.⁵⁰ The majority of scholars today follow Fishbane in viewing the text as a unity, possibly with some supplemental additions.⁵¹ I find this reading most convincing, primarily because the passage is intelligible as a unity, without recourse to multiple source divisions. In the discussion that follows, the passage will be read as a final-form text.

But the interpretations of key passages are in themselves problematic; in particular, the consequences laid out in vv. 21 and 22, in which the woman is threatened with having ירכך נפלת (*y'rekek nopelet*) and בטנך צבה (*bitnek tzavah*). Literally, the two phrases indicate the woman's "thigh falling" and her "belly swelling," but most scholars agree that the woman's reproductive functions are in view. However, the specifics are still disputed. Timothy Ashley, for example, sees this as indicating only the preclusion of further pregnancies.⁵² However, Gray cautiously suggests that the water "may have been regarded as affecting the offspring of a guilty intercourse, so that, though the woman grows great with child ('the swelling of the belly'), the birth is abortive."⁵³ Baruch A. Levine suggests that the wife's pregnancy is likely the precipitating factor for the husband's jealousy, indicating that a miscarriage will be the result of a failed ordeal.⁵⁴ The question still remains as to whether a miscarriage is the end of the punishment, or if the woman's future fertility is affected. While the details might be obscure, the overall thrust is clear: if the woman has transgressed in matters of sexuality, her reproductive capacity will be threatened.⁵⁵

While the opening passage of the law is a convoluted series of כי (here rendered most accurately as "if") clauses, the last hypothetical is the most telling: if a husband is (וקנא את־אשתו, *qin'ah et-ish'to*) "jealous of his wife," whether or not she has actually committed an act of infidelity (Numbers 5:14).⁵⁶ In the words of Diana Lipton, "the formulation of Num. 5.14 . . . makes the woman's guilt effectively irrelevant."⁵⁷ What matters is the husband's jealousy, which is to be taken *primo facie* as evidence enough to subject the woman to this harrowing and humiliating ritual. At the end of the ritual, the text repeats that these are the steps to be followed if the woman has actually been engaged in adulterous behavior, or if her husband is jealous without warrant (5:29–30).

The intervening verses lay out the ritual in detail. The husband brings his wife and an offering to the priest (5:15). The priest then uncovers (פרע, *phara'*) the woman's head (5:18), clearly an act of shaming.⁵⁸ The woman is then made to take an oath and given the מי המרים (*may hamarim*; water of bitterness) to drink. If the woman is innocent, this water will cause great pain (5:24), but she will still be able to bear children afterwards.⁵⁹ A woman who is guilty of adultery is less fortunate.

Many scholars have noted the problematic gender imbalance of this legislation; these procedures cover a husband who is jealous of his wife's suspected infidelity, but no parallel procedures address a jealous wife. But the problematics of gender exhibited by the text run much deeper than this. As noted above, many scholars note that this ordeal seems to be a special case for a situation outlined elsewhere in the legal codes. If adultery can be proven by witnesses, the woman and her partner in adultery are subject to the death penalty (Leviticus 20:10; Deuteronomy 22:22–27). This is in keeping with the legal practice of only permitting capital punishment in circumstances where witnesses are available (Deuteronomy 17:16, 19:15; Numbers 35:30). But it is only in the case of suspected adultery where a procedure must be outlined for if no witnesses were present. Implicitly, the text seems to imply that other crimes may go unpunished. If no witnesses were present for the crime, then the community must drop their suspicions and continue. This is unfortunate, but it is not possible for all crimes to be punished; sometimes, there is simply a lack of evidence.

However, in the case of a woman's adultery, this is unacceptable. Numbers 5:11–31 views this as a crime so severe that if the husband's suspicion is the only evidence, YHWH must be brought into the situation as judge. Apparently, the risk to the community is so great that a woman's adultery cannot go unpunished, whether there is evidence present or not. If a trial is not possible due to a lack of witnesses, then the community still has further recourse to enlist YHWH's aid through the ordeal of the bitter waters. This seems to imply that the power of woman's sexuality is so great that the community cannot rely only on their husbands to contain it: YHWH can be called in to provide assistance.

In *Carrie*, the protagonist undergoes a pair of *sotah* ordeals. In both scenarios, blood is linked to a public ritual of shaming, which is then interpreted as a statement regarding Carrie's sexuality. The first instance is the opening shower scene, discussed briefly above. The onset of Carrie's menstruation turns Carrie into an object of ridicule, with the other girls in the locker room responding by throwing tampons at her and chanting "Plug it up!" An interpretation linking the onset of menses to sexual impurity is provided by Carrie's mother, the fundamentalist Mrs. White. When Carrie returns home, her mother opens a tract to a chapter entitled "The Sins of Women," and reads: "And God made Eve from the rib of Adam. And Eve was weak, and loosed the raven on the world. And the raven was called sin." Mrs. White concludes the reading by hitting her daughter with this book, then forcing her to repeat, "The raven was called sin!" For Mrs. White, there is only one possible outcome for the ritual that Carrie has just endured: for entering into womanhood, she is judged guilty. Mrs. White continues with her theology by identifying the first sin as "intercourse" and identifying "the curse" that entered the world after Adam and Eve ate the forbidden fruit with "the blood." In Mrs. White's worldview, menstruation isn't simply unclean, it is a direct result of sin and leads inevitably to sin. Carrie protests, "I didn't sin, Mama!" but her protests go unheeded. Mrs. White concludes the encounter by praying, "Oh Lord, help this sinning woman see the sin of her days and ways."

This scene finds its echo near the film's conclusion, as Carrie is offered a date to the senior prom by popular Tommy. While Tommy has asked Carrie in a (perhaps misguided) gesture of kindness, some of Carrie's classmates have other ideas: they plan to rig the voting for prom king and queen, ensuring that Carrie will win, in order to humiliate her in front of the school. Mrs. White once again provides the exegesis for this event, as she forbids Carrie to go to the prom: "After the blood come the boys, like sniffing dogs!" Mrs. White warns her daughter. Mrs. White continues the connection between menstruation and sexuality that she began in the earlier scene, once again linking both to sin. Carrie disregards this in addition to her mother's prescient warning that "They're all gonna laugh at you!" and goes to the prom with Tommy. But after she is named prom queen and brought up on the stage, she and Tommy are doused with a bucket of pig's blood. The ritual of senior prom is turned into another kind of *sotah*, in which Carrie is once again judged unclean. And to ensure that the viewer makes the connection between this scene and Carrie's earlier ordeal in the shower, Carrie hears both her mother's voice in her mind, repeating "They're all gonna laugh at you!" as well as her peers in the locker room chanting "Plug it up!" This is what finally triggers Carrie's telekinetic powers to reveal their full force, as she turns the school gymnasium into a bloodbath. Carrie decides not to accept the verdict of this final *sotah*.

These ordeals share much in common with the biblical trial. They are both public ordeals, in which the woman's private life is put on full display and judged by the community. Nicole Ruane sees this public aspect as being central to the biblical impurity system, as a means to monitor "the sexuality and reproductive status of its members."[60] Questions of sexuality cannot be controlled if they are kept private. These rituals also have an authority aside from the community serving as judge: YHWH, in the biblical text, and Mrs. White, as *Carrie*'s priestly stand-in. They are both linked to the woman's sexuality by the suspicion of adultery in the *sotah* and Mrs. White's conviction that the natural state of women is sin, with menstruation leading naturally and inevitably to "intercourse."

While the *sotah* ordeal is clearly a ritual of shaming and male dominance, it also reveals the community's deep anxiety concerning women's sexuality. As in a number of modern horror films, such as *The Brood* or *Carrie*, woman is viewed as being a dangerous presence within the community, one which could sow the seeds of its destruction at any time. As such, a constant vigil must be kept around woman's sexuality, lest this power be unleashed. All of the men of the community must be on guard and listen closely to their feelings of suspicion so that YHWH can be called at the first hint of danger. Woman, by virtue of the power of her sexuality, is a dangerous threat that all of the community's power must be marshalled to corral it. If the death penalty is not practical, calling for YHWH as backup is the next step.

Woman as the Monstrous Abject

Along with being a potentially devastating threat to the community, women also fulfill the role of the monster by their uncategorizable nature. Throughout the Hebrew Bible, women are on the margins of a variety of categories, never fitting quite cleanly into one or the other. French linguist and psychoanalytic theorist Julia Kristeva has created the term "abject" to describe this state of existing on the boundaries of a variety of categories; this section will explore the ways in which the Hebrew Bible, in particular its legal traditions, view women as existing in this state of abjection.

Kristeva has described the state of being neither subject nor object as the state of abjection. She introduces this theory in her seminal work *Powers of Horror: An Essay on Abjection*, a beautifully poetic and maddeningly obtuse text.[61] Kristeva writes, "It is thus not lack of cleanliness or health that causes abjection, but what disturbs identity, system, order. What does not respect borders, positions, rules. The in-between, the ambiguous, the composite."[62] Kristeva offers as examples of the abject a corpse, excrement, and, what she considers the ultimate abject, the maternal body.

In Kristeva's theory (building on the work of Jacques Lacan), the newborn infant does not distinguish between its own body and the body of its mother. When the infant finally discovers that these two bodies are distinct, the infant begins the painful process of separation, which Kristeva terms "matricide."[63] This involves a symbolic killing of the mother, as the infant rejects the realm of the maternal to enter into the symbolic order, the world of language rather than signs, governed by the father.

While abjection is the state of women as portrayed in much of the Hebrew Bible, this section will focus on one specific aspect of abjection: the legal code's undecidability as to whether the female members of the community are being spoken to by the law, or if their relationship to the law is only mediated through the male members of the community.[64] Are they subject or object? What is their relationship to the law, and, hence, to the community? While this would seem a straightforward question, the text itself presents a high degree of ambiguity.

These questions are foregrounded in the decalogue, in both its priestly version (Exodus 20:1–17) and the version in Deuteronomy (Deuteronomy 5).[65] From the decalogue's beginning, the verbs are all in second person masculine forms. This in itself isn't surprising, as the masculine form frequently also stands in as the generic form for both males and females.⁶⁶ But a more careful examination makes it difficult to tell if women are, in fact, being spoken to at all by these laws. Most clear in this regard is Exodus 20:17, admonishing the listener: "You shall not covet your neighbor's house; you shall not covet your neighbor's wife, or male or female slave, or ox, or donkey, or anything that belongs to your neighbor." Two points stand out in this passage. First, the wife has been included in a list of items that are primarily construed as property.⁶⁷ While the hearer's wife is not directly labeled as property, the force of the concluding descriptor is clear: "or anything that belongs to your neighbor" (וכל אשר לרעך, *v'kol asher l're'eka*). In this instance, the man's wife is portrayed as one of a man's belongings in a list including his house and animals. Perhaps even more telling is what this text reveals about who it is speaking to. There is no subsequent warning not to covet a neighbor's husband—unless we are to assume that the text did not view female desire as a possibility, this text is speaking only to men. This leads to a challenging question: did the decalogue assume that its only audience was the males of the community, or is 20:17 an exception?

A clue is found in the introduction to the priestly decalogue in Exodus 19. In this chapter, YHWH tells Moses to prepare the people⁶⁸ to receive the commandments. This includes instructions to consecrate themselves, so they will be prepared for the third day (והיו נכוים ליום השלישי, *v'hayo n'konim layom hash'lishi*; Exodus 19:11), on which YHWH will appear. After Moses follows these instructions from YHWH and has the people consecrate themselves, Moses adds a statement of his own. Exodus 19:15 reports: "And he [Moses] said to the people, "Make yourselves prepared for the third day. Do not approach a woman."⁶⁹ As in 20:17, this verse assumes that the audience is male.

We are left with two choices. Either women are objects of the law, not subjects, or women are in a more ambiguous status, one in which they waver between subject and object depending on the particular law. With support from further legal texts below, it will become clear that the status of women under the law is shifting and ambiguous. Israelite women are supposed to follow the laws, as are the men. But their relationship to the legal texts remains unclear.

The decalogue is not the only legal code to have a tenuous hold on the status of women in the Israelite community. The Holiness Code reveals a similar ambiguity, particularly in its sexual prohibitions. As was observed above, Leviticus 15 (P) discusses the bodily emissions of both males and females in a relatively equal manner. Similarly, the language used to describe these emissions places men and women in the same status as subjects of the law. The law is delivered by Moses to "the people of Israel,"⁷⁰ and there are then instructions to be followed for a man's behavior (introduced by the phrase איש איש, *ish ish*, "any man") and a woman's behavior (introduced by ואשה, *va'isha*, "when a woman").

Moving to the Holiness Code, however, the text is much more ambiguous regarding its addressee. Chapters 18 and 20, discussed briefly above, serve as interesting examples. In Leviticus 18, vv. 1–5 are addressed as broad, overarching commands to the people as a whole.[71] All of Israel is intended to abstain from the practices of Egypt and Canaan (18:3) and follow the statutes of YHWH (18:4–5). After this, however, the commands are directed to men specifically. The relationships described as being forbidden are all those that a man might be tempted to engage in: the vast majority of the passage centers on mothers, daughters, and sisters of various relationships to the man.[72] Rather than the descriptive laws of chapter 15 ("if a man" does this), these laws are all in 2ms form: "You shall not." Given the actions described, it is clear that the reader is to take the masculine grammatical form in its most literal sense. This becomes most apparent in v. 23. In this verse, both men and women are forbidden from having sexual intercourse with animals. However, the masculine side of this equation is addressed to the listener, through the 2ms verbal form and 2ms suffix.[73] In the half of the law corresponding to Israelite women, the verbal forms shift not to 2fs, but to the third person. In verse 24, the addressee shifts back to all of Israel. The people are reminded not to partake in "any/all" (כל) of these things, which would include the sexual practices that were forbidden to women in v. 23. Now, both genders are expected to be listening again.

Clear examples like these call into question our readings of the rest of the legal codes. When we have clear documentation that the women of Israel are sometimes excluded from being spoken to by the law, what allows us to infer that at other times they are being spoken to? The clearest signal seems to be that many of the laws are universal, laws that all Israelites are expected to follow regardless of gender. But we have seen how quickly the decalogue can shift from speaking universally, to all Israelites, to assuming an audience that is male. This, by itself, is enough to raise the question of when Israelite women are being spoken to by the legal texts, and when they are not.

CONCLUSION

As discussed above, earlier generations of horror films, both American and British, frequently conceived of the monster as a malevolent force from outside the community. But in more recent horror films, particularly those released since the 1960s, the terror is more often one from within, as monsters come from our own communities, from our own families, from within ourselves. Just when we expect the killer to be menacing us from outside, we learn that "The calls are coming from inside the house!" Instead of being a threat from outside, the monster is within.

The Israelite female serves a similar function in the Hebrew Bible. She is the destabilizing element within the community, the family member who threatens to make everything unravel. By virtue of her dangerous sexual power and her existence in a state of abjection, the Israelite woman fits nicely alongside her monstrous-feminine compatriots. A wide variety of texts from the Hebrew Bible, found in numerous layers of composition and at various times throughout biblical history, attest to woman's power to threaten male pride and the purity system. While many of the Israelites' enemies (whether based in historical fact or textual creations) are external—the Canaanites, the Ammonites, the Midianites—the persistent and unique power of women to threaten the male ego is attested by the attention they are given in these legal texts. And the inability of the texts to decide on their relationship to Israelite women—whether they are subject or object—moves women further into the category of the monstrous.

The calls are, indeed, coming from inside the house, and the patriarchal society of ancient Israelite is unsure about what to do other than to create legislative boundaries around this threat. But even this effort is undone as the texts are unable to decide whether the women are being spoken to or spoken about. The transformation of woman into monstrous abject is then complete.

NOTES

1. Miriam Forman-Brunell, *Babysitter: An American History* (New York: New York University Press, 2009).
2. Amy Kalmanofsky, *Dangerous Sisters of the Hebrew Bible* (Minneapolis, MN: Fortress, 2014), 5–6.
3. In a somewhat different vein, yet with similar connotations, Ken Stone has explored the manner in which some women in the Hebrew Bible are connected with domestic animals, using Jepthah's daughter as a test case; see "Animal and Sexual Difference, and the Daughter of Jephthah," *BI* 24 (2016): 1–16. Stone remarks: "Isaac is spared when his place is taken *by* an animal, while Jephthah's daughter is sacrificed *like* an animal" (5, italics original). In the narratives Stone highlights, the value of women is precariously situated between that of the males of the community and property.
4. Carroll, *Phlosophy of Horror*, 21–23; See also Grafius, "Text and Terror," 38–39.
5. The monster is definitely portrayed as female throughout the series. See Barbara Creed's discussion in *The Monstrous-Feminine: Film, Feminism, Psychoanalysis* (New York: Routledge, 1993), 16–30.
6. The monster's drool becomes a focal point at various points throughout the series, as it proves to be highly acidic. In this instance, the deadly and disgusting are merged into one element.
7. Erin Harrington, *Women, Monstrosity and Horror Film Gynaehorror* (Film Philosophy at the Margins 2; New York: Routledge, 2018), 229. Harrington also discusses the Canadian film *Ginger Snaps* as an excellent example of the uses of menarche in horror.
8. The film's full title is *South Park: Bigger, Longer, and Uncut* (1999), ensuring that the horrific humor of reproduction is in the foreground.

9. Creed, *The Monstrous-Feminine*, 105–122. As Creed points out, this concept is not directly discussed by Freud, even though he discusses the vagina as an object of horror and "teeth dreams," which frequently seem to contain imagery (such as rooms and passageways) that Freud elsewhere connects with the vagina. Creed's readings of horror films utilizing this concept have proven highly influential. Otero Solimar, "'Fearing Our Mothers': An Overview of the Psychoanalytic Theories Concerning the Vagina Dentata Motif," *American Journal of Psychoanalysis* 56.3 (1996): 269–288, provides an overview of this motif with references to both film and folklore. The most explicit use of this motif in horror is, perhaps, *Teeth* (2007), in which a high school girl discovers that her vagina does, in fact, have teeth, much to the chagrin of her potential partners (and rapists). Erin Harrington discusses the *vagina dentata* motif in horror generally, and in *Teeth* specifically, in her monograph *Women, Monstrosity and Horror Film*, 52–75. Another scholarly treatment of *Teeth* is provided by Casey Ryan Kelly, "Camp Horror and the Gendered Politics of Screen Violence: Subverting the Monstrous-Feminine in *Teeth* (2007)," *Women's Studies in Communication* 39.1 (2016): 86–106.

10. Writer-director David Cronenberg has famously referred to *The Brood* as "Like *Kramer vs. Kramer*, but more realistic." Barbara Creed discusses *The Breed* as the paradigm of "woman as monstrous womb." *Monstrous-Feminine*, 43–58.

11. Amy Kalmanofsky has explored this dynamic of how the "male monster meets female victim thereby making female monstrous victim" in the book of Jeremiah in her article "The Monstrous-Feminine in the Book of Jeremiah," *Lectio Difficilior*, edition 1/2009. Accessed August 29, 2018. http://www.lectio.unibe.ch, accessed 8.29.18.

12. Creed, *Monstrous-Feminine*, 73–83, connects these powers to the tradition of the witch, also associated with dangerous female sexuality. Robert Eggers' more recent film *The Witch* (2015) offers an extremely provocative exploration of cultural constructs of the figure of the witch.

13. Nicole J. Ruane, *Sacrifice and Gender in Biblical Law* (New York: Cambridge, 2013), 3.

14. Jacob Milgrom, "The Dynamics of Purity in the Priestly System," in *Purity and Holiness: The Heritage of Leviticus*, ed. M. J. H. M. Poorthuis and J. Schwartz (Leiden, NL: Brill, 2000), 29–32, here 29.

15. Milgrom, "Dynamics of Purity"; Milgrom explores these ideas in more detail in his Anchor Bible Commentary, *Leviticus 1–16: A New Translation with Introduction and Commentary* (AB 3; New York: Doubleday, 1991), esp. 763–766, 1000–1004. Other recent explorations of Israelite conceptions of purity include Jacob Neusner, *The Idea of Purity in Ancient Judaism* (Studies in Judaism in Late Antiquity, volume 1; Leiden, NL: Brill, 1973); Jonathan Klawans, *Impurity and Sin in Ancient Judaism* (Oxford: Oxford University Press, 2000); and the essays included in *Perspectives on Purity and Purification in the Hebrew Bible*, eds. Baruch J. Schwartz, David P. Wright, Jeffrey Stackert, and Naphtali S. Meshel (LHBOTS 474; New York: T&T Clark, 2008).

16. Baruch J. Schwartz, "Israel's Holiness: The Torah Traditions," in *Purity and Holiness*, 47–59. Schwartz has also discussed the relationship between impurity and sin in "The Bearing of Sin in the Priestly Literature," in *Pomegranates and Golden Bells: Studies in Biblical, Jewish, and Near Eastern Ritual, Law, and Literature in Honor of Jacob Milgrom*, eds. David P. Wright, David Noel Freedman, and Avi Hurvitz (Winona Lake, IN: Eisenbrauns, 1995), 3–21.

17. Schwartz, "Israel's Holiness," 49

18. Much work has been done on the relationship between the rituals in P and their relationship to states of purity/impurity. See, for example, Hyam Maccoby, *Ritual Morality: The Ritual Purity System and Its Place in Judaism* (New York: Cambridge University Press, 1999); Cranz, *Atonement and Purification*.

19. Marcel Poorthuis and Joshua Schwartz, "Introduction," 3–26 in *Purity and Holiness*, 9. While I imagine the use of the term *man* was meant in a gender-neutral sense, its usage in this quotation is quite interesting and connects with the points this chapter will make further on.

20. Mary Douglas, *Purity and Danger: An Analysis of Concept of Pollution and Taboo* (New York: Routledge & Kegan Paul, 1966), esp. 51–71. In Douglas's later work, she revised her claims regarding Leviticus; in *Leviticus as Literature* (New York: Oxford, 1999), vii–viii,

she suggests that the Hebrew Bible is unique in attempting to construct a theological system rather than a social system. Responses to Douglas's work within the field of biblical studies include Bryan, *Cosmos, Chaos and the Kosher Mentality*, 154–167; Milgrom, *Leviticus 1–16*:718–736; Walter Houston, *Purity and Monotheism: Clean and Unclean Animals in Biblical Law* (JSOTSup 140; Sheffield, UK: Sheffield Academic Press, 1993), 93–102; James W. Watts, *Ritual and Rhetoric in Leviticus: From Sacrifice to Scripture* (New York: Cambridge, 2007), 15–27; Ruane, *Sacrifice and Gender*, 156–164.

21. Douglas, *Purity and Danger*, 44.
22. Ruane, *Sacrifice and Gender*, 158.
23. Carroll, *Philosophy of Horror*, 43.
24. Ibid., 46, italics original.
25. For example, Jacob Milgrom's discussion in *Leviticus 1–16: A New Translation with Introduction and Commentary*; Tarja Phillip, "Priestly Matters: Priestly Writing on Impurity," in *Embroidered Garments: Priests and Gender in Biblical Israel*, ed. Deborah W. Rooke (Hebrew Bible Monographs 25; Sheffield, UK: Sheffield Phoenix, 2009), 40–59; in the same volume, Elizabeth Goldstein, "Genealogy, Gynecology, and Gender: The Priestly Writer's Portrait of a Woman," 74–86. Wilfried Warning, *Literary Artistry in Leviticus* (BI 35; Leiden, NL: Brill, 1999), 106–107, discusses the passage from a purely literary/structural perspective, and identifies a similar chiasm. In spite of the degree of literary artistry identified by other scholars, Jason M. H. Gaines, *The Poetic Priestly Source* (Minneapolis, MN: Fortress, 2015) does not discuss this passage in connection with his "poetic priestly stratum," as he is concerned exclusively with narrative texts.
26. Philip, "Priestly Matters," 42–43.
27. Scholars of various cultures have noted that while many cultures share a concern with questions surrounding menstruation, there is seldom a reason given for this. Lesley Dean-Jones, in discussing classical Greek culture, opines, ". . . menses come in the form of blood, which when shed involuntarily usually signifies some injury or disease—often life-threatening; yet menstrual blood flows regularly from the woman's genitals (the source of life itself) without causing her any appreciable weakening," *Women's Bodies in Classical Greek Science* (New York: Oxford, 1994), 232. This statement makes the ancient Greeks sound rather similar to *South Park*'s Mr. Garrison.
28. Most contemporary scholars differentiate between the P source and a later H source, with H being entirely responsible for Leviticus 17–26. Christian Feucht, *Untersuchungen zum Heiligkeitsgesetz* (Theologische Arbeiten XX; Berlin: Evangelische Verlagsanstalt, 1964) sees a two-stage edition of H, composed prior to P. Israel Knohl's work, in particular, has been highly influential, though few scholars follow either his extremely early date for H (during the reign of Hezekiah, between 743 and 701), or the large number of H additions found outside of Leviticus 17–26. Knohl's argument for H as preceding P is found in *The Sanctuary of Silence: The Priestly Torah and the Holiness School*, trans. Jackie Feldman and Peretz Rodman (Minneapolis, MN: Fortress, 1995), 111–123. For further discussions on the relationship between H and P and histories of scholarship, see Jan Joosten, *People and Land in the Holiness Code: An Exegetical Study of the Ideational Framework of the Law in Leviticus 17–26* (VTSup LXVII; Leiden, NL: Brill, 1996), 5–8; Wilfriend Warning, *Literary Artistry in Leviticus* (BibInt 35; Leiden, NL: Brill, 1999), 8–14; Christophe Nihan, *From Priestly Torah to Pentateuch: A Study in the Composition of the Book of Leviticus* (FAT II/25; Tübingen, DE: Mohr Siebeck, 2007), 1–11; Gaines, *Poetic Priestly Source*, 276–282. A few scholars have not accepted P's priority to H; Baruch Levine, for example, uses Lev 23 to argue that P consistently adapts the rites of H "to a later mode, which became normal thereafter." Baruch Levine, "Leviticus: Its Literary History and Location in Biblical Literature," in *The Book of Leviticus: Composition and Reception*, eds. Rolf Rentdorff and Robert A. Kugler (VTSup XCIII; Leiden, NL: Brill 2003), 11–23. The question of H's relationship to D is also vexing, with most scholars seeing D as the earlier source, but some arguing for at least portions of H as prior to D; see, for example, Jacob Milgrom, *Leviticus 17–22: A New Translation with Introduction and Commentary* (AB 3A; New York: Doubleday, 2000), 1357–1361; Jean-Louis Ska, *Introduction to Reading the Pentateuch*, trans. Sr. Pascale Dominique (Winona Lake, IN: Eisenbrauns, 2006), 187–191; Michael Fishbane, *Biblical Interpretation in Ancient Israel* (New York: Oxford University Press, 1985),

55–63, 175–177; and the book-length study by Alfred Cholewinski, *Heiligkeitsgesetz und Deuteronomium* (AnBib 66; Rome: Biblical Institute Press, 1976).

29. Goldstein, "Genealogy, Gynecology, and Gender," as well as her more fully developed argument in her subsequent monograph, *Impurity and Gender in the Hebrew Bible* (Lanham, MD: Lexington Books, 2015).

30. This shift is one of the factors Thomas Kazen points to in support of a Persian-period origin for the Holiness code, noting its similarities to the Vendidād. "Purity and Persia," in *Current Issues in Priestly and Related Literature: The Legacy of Jacob Milgrom and Beyond*, eds. Roy E. Gane and Ada Taggar-Cohen (Resources for Biblical Study 82; Atlanta: SBL, 2015), 435–462, esp. 451–453.

31. Goldstein, *Impurity and Gender*, 52. Goldstein traces the use of טמא to describe menstruation in both H and Ezekiel, a prophetic text that demonstrates a high level of congruity with H's worldview.

32. Amy Kalmanofsky has made a similar observation with regard to the motif of childbirth in prophetic literature. See her article "Israel's Baby: The Horror of Childbirth in the Hebrew Prophets," *BibInt* 16.1 (2008): 60–82.

33. Freud has explored the male fear of female sexuality; see, for example, his essay "Analysis of a Phobia in a Five Year Old Boy" (known more popularly as "Little Hans"), in which Freud posits that males view women as objects of fear because they understand them as having been castrated. This essay is found in *The Standard Edition of the Complete Psychological Works of Sigmund Freud*, trans. James Strachey (London: Hogarth, 1953–1966), 10.1–50. Creed examines this theory in *Monstrous-Feminine*, 88–104.

34. I have explored this film more fully in a blog post, "Single Moms in Horror: Progressive and Conservative Ideologies Beneath the Surface," *Monstrous Times*, May 5, 2017. Accessed August 16, 2018. https://monstroustimes.wordpress.com/

35. The question of "maternal instinct" is a fraught one. Grafius, "Ideas of Maternity," provides an overview of the contemporary debate; the philosophical work of Elisábeth Badinter, in texts such as *Mother Love: Myth and Reality*, trans. Francine du Plessix Gray (New York, McMillan: 1980) has been influential in questioning the patriarchal assumptions lying behind the concept of maternal instinct. Another fascinating discussion is found in Rozsika Parker, *Torn in Two: The Experience of Maternal Ambivalence* (New and Revised ed.; London: Virago Books, 2005).

36. Grafius, *Reading Phinehas*, 88–94, discussing the work of Clover, *Men, Women, and Chain Saws*, and Dika, *Games of Terror*.

37. Eve Levavi Feinstein, *Sexual Pollution in the Hebrew Bible* (New York: Oxford University Press, 2014), argues that concepts of pollution underlie this anxiety; women are viewed as being contaminated by sexual contact, and this contamination can then be spread to subsequent sexual partners. While quite convincing, I find it fascinating that this needs to be mined so carefully from the biblical text. Rather than being stated directly, it lies under the surface as an unstated assumption.

38. Much literature has been written on the story of Dinah and her brothers. For an excellent overview to the myriad ways in which the text has been contorted by its interpreters into a narrative in which Dinah can be blamed, see Joy A. Schroeder, *Dinah's Lament: The Biblical Legacy of Sexual Violence in Christian Interpretation* (Minneapolis, MN: Fortress, 2007).

39. Here, the word to describe these women is פלגש, not נשי as was used in 2 Samuel 12:11. The difference might indicate a lack of respect for the women of David's household.

40. He describes this action as being effective because it will "make Absalom odious" (*niphal* of באש) to his father.

41. Feinstein, *Sexual Pollution*, 138, sees this act as Absalom's "deliberate effort to dishonor his father."

42. Stone, *Sex, Honor, and Power*, 121.

43. The idea of gender as a performance, judged as successful or unsuccessful by its adherence to appropriate cultural norms, comes from the influential book of Judith Butler, *Gender Trouble: Feminism and the Subversion of Identity* (New York: Routledge, 1990), particularly 185–193.

44. Stone, *Sex, Honor, and Power*, 121.

45. For a history of scholarship and an argument for this as the most fitting translation, see Eve Levavi Feinstein, "The 'Bitter Waters' of Numbers 5:11–31," *VT* 62 (2012): 300–306.

46. The Mishnah includes a tractate entitled *Mishnah Sotah*, Hebrew סוטה.

47. Other scholars have also read this case in conjunction with the requirement for witnesses. See Phillip J. Budd, *Numbers* (WBC 5; Nashville: Thomas Nelson, 1984). Jacob Milgrom, *Numbers* (JPS Torah Commentary; Philadelphia: Jewish Publication Society, 1990), 38, oddly remarks that capital punishment is usually not permitted without multiple witnesses, but that Numbers 5:13 "implies that the case of an adulteress is an exception." Here, Milgrom seems to overlook that this ritual is intentionally constructed to invite YHWH to participate as judge, as a way to solve this very dilemma.

48. Martin Noth, *Numbers: A Commentary*, trans. James D. Martin (OTL; Philadelphia: WJK, 1969), 48, refers to this as the "most exhaustive law procedure that has been preserved in the Old Testament for the carrying out of a so-called divine judgment." George Buchanan Gray, *Numbers: A Critical and Exegetical Commentary* (ICC; Edinburg: T&T Clark, 1903), 48, notes that this ritual helps the community to feel confident that "the judgment [is] due to Yahweh's activity."

49. Timoth Ashley, *The Book of Numbers* (NICOT; Grand Rapids, MI: Eerdmans, 1993), 120.

50. D. B. Stade, "Beiträge zur Pentateuchkritik," *ZAW* 15 (1895): 166–175, is usually credited as being the first to propose dividing this passage into two sources. For a more recent argument in favor of this solution, see Jaeyoung Jeon, "Two Laws in the Sotah Passage (Num. v 11–31)," *VT* 57 (2007): 181–207. Jeon argues for two strands based on the Laws of Hammurabi 131 and 132.

51. Michael Fishbane, "Accusations of Adultery: A Study of Law and Scribal Practice in Numbers 5:11–31," *HUCA* 45 (1974): 24–45; see also Jacob Milgrom, "The Case of the Suspected Adulteress, Numbers 5:11–31: Redaction and Meaning," in *The Creation of Sacred Literature*, ed. R. E. Friedman (Berkley: University of California Press, 1981), 69–79; Tikva Frymer-Kensky, "The Strange Case of the Suspected Sotah," *VT* 34 (1984): 11–26. Fishbane, in particular, has argued that the repetitions are common in ANE legal texts and frequently serve as a means of clarification and emphasis. A brief summary of this debate is found in Ashley, *Numbers*, 119–120.

52. Ashley, *Numbers*, 131–132. Ashley sees nothing in the text to indicate that the woman must be pregnant, so he rules out miscarriage as a possible punishment.

53. Gray, *Numbers*, 48.

54. Baruch A. Levine, *Numbers 1–20: A New Introduction with Translation and Commentary* (AB 4A; New York: Doubleday, 1993), 203. Levine then proceeds to suggest that this indicates a "pro-choice" view held by the priestly class, as if forced miscarriages had anything to do with a free choice. I find this suggestion to be in poor taste, at best.

55. Ashley, *Numbers*, reads this ordeal as an instance of the severe threat brought about by contact between the impure and the holy; if the woman is, in fact, impure, this "brings disaster" (124). He further summarizes: "One who is unclean is in great danger in the presence of the holy" (129).

56. The Hebrew phrase referring to infidelity is נטמאה, a niphal form of the verb that usually means "to defile." By using the niphal form, the implication is that the woman has brought this condition upon herself; her sexual partner (real or imagined) escapes culpability in this ritual.

57. Diana Lipton, "Feeding the Green-Eyed Monster: Bitter Waters, Flood Waters, and the Theology of Exile," in *Embroidered Garments: Priests and Gender in Biblical Israel*, ed. Deborah W. Rooke (HBM 25; Sheffield, UK: Sheffield Phoenix, 2009), 102–118, here 111.

58. Among the commentators, Levine, *Numbers*, 206, makes specific mention of this as an act of shaming; Ashley, *Numbers*, 129, also points out that Mish *Sotak* 2:5–6 adds further elements of shame to this ritual, specifying that the woman be bound and have her breasts bared. Perhaps the most well-known biblical passage in which uncovered hair is associated with shame is 1 Corinthians 11:2–16. The literature on this passage is vast, much of it focusing on Paul's usage of kefalh\, "head" or "glory," and what this phrase means for the relationship between men and women, which is outside of the scope of this article. For an overview, see, for example, Michael Lakey, *Image and Glory of God: 1 Corinthians 11:2–16 as a Case Study in*

Bible, Gender and Hermeneutics (LNTS; New York: T&T Clark, 2010), 6–36; David E. Blattenburger III, *Rethinking 1 Corinthians 11:2–16 Through Archaeological and Moral-Rhetorical Analysis* (Lewiston, NY: Edward Mellen, 1997), 1–8; and, from an evangelical perspective, Thomas R. Schreiner, "Head Coverings, Prophecies, and the Trinity: 1 Corinthians 11:2–16," in *Recovering Biblical Manhood and Womanhood: A Response to Evangelical Feminism*, eds. John Piper and Wayne Grudem (Wheaton, Ill: Crossway Books, 1991), 124–139. See also the Testament of Job 23–26, in which Job's wife is tricked by a disguised Satan into allowing him to cut her hair and responds with horror at his wife's humiliation. This episode is discussed in Robert A. Kugler and Richard L. Rohrbaugh, "On Women and Honor in the *Testament of Job*," *JSP* 14:1 (2004): 43–62; and Maria Haralambakis, "'I Am Not Afraid of Anybody, I Am the Ruler of this Land': The Portrayal of Job in the *Testament of Job*," in *Men and Masculinity in the Hebrew Bible and Beyond*, ed. Ovidiu Creanga (Sheffield, UK: Sheffield Phoenix, 2010), 127–144.

59. Budd, *Numbers*, 67, argues that there is "little danger to the innocent in such a procedure," since YHWH is understood as the arbiter; the "great pain" inflicted by the water, regardless of the woman's guilt or innocence, does not seem to rise to the level of "danger" for Budd.

60. Ruane, *Sacrifice and Gender*, 159.

61. Julia Kristeva, *Powers of Horror: An Essay on Abjection*, trans. Leon S. Roudiez (New York: Columbia University Press, 1982). Thea Harrington has provocatively explored the poetic qualities of Kristeva's essay and its refusal to adhere to standard philosophical format. She argues that *The Powers of Horror* is an abject text within the discipline of philosophy, mirroring Kristeva's own position as abject. Since Kristeva is simultaneously part of the traditions of Hegel and Lacan, and a critic of these traditions, she can be situated neither completely inside nor outside, resulting in an ambiguous status. Harrington writes: ". . . the performative nature of her work reveals her own enactment of a practice that critiques these traditions" (140). Thea Harrington, "The Speaking Abject in Kristeva's *Powers of Horror*," *Hypatia* 13.1 (1998): 138–157. Other surveys of Kristeva's conception of the abject are found in Grafius, *Reading Phinehas*, 82–86; Gail Weiss, "The Abject Borders of the Body Image," in *Perspectives on Embodiment: The Intersections of Nature and Culture*, eds. Gail Weiss and Honi Fern Haber (New York: Routledge, 1999), 41–59. More general introductions to Kristeva's thought include Kelly Oliver, *Reading Kristeva: Unravelling the Double-Bind* (Bloomington: Indiana University Press, 1993) and Sara Beardsworth, *Julia Kristeva: Psychoanalysis and Modernity* (Albany: SUNY University Press, 2004). Kristeva's theory has been applied to a variety of other disciplines with fascinating results. Noëlle McAfee, for example, has read our relationship to the foreigner through the lens of abjection in "Abject Strangers: Towards an Ethics of Respect," in *Ethics, Politics, and Difference in Julia Kristeva's Writing*, ed. Kelly Oliver (New York: Routledge, 1993), 116–134. Closer to this current chapter's field of exploration is Creed, *Monstrous-Feminine*; another interesting use of the abject in analysis of film is Fran Pheasant-Kelly, "Cinematic Cyborgs, Abject Bodies: Post-Human Hybridity in *T2* and *Robocop*," *Film International* 53: 54–63.

62. Kristeva, *Powers of Horror*, 2.

63. In addition to *The Powers of Horror*, Kristeva also discusses matricide in *Black Sun: Depression and Melancholia*, trans. Leon S. Rudiez (New York: Columbia University Press, 1989), in which she argues that an incomplete separation from the maternal figure is the root of melancholia. On Kristeva's concept of "matricide," see Miglena Nikolchina, *Matricide in Language: Writing Theory in Kristeva and Woolf* (New York: Other Press, 2004), 85–88; Allison Stone, "Against Matricide: Rethinking Subjectivity and the Maternal Body," *Hypatia* 27.1 (2012): 118–138. On reading horror films with Kristeva's concept of matricide, see Brandon R. Grafius, "*Mama* and Kristeva: Matricide in the Horror Film," *Post Script* 36.1 (2017): 52–63.

64. Jacques Derrida has undergone a similar exploration in his two-volume series of essays, *The Beast and the Sovereign*. The guiding question of these essays is the relationship to the beast and the sovereign, the animal and the king. Derrida asserts that both are outside of the law: the king above it, the beast below it. By virtue of not being a subject to the law, beast and

sovereign share a surprising amount of similarities. See *The Beast and the Sovereign*, trans. Geoffrey Bennington (Chicago: University of Chicago Press; vol. 1, 2009; vol. 2, 2011).

65. As with many questions of historical development, there is little scholarly consensus regarding the date or authorship of these texts. As briefly described by Douglas A. Knight in *Law, Power, and Justice in Ancient Israel* (Library of Ancient Israel; Louisville, KY: WJK, 2001), the decalogue is "the wild card in this historical progression of legal codes" (24), with some scholars dating it as the earliest of Israelite law, and others placing it much later in the process. An excellent overview of the scholarship is provided by David H. Aaron, *Etched in Stone: The Emergence of the Decalogue* (London: T&T Clark, 2006), 13–40. Aaron himself sees the decalogue as "written by a group of postexilic authors . . . based upon earlier attempts to create a covenant scene that would serve to unite the Israelite people at a time of political and social discord" (1). For Aaron, the repetitions of the decalogue are a product of literary concerns rather than indicating a source-critical question. While there are significant differences in the two versions of the decalogue, this discussion will refer primarily to verse numbers from Exodus; as will be clear below, the only differences relative to this discussion will be found in Exodus's frame narrative.

66. See, for example, Bruce K. Waltke and M. O'Connor, *An Introduction to Biblical Hebrew Syntax* (Winona Lake, IN: Eisenbrauns, 1990), §6.5.3, and the examples cited where both 2ms and 3ms forms are clearly meant to indicate men and women together; Exodus 20:10 is among their examples.

67. T. M. Lemos, "Were Israelite Women Chattel? Shedding New Light on an Old Question," in *Worship, Women and War: Essays in Honor of Susan Niditch*, eds. John J. Collins, T. M. Lemos, and Saul M. Olyan (BJS 357; Providence, RI: Brown Judaic Studies, 2015), 227–241, argues that women are never described as property in the Hebrew Bible, although their status is certainly lower than that of men. This essay does not address this passage from the decalogue. Lemos has further explored the question of whether brides were purchased as property in a wide range of ancient near eastern contexts in her monograph *Marriage Gifts and Social Change in Ancient Palestine, 1200 BCE to 200 CE* (New York: Cambridge University Press, 2010).

68. Here, העם is used, which should erase any ambiguity that might arise from the phrase בני ישראל. However, it is clear that this is not sufficient to identify the text's intended audience.

69. ויאמר אל–העם היו נכנים לשלשת ימים אל–תגשו אל–אשה. For תגשו as referring to sexual activity, see *HALOT*, "נגש."

70. Technically the "sons of Israel" (בני), another instance of continued ambiguity. It seems likely that in this instance the use of בני is merely an instance of the grammatical masculine form being primary, but it is difficult to determine for sure whether the text intends that this law is spoken to all of Israel, or only the men.

71. At least it seems that all people are being addressed. However, note that the passage is once again addressed to בני ישראל, leaving open the question as to whether this is simply a grammatical form, or if it is intentionally indicating that only the men are being spoken to.

72. Although see the vexing 18:7, in which the nakedness of the listener's father is not to be uncovered. On this verse, see Milgram, Leviticus 17–22, 1536–1538.

73. ובכל–בהמה לס–תתן שכבתך.

Chapter Six

The Monstrous YHWH

On his way home from work, a single father in Texas (named only "Dad Meiks" in the film's credits) has a revelation. A light from the heavens leads him to an axe, and a message from an angel tells him that he and his two young boys will be given a task to accomplish. This task turns out to consist of murdering the names on a list, which Dad claims was given to him by God. His young sons Fenton and Adam Meiks become accomplices in his killing spree, with varying degrees of willingness. But when the two children are grown, long after their father has passed away, the murders are continuing. The final twist comes when Adam kills the investigating officer, and we are given a glimpse of what Adam sees, and what the officer knows to be true: the officer murdered his mother many years before, a crime which Adam could not possibly have been aware of on his own. The implication is clear: like his father before him, Adam is, indeed, receiving revelation from the divine, and their murders have truly been exacted at the command of God. As viewers, the horror we are left with is the possibility that God is a monstrous God of vengeance, one who has no qualms about using children to enact bloody retribution.

GOD THE GREAT AND TERRIBLE

In his book *The Bible Tells Me So . . .*, Peter Enns suggests that one of the biggest problems the modern reader has in approaching the Bible, particularly the Hebrew Bible, is that it isn't the kind of book we expect it to be.[1] "When you read the Bible on its own terms," Enns writes, "you discover that it doesn't behave as a holy rulebook should."[2] Instead of offering "Truth downloaded from heaven,"[3] the Bible is frequently perplexing, mystifying, and, as we've seen in this book so far, frightening. Perhaps nowhere is this more apparent than in the Hebrew Bible's portrayal of God.

YHWH has tender moments, certainly: we think of YHWH's walks with Adam in the garden, the deep conversations with Moses, the beautiful relationship with David, and the care God shows for so many people in the Hebrew Bible. (However, given the previous chapter's subject matter, one might note that the vast majority of these examples involve YHWH's relationship with male characters.) But there are also times when YHWH is ornery, angry, and maddeningly inconsistent.[4]

We can start with a brief discussion of YHWH's anger. While YHWH's anger can be an uncomfortable emotion for readers of the Bible to wrestle with, after closer inspection this emotion ends up being less troubling than it might at first appear. For example, when YHWH threatens judgment on Jerusalem and the nations in the prophetic books, it's usually the case that YHWH's anger is the result of some terrible behavior on the part of the people, frequently in the realm of social justice. Theologian Miroslav Volf, for example, has argued that wrath is a necessary component of a God who cares deeply enough to desire justice.[5] Even if this makes us uncomfortable, we understand. Anger at injustice is rational. We want to see this anger balanced with mercy and love, but there are enough passages in both testaments to allow us to do this without much difficulty.

But those aren't the instances of YHWH's behavior that are most troubling. What's more complicated is when YHWH suddenly becomes furious at Moses and Aaron, seemingly because they didn't follow YHWH's instructions to the letter when trying to get water for the people at Meribah (Numbers 20:2–13).[6] Or when YHWH decides to harden Pharaoh's heart so that Pharaoh will not let the Israelites go, so that YHWH will get to perform more violent miracles (Exodus 4:21; 7:3; 14:4). And there seems to be something about the ark that puts YHWH in a foul mood; in 1 Samuel 6:19, the people of Jeconiah didn't rejoice sufficiently when the ark came through their village, so YHWH killed seventy of them. Or when Uzzah makes the mistake of touching the ark and is struck dead on the spot (2 Samuel 6:7).[7] In these cases, and in many others, it's not just that God gets angry when people behave poorly. It's that YHWH is not rational. The rules are difficult (if not impossible!) to determine in advance, and the punishment seems arbitrary, as if YHWH is responding to whims of which humans aren't privy to. In these passages, God is completely unpredictable.

In the early part of the twentieth century, Rudolf Otto argued that this irrational side of God is key to our experience of the divine.[8] Otto refers to this side of God as "the numinous," and argues that this experience of God is one of the foundational emotions of religion. This inability to comprehend, this overwhelming feeling of a universe that doesn't adhere to any recognizable rules, is for Otto at the heart of what it means to approach God. Otto describes the experience of "creature-feeling," in which the subject experiences a profound sense of smallness in the face of the vastness of the universe.[9] The subject understands how vulnerable he or she is, and is acutely aware of his or her helplessness.[10] Otto understands the ground of religious feeling to be this experience of terror at the overwhelming nature of the divine. So for Otto, religious expression does not stem from feelings of gracious love, but from feelings of fear. In Otto's understanding, as our religions have developed, our rituals attempt to sublimate this fear.[11]

I would suggest that the God Otto offers to us, while far less comforting than the God we have often been presented with, is a God who explains a good deal more of our experiences. The universe is not always a kind place. It sometimes feels as if we are being punished for small infractions, while others commit malicious acts of much greater consequence and skate away without penalty. The world often doesn't make sense to us, and it's this irrational, sublime God who governs these incongruities, who oversees the times when the simple choices of Proverbs don't work out.

Horror movies have picked up on this possibility of God as holding more terror than comfort as well. In addition to the film *Frailty*, discussed briefly at the chapter's beginning, a highly relevant example is Frank Darabont's *The Mist*, adapted from a Stephen King novella of the same name.[12] In both the novella and the film adaptation, a mist descends upon a small town in rural Maine; the mist harbors vicious monsters that turn anyone caught out in the mist into quick prey. David and his young son, Billy, are trapped in a grocery store with a group of other scared customers, debating whether the smartest move is to hunker down and try to wait until the mist passes, or develop a more daring plan to seek help. Tensions rise in the supermarket, however, when one of the local women, Mrs. Carmody (played with a wonderful sense of both dread and mania by Marcia Gay Harden), starts preaching that these are signs of the end times, and that everyone needs to repent if they hope to be saved. At first, she is only annoying. But as the situation worsens, Mrs. Carmody starts to gather followers and turns her preaching towards the contents of a new revelation she has received: the necessity of a blood sacrifice. (Without having done a quantitative study, I'm confident that this film uses the word "expiation" with greater frequency than any other Hollywood film.) Eventually, she identifies Billy as the innocent blood that must be shed.[13] This forces David, Billy, and a few other followers to make a dash for David's SUV, with a plan to see if they can drive far enough to leave the Mist behind.

Up until this point, the film follows the novella faithfully.[14] But their endings diverge dramatically. In King's novella, the small band drives and scans their radio, but finds no signs of the mist coming to an end. The novella ends with them camped in an abandoned motel, trying to hold onto hope. The film offers a much more definite conclusion, but one which sheds disturbing new light on Mrs. Carmody's rantings.

In the film, the less-than-merry band drives until their SUV runs out of gas. Alone in the woods, they wordlessly agree that death by gunshot is preferable to becoming food for the beasts of the mist; however, young Billy is asleep and unaware of this decision. As the group's patriarchal protector, David shoots his passengers, including Billy, in what he views as an act of mercy. He then turns the gun on himself, only to find that he has run out of bullets. Opening his car door and striding into the mist, understandably distraught from having just killed his son, he calls out for the monsters to come and take him. Instead, he is greeted by a military convoy rolling through the woods with flamethrowers to dispatch the monsters; the mist dissipates behind them. As society starts to return to normal, David falls to his knees, devastated.

While the film's ending is far from definitive, one strong implication is that Mrs. Carmody's rantings about expiation were, in fact, a reflection of the divine will. Mrs. Carmody had called for Billy's sacrifice as the necessary cost for deliverance from the mist. At the film's conclusion, we see the mist disappearing only after Billy has been killed. The film seems to embody Tzvetan Todorov's theory of the Fantastic, in which the narrative refuses to give definitive evidence for either supernatural or mundane explanations for events.[15] While the film's monsters are definitely real, plausible explanations for their appearance can be found both in the experiments of military stationed nearby, as well as in Mrs. Carmody's claims that the events are the result of God's wrath. If the beasts are purely the result of a military experiment gone wrong, then the film presents a world that we can understand. In fact, this would be the world of films as far back as the 1931 version of *Frankenstein*, and practically every science-fiction film of the 1950s, where pushing beyond the boundaries of human knowledge leads to terrible consequences. But if the film is interpreted to mean that God bears responsibility for unleashing these horrible monsters upon the world, then we are in a much less comfortable space. While the film's ending might be experienced as a deep tragedy, in which David and his companions gave up on hope just a few moments too quickly, the film also lends support to the idea that Mrs. Carmody's conception of God was the correct one, and that Billy's death is what allowed the mist to vanish.

This image of God as irrational and monstrous is often too terrible to consider. So readers often ignore passages in which God does not behave how one would like God to behave, or they try to shoehorn passages into our ideas of a God who acts calmly, rationally, and with humanity's best interests in mind. While this is a much more comforting God to believe in, it is not always the God experienced by the biblical writers. Sometimes God is irrational in the Hebrew Bible, and sometimes downright monstrous.

As with much of the Hebrew Bible, this presentation of YHWH is not uniform; some traditions lean on the irrationality of YHWH more heavily than others. For the Deuteronomist, YHWH's adherence to the deeds-consequence nexus is very important. We see over and over in Deuteronomy,[16] the Deuteronomistic History (particularly Judges and 1–2 Kings),[17] and the prophetic works who draw most heavily from the Deuteronomistic tradition (Jeremiah in particular[18]) that actions are rewarded with consequences, whether for good or ill. This is one of the Hebrew Bible's answers to the question of theodicy, or why bad things happen in the world: people make choices that bring consequences. As has been thoroughly discussed by biblical scholars, when faced with questions regarding Babylon's destruction of Jerusalem and the temple, the answer from the Deuteronomistic school is that the people deserved it for their idolatry and mistreatment of one another.

But that's not the only answer the Hebrew Bible gives. In other places, particularly in priestly texts and in Job, the answer isn't nearly so simple. Sometimes, the Hebrew Bible portrays a God who is sublime, irrational, and outside of all frames of references humans have. And in some places, the comparisons between God and monster are much more direct, as in several passages where YHWH is portrayed as a chaos monster. First, we'll explore a pair of passages in which the terrifying, irrational side of YHWH takes center stage, then we will move into discussing the passages in which YHWH becomes a monster of chaos.

The Irrational God

This section will first examine the brief (yet immensely befuddling!) pericope of Exodus 4:24–26, then move into a discussion of the portrayal of YHWH in the theophanic speeches at the conclusion of Job. Both passages have baffled exegetes for centuries. I will argue that, while by no means removing all difficulties, a reading of these passages that acknowledges the irrational, terrifying side of YHWH as a deeply felt reality for the authors of the Hebrew Bible will help us move beyond questions of the ethics of YHWH's character into a more fruitful discussion of how these passages attest to a common religious experience.

Exodus 4:24–26 occurs during the end of Moses's time in Midian, when he is returning to Egypt. Moses has married Zipporah, a Midianite woman, and has had children with her.[19] While in Midian, Moses encounters YHWH in the burning bush[20] and is given his commission to return to Egypt and free the people. As Moses is departing, YHWH tells him to say to Pharaoh: "Thus says YWHW: Israel is my son, my firstborn. I said to you, 'Release my son that he may serve me.' But you refused to release him; now I myself am killing your son, your firstborn" (Ex 4:22–23). We move immediately from this threat against the child of Pharaoh to a laconic statement from the narrator: "On the road, at an inn, YHWH met him and tried to kill him" (Ex 4:24). The tone is so matter-of-fact that it's easy for readers to gloss over what is happening. But we've just spent two chapters with YHWH promising to deliver the people of Israel from Pharaoh, with Moses as God's own chosen representative, and now in a single verse YHWH is trying to kill him.[21] This comes completely out of the blue, without any reason. Apparently, YHWH doesn't need a reason. Here, the monstrous, terrifying side of YHWH is dominant.

Zipporah thinks quickly and is able to save Moses, although her actions don't do much to lend clarity to the story in and of themselves. She takes a flint, cuts off her son's foreskin, and touches Moses's feet (רגלים, *reglayim*) with it. She cryptically says (to Moses?), "For you are a bridegroom of blood to me" (4:25). Something in this action pacifies YHWH, and the attack ends just as quickly, and understatedly, as it began. The narrator tells us simply, "And he left him alone."[22] The short passage concludes with a brief note that, after this, Zipporah says, "a bridegroom of blood on account of circumcision" (4:26).

It's easy to wonder what in the world is going on here. And while it seems like some of the details are lost to history, or perhaps to an accident of textual transmission, the framework we are left with gives us enough to indicate the basic structure of the narrative. Even if it's an extremely uncomfortable narrative. YHWH tries to kill Moses, but YHWH's bloodlust is satiated when Zipporah circumcises their son.

Throughout the centuries, a wide range of interpretations have been offered, with none reaching the status of consensus.[23] In a common scholarly reading, Zipporah's act of circumcision is the narrative's most important element, and the narrative serves as a kind of etiology for this practice.[24] In another, YHWH's attack is a sort of "rite of passage" for Moses, standing at the end of Moses's call narrative.[25] William Propp has argued that Moses is attempting to return to his homeland "bearing unexpiated bloodguilt," such that YHWH serves as the avenger.[26] In a similar vein, John T. Willis argues that Moses was conflicted about returning to Egypt, and YHWH's attack is a demonstration of his power in an attempt to persuade Moses.[27] Some scholars focus primarily on attempting to unravel Zipporah's enigmatic actions,[28] while others have suggested that this is the remnant of a Midianite or Kenite tale.[29] Rhiannon Graybill reads the text through a queer lens, seeing in this narrative a wounded, "fluid," prophetic body, made unmasculine in its vulnerability and rescued by a foreign woman.[30]

Fewer scholars, however, have read this as a narrative in which the primary question is one of YHWH's character.[31] Those who spend too much time with YHWH focus on ways to explain these actions, as if attempting to kill the man YHWH has just commissioned to lead the Israelites out of slavery could somehow be a rational action. Terence Fretheim, for example, places great weight on the compound verbal construction of 4:24: "YHWH *sought* to kill him."[32] In Fretheim's reading, if YHWH had truly wanted Moses dead, there would be no "seeking." Instead of a "single-minded divine intention for death," God makes a "threat" and then *"decides"* to let Moses live.[33] This attack, then, is merely a "divine demonstration of the seriousness of the matter upon which God and Moses are about to embark," rather than an earnest attempt on the part of YHWH to kill Moses.[34]

This reading contains a good deal of special pleading on behalf of YHWH, suggesting motives that seem at odds with what the text plainly states. If we start with the plain language of the text, we're left with a stark narrative: YHWH tried to kill Moses, then backed away after Zipporah's action of circumcision, for reasons unknown. Thomas Römer, connecting this narrative with Jacob's nighttime wrestling match with a divine foe in Genesis 32, states succinctly: "From the beginning, the aggressor is identified as being YHWH, whose motive is clearly to kill."[35] Attempting to kill someone doesn't merely demonstrate seriousness of purpose, it's an action of severe hostility. Divine freedom may be one of the issues under consideration,[36] but this passage primarily consists of YHWH trying to kill the person YHWH had just chosen to deliver a divine message to Pharaoh. This might help us to understand why prophets, from Isaiah to Jeremiah to Ezekiel, attempt to decline YHWH's offer of becoming a prophet; not only are they likely to face scorn from the people due to their unpopular message, but they risk becoming a target of irrational divine wrath as well.

The obvious reading of this passage is also the most uncomfortable. YHWH can be a liberator of YHWH's people; YHWH can also persecute us in the night, with no prior warning, with no reason given. It's a portrait of God very similar to that described by Rudolf Otto, in which God is far enough outside of human experience to be truly, deeply terrifying. It's a portrait of YHWH that many of the psalmists would recognize, before they return to the position of faith and trust that (usually) characterizes the ending section of each psalm.

Job experiences God in a similar way. Even setting aside the prose framework of the book, in which YHWH agrees to a wager with the satan—with Job (and his family and servants) as an unknowing guinea pig—Job accuses God throughout the poetic dialogues of irrationally persecuting Job. And when YHWH finally arrives in the whirlwind to answer Job's complaints, YHWH's speech confirms Job's worst fears.

From the beginning, the reader knows that YHWH has willingly entered into a wager with the satan,[37] in which YHWH allows the satan to inflict great calamity on Job in order to allow Job to demonstrate his faithfulness. The question is whether Job's faith is disinterested: "Does Job fear YHWH for nothing?" the satan asks, implying that Job only fears YHWH because his life is without trouble.[38] As soon as YHWH afflicts Job, the satan says, "he will curse[39] you to your face" (1:11). The question at the heart of this debate is not whether Job reveres God; the question is whether he does it for reasons that are sufficiently flattering to God's ego. It was, after all, YHWH who first brought up Job's righteousness in a conversation with the satan. So because of YHWH's pride, Job suffers the loss of his house and all of his wealth, the death of his children and servants, the estrangement of his wife, and even the health of his own skin.[40] YHWH's pride is an important characteristic throughout the Hebrew Bible;[41] here, YHWH is willing to sacrifice a great number of innocent people to defend against the satan's charge.[42]

Throughout the poetic dialogues, Job experiences God not as a protector or helper, but as a divine persecutor. In 6:4, Job proclaims, "The almighty's arrows are in me, whose wrath my spirit drinks. The terrors of Elohim are against me." While Job was not privy to the discussion between YHWH and the satan, Job identifies YHWH as the source of his persecution.[43] This motif of persecution intensifies in 7:17, in which Job parodies Psalm 8: "What are humans, that you magnify them, that you set your heart on them?" In the subsequent verses (18–20), Job continues to levy this charge against YHWH. Job does not experience YHWH as absent; on the contrary, he experiences YHWH as too deeply present, too involved in human affairs. Job is not asking for YHWH's help or intervention. He just wants YHWH to leave him alone.

Job develops the experience of YHWH's persecution into a desire to justify himself before YHWH in ch. 9. However, Job also knows that he will not be able to contend with YHWH, and that Job will be proven in the wrong even though he is innocent. "Though I am righteous," Job proclaims in 9:19, "my mouth will condemn me." The courtroom that Job imagines is a mockery, where YHWH uses YHWH's might to intimidate and overpower all others. Even if YHWH appeared in response to Job's call, Job says, "I do not trust that he would hear my voice" (9:16). This will prove true in the final theophanic speeches, when YHWH overwhelms Job to where Job can barely offer a response.

The accusations against Job mount throughout Job's discourse. Job feels hunted by YHWH (10:16) and hated (16:9), and in a remarkably violent passage, Job describes himself being broken, shattered, and having his kidneys cleaved open by YHWH (16:12–13). This is a deity who has no conception of justice, delights in persecuting the innocent, and only understands the language of power and domination.

Now, this is not to say that this is the final verdict of the book of Job. While some scholars have read the divine speech in such a way, many more have understood YHWH's appearance as indicating a sense of justice that is deeper and more complex than Job had imagined; YHWH is more involved with all of creation than Job was aware and therefore YHWH was not focused solely on Job.[44] But for much of the book of Job, the book's protagonist experiences YHWH in this manner, and this experience is preserved in the text. It's a strong enough counter-voice to complicate the depiction of YHWH as just, benevolent ruler. And it's in keeping with both Otto's understanding of the Holy and contemporary monster theory: the monster and the hero are never as far apart as they seem.

While it might be easy to write off Exodus 4:24–26 as an odd remnant from an earlier tradition, and the laments of Job as the perspective of a single character that proves to not be the final vision of the book as a whole, there are other places where YHWH's monstrous nature is much more difficult to discount. In our next section, we'll turn to the flood narrative and the Sea of Reeds, particularly in the P source, in which YHWH employs the forces of chaos as YHWH's own weapons.

YHWH the Chaos Monster

Friedrich Nietzsche's epitaph about becoming the monsters we fight against has become so common as to become a cliché.[45] But this dynamic has been present in the interplay between monster and hero many centuries before Nietzsche. As discussed in chapter 2, Safwat Marzouk has explored a similar relationship between Tiamat and Marduk. Marduk battles the chaos monster, while also harboring characteristics of the same monsters he fights against. In traditional readings of these *Chaoskampf* myths, order and chaos are binary options; each character in the narrative is on one side or the other. Hence, C. L. Crouch can discuss the frequent use of these myths in royal inscriptions, in which the king is aligned with the forces of order, and the enemy armies are depicted as forces of chaos.[46]

It's a small step from Marduk to YHWH; both of them fight chaos, and both of them, at times, participate in that which they fight against. Building off of this work of Beal and Marzouk, this essay now turns to passages in the Pentateuch, with a particular focus on the P source, in which the image of YHWH as warrior against the evil forces of chaos blurs into YHWH as chaos monster.

CHAOS IN THE FLOOD NARRATIVE

Chapter 2 has already explored the scholarly history of God as dragon slayer, as depicted in the narratives of many ancient cultures and preserved (and modified) within the Hebrew Bible. But even when the dragon is not explicitly present, her echoes remain in the presence of the sea.

Many scholars have noted that the priestly creation account of Genesis 1 responds to the chaos creation battles of other ANE texts, in particular the *Enuma Elish*. While YHWH's creation of the world is not explicitly portrayed as combat in Genesis 1, the world begins in a state of chaos (the *tehom* of Genesis 1:2)[47] over which YHWH exerts dominion through the power of YHWH's word. The state of the world before YHWH begins the act of creation is that of a watery chaos, similar to the chaotic waters of *Enuma Elish*. YHWH's first act is to create light, which YHWH can then "divide" (בדל, *badil*) from the preexisting darkness. This motif of "dividing" will continue throughout Gen 1, culminating in YHWH "dividing" the waters under the dome from the waters above the dome to form the ocean and the sky in Gen 1:7. Similarly, after Marduk has defeated Tiamat, he "divides" the monster's body into the earth and the sky. And as Bernard Batto has further noted, while many ANE creation myths, such as the Ba'al cycle, end with the victorious god building a palace, the *Enuma Elish* myth ends with Marduk resting.[48] These parallels point to YHWH as waging a similar battle against chaos in the act of creation; however, instead of defeating chaos through violence, YHWH defeats chaos through the sheer power of YHWH's word. In this passage, YHWH is on the side of order, shaping the primordial chaos into a created world.

Both the flood narrative of Gen 6–9 and the Exodus narrative also employ motifs from ANE creation myths, as has often been noted. What has been less frequently remarked, however, is the change in YHWH's role in these two stories. Instead of mastering chaos in the service of providing order to the world, these two narratives portray YHWH as being on the side of chaos, destroying what had previously been ordered. In these two passages, YHWH takes on the role of a chaos monster.

As is well known, the flood narrative shows evidence of being a blend of the P source and J source.[49] While both the J and P sources contain the basic narrative of God using the destructive power of water, the P source's connections with Gen 1 have the effect of portraying YHWH as a chaos monster, a theme which is not as strongly present in the J source. This is consistent with the P creation narrative's employment of the *Chaoskampf* motif in Gen 1. In the J text of 6:5–8, YHWH grieves over YHWH's creation of humanity; YHWH decides to destroy humanity and the animals, to "wipe out" life from the face of the earth. While YHWH plans to destroy life, the earth itself remains unthreatened. The P text of 6:9–13 introduces a further development of this plan. Not only does YHWH seek to destroy "all flesh," but YHWH plans to destroy the earth as well. The living things (all flesh) have filled the earth with violence: as a response, YHWH is going to "destroy them along with the earth" (6:13). This declaration introduces a note absent from J; YHWH's complaint is not simply with humans, or even with all living things. It is a complaint against the very earth itself, against the entirety of creation.

This is precisely how the chaos monster functions in the *Chaoskampf* myth. When Marduk battles Tiamat, there is no humanity to protect. Marduk is fighting for the integrity of creation, or at least his preferred vision of creation.[50] The patron God of the earth fights against the chaos monster who threatens to create a different world. But in Gen 6:13, YHWH assumes the role of Tiamat, threatening to undo the creation of the world described in Gen 1 and plunge creation back into formless chaos. YHWH functions as both heroic God and monstrous adversary.

By contrast, in the J narrative YHWH does not mention his plan to destroy the earth until 7:4. And here, rather than a flood upon the earth (the *mayim* of the P source), YHWH threatens to bring "rain" (ממטיר, *mamatir*) to destroy the earth's creatures. Throughout the J source, the waters are portrayed as emanating from the rain (7:4, 12; 8:2b), whereas in the P narrative the waters emanate from both the "spring of the deep" (*tehom* again, as in Gen 1:22) and the window of heaven. By bringing up water from the *tehom*, this flood is directly linked with the chaos that YHWH had subdued in the P creation account. But here, YHWH calls forth this watery chaos once again, this time to plunge the world back into its pre-creation state. YHWH seems equally willing to destroy as YHWH is to create. And when YHWH destroys, YHWH prefers to use the weapons of the chaos monster.

Chaos in the Exodus Narrative

The *Chaoskampf* motif is used in two major sections within the Exodus narrative: the "signs and wonders" of Ex 7–11, and the crossing of the Sea of Reeds in Ex 14. In both of these cases, the passages usually identified as P display a greater interest in the *Chaoskampf* motif than their non-P counterparts, and they present a stronger portrait of YHWH as using the forces of chaos as a weapon against YHWH's adversaries. In employing these forces of chaos, YHWH's role as creator god blurs with YHWH's role as chaos monster.

In the first sign of Ex 7:8–13,[51] YHWH says to Aaron and Moses, "When Pharoah speaks to you, saying 'make for yourselves a sign'," then Aaron is to throw down his staff, which will turn into a "sea monster" (the *tannin* of Gen 1:21). Here, YHWH's power is displayed as the ability to create sea monsters, the very embodiment of chaos in the ANE combat myths, and unleash them upon the world. Pharoah's advisors follow suit, also causing their staffs to turn into sea monsters, but the sea monster from Aaron's staff swallows them up. As is a recurring theme throughout this section, YHWH is proven to be the God over all creation, both Israel and Egypt; however, in this instance, YHWH proves YHWH's lordship by employing the forces of chaos.

The second, third, and fourth signs of the P traditions function in similar ways to the flood narrative of Gen 6–9. YHWH is Lord over all creation, but YHWH also exhibits a willingness to return YHWH's creation back to the preordered state by unleashing the forces of chaos. In the second sign, the waters (again, a symbol of the potential chaos within the ordered world) are turned into blood. The earlier non-P source presents only the waters of the Nile as being turned to blood (7:17–18); in the P tradition, this has been expanded to include the waters of all of Egypt (7:19).[52] What was originally conceived of as a sign demonstrating YHWH's power to Pharaoh has been transformed by the P tradition into an act that plunges all of Egypt into primordial chaos. This chaos extends "throughout the whole land of Egypt," even into drinking vessels (7:19). The extension through "the whole land of Egypt" is repeated again in 7:21. The third sign also involves the waterways; in this sign, frogs burst out of the boundaries of the waters and come up on the land. Again, the boundaries that were established in Genesis 1 are shattered, such that the distinctions between water and land are becoming meaningless. Again, YHWH reverses his role as God of creation in Genesis 1 to become a god of chaos. The land is similarly devastated by the plague of flies in Exodus 8:20 (ET 8:24): "in all the land of Egypt, the land was destroyed because of the swarm." The emphasis here is not only on Pharaoh and his officials, but on the land itself.

The other sign that shows the greatest degree of shaping by P is the plague of boils in Ex 9:8–12. This plague also portrays YHWH as undoing creation by removing the boundaries that YHWH had placed against chaos. Moses is directed to take soot (פיח, *piach*) from the kiln and throw it into the air in front of Pharaoh. This soot will become dust,[53] which will cover "all of the land of Egypt" (9:9) and cause painful boils to cover all of the humans and animals. (In 9:11, this is qualified to reveal that only the Egyptians suffer this calamity.) Whereas the earth suffered under the previous plagues, here the earth becomes an active participant in YHWH's violence. Creation itself is employed in YHWH's battle against Egypt.[54]

The *Chaoskampf* motif is most clearly utilized in the miracle at the Sea of Reeds in Exodus 14. Once again, the P narrative demonstrates the clearest connections with this mythic background, and hence gives the clearest portrayal of YHWH as a chaos monster.

In the non-P narrative, YHWH makes the sea go back (*hiphil* of הלך, *halak*); in the morning, after the Israelites have crossed, the sea returns to normal, and the Egyptians flee. In contrast, the P narrative is much more explicit about YHWH "dividing" the waters. The verb used is בקע (*baqa'*), not בדל as in Genesis 1, but the image is consistent enough that this still seems a likely connection. But furthermore, the P source describes the sea in contrast with the "dry ground" (ביבשה) on three separate occasions in 14:16, 22, and 29; this is the same word used in Genesis 1:9 and 10 to describe the newly formed earth arising from the separated waters.

So the imagery of Exodus 14 bears important similarities to that of Genesis 1; YHWH orders the world by dividing the waters to make the dry land emerge from its mist, just as YHWH divides the waters of the Sea of Reeds to allow the Israelites to walk through on dry land. But in Exodus 14, YHWH immediately reverses this new creation, plunging it back into chaos at the expense of the armies of Pharaoh. Again, whereas YHWH acts as the God of order in the priestly creation narrative, here YHWH aligns with the forces of chaos and willingly undoes the order of creation.

In these texts, YHWH is portrayed as both the God who creates and the God who destroys, and these roles can often blur together. Whereas the God of Genesis 1 separates the water and binds it, keeping it separated from the dry land, the God of Genesis 6–9 and Exodus 14 uses this very same water as a tool of destruction. While readers might be comforted by the fact that YHWH rebuilds the world after destroying it with the floods of Genesis 6–9, and the fact that YHWH uses the waters to defeat the armies of Pharaoh in Exodus 14, the uncomfortable, monstrous image of God in these texts lingers.

CONCLUSION

One of the great achievements of the Hebrew Bible is its rich, multifaceted portrayal of God. Throughout these texts, YHWH is portrayed as generous and harsh, loving and brutal, forgiving and merciless, self-giving and vain. YHWH's character encompasses the entire range of our experience with the world. It has often been remarked that the two creation narratives present very different visions of God—one who is transcendent (the P account of Genesis 1:1–2:4a), and one who is imminent (the J or non-P account of Genesis 2:4b–3:24)—and that a portrait of God would not be complete without each of these conflicting presentations. Similarly, depicting God as purely benevolent does not allow for a full picture of the totality of the divine and does not encompass our full experience as humans. At times, the world is a monstrous place. Likewise, the biblical text depicts a God who is sometimes monstrous.

The P text wrestles with this by depicting God as existing on both sides of the order/chaos dichotomy and controlling the forces from each side. In the creation narrative of Gen 1, we see a God who controls chaos, keeping it at bay so that the order of the world may emerge. But in the flood narrative, the signs and wonders, and the miracle at the Sea of Reeds, we see a God who does not hesitate to use these same forces to plunge the world back into chaos.

While our understanding of the divine can never reach totality, the P authors understood that the world sometimes feels like a beautifully ordered place, and sometimes feels like a threatening mess of chaos. Incorporating all of these as elements of God's character helps the biblical text to present a picture of God that encompasses these diverse sets of experiences.

The monstrous portrayal of God leads us to a place similar to horror films of cosmic dread, such as *Frailty* or *The Mist*. While the Hebrew Bible tempers this frightening portrayal of YHWH with much that is kind and loving, the monstrous still lurks beneath the surface, teeming through all of our interactions with the divine. It is a depiction of a world that is less safe and comforting than the one we were presented as children in Sunday school, but also one that is much more rich and honest and encompasses a wider range of our experiences of the world.

As we have seen repeatedly in our discussions of horror films, monsters are receptacles for the anxieties of the cultures who create them. Their monstrous bodies are stitched together out of the fears and dread that permeate daily life, and their drive and movements are centered around dramatizing these actions. In this discussion of the monstrous aspects of YHWH, I suggest that the writers of the Hebrew Bible have constructed the character of God in a similar fashion. YHWH is the embodiment of the hope for the universe's benevolence—and the fear that the universe is not so kind, and that the daily anxieties and dreads we carry with us are the only meanings the universe has to offer to us. Out of these contradictory hopes and fears emerges the paradoxical, unfinalizable character of YHWH.

NOTES

1. Tod Linafelt has read YHWH in conversation with the "Great and Terrible" Oz in "The Wizard of Uz: Job, Dorothy, and the Limits of the Sublime," *BibInt* 14.1–2 (2006): 94–109.

2. Peter Enns, *The Bible Tells Me So . . . : Why Defending Scripture Has Made Us Unable to Read It* (New York: Harper One, 2014), 4.

3. Ibid., 3.

4. The so-called "New Atheists" have filled many pages cataloguing YHWH's unpleasant characteristics; Richard Dawkins, in *The God Delusion* (New York: Houghton Mifflin, 2006), has famously remarked that "The God of the Old Testament is arguably the most unpleasant character in all fiction: jealous and proud of it; a petty, unjust, unforgiving control-freak; a vindictive, bloodthirsty ethnic cleanser; a misogynistic, homophobic, racist, infanticidal, genocidal, filicidal, pestilential, megalomaniacal, sadomasochistic, capriciously malevolent bully." Paul Copan offers an apologetic evangelical response in *Is God a Moral Monster? Making Sense of the Old Testament God* (Grand Rapids, MI: Baker, 2011). Thomas Römer also wrestles with these same questions from a historical-critical perspective in *Dark God: Cruelty, Sex, and Violence in the Old Testament* (Mahwah, NJ: Paulist Press, 2013).

5. Miroslav Volf, *Free of Charge: Giving and Forgiving in a Culture Stripped of Grace* (Grand Rapids, MI: Zondervan, 2005), 138–140. For a historical overview of doctrines of God's wrath, see Stephen Butler Murray, *Reclaiming Divine Wrath: A History of a Christian Doctrine and Its Interpretation* (Studies in Theology, Society, and Culture 8; New York: Peter Lang, 2011).

6. The history of interpretation of this passage is lengthy, with scholars still disagreeing over the basic question of what Moses did to make YHWH so angry; suggestions include unbelief (Noth, *Numbers*, 145–147); Moses's own anger against the people (Eugene Arden, "How Moses Failed God," *JBL* 76 [1957]: 50–52); and disobedience (Pierre Buis, "Qadesh, un Lieu Maudit?" *VT* 24 [1974]: 268–285). A recent argument for this passage's role in structuring the Priestly narrative is found in Suzanne Boorer, "The Place of Numbers 13–14* and Numbers 20:2–12* in the Priestly Narrative (Pg)," *JBL* 131.1 (2012): 45–63.

7. An excellent study of the ark traditions in the books of Samuel is still Patrick D. Miller, *The Hand of the Lord: A Reassessment of the Ark Narrative in 1 Samuel* (New York: John Hopkins, 1977).

8. Rudolf Otto, *The Idea of the Holy*, trans. John W. Harvey, second ed. (New York: Oxford, 1950). Of course, much of Otto's work is open to critique along the lines of those levied against the "History of Religions" scholarship of the early twentieth century, but, as I will argue below, there is still much from Otto's thesis that is useful.

9. Ibid., 12–24.

10. Otto compares this with Friedrich Schleiermacher's "feeling of dependence" (Otto, *The Idea of the Holy*, 8–11), but finds Schleiermacher's concept rooted too deeply in rational, analytical categories of thought.

11. This type of evolutionary approach to religious development is one idea of Otto's that has not held up well over the last century; nevertheless, I find his uncovering of fear as a central component of religious expression to be a profound insight.

12. The novella can be found in King's 1985 collection of stories *Skeleton Crew* (Scribner Paperback trade edition; New York: Scribner, 2016), 1–152.

13. There are certainly some inconsistencies in Mrs. Carmody's theology; her apocalyptic dispensationalism seems at odds with her call for a blood sacrifice. And she would be unlikely to make the mistake of referring to the book of "Revelations" in the plural, as Mrs. Carmody does in the film.

14. The more recent, and much less interesting, Paramount television miniseries of *The Mist* is much freer in adapting the source material; it only bares a passing resemblance to the novella and film. I have written on the differences in the religious worldviews of the two adaptations in an article for *Horror Homeroom*, "Apocalyptic Religions in the Mist."

15. Todorov's theory is found in *The Fantastic: A Structural Approach to a Literary Genre*, trans. Richard Howard (Ithaca, NY: Cornell, 1975). Todorov argues that much gothic fiction begins in the realm of the Fantastic, in which the events could be explained either with or without resorting to ideas of the supernatural. By their conclusion, most narratives offer explanations that are either supernatural (the marvelous) or not (the uncanny). However, some narratives, such as Henry James "The Turn of the Screw," refuse to settle questions regarding the supernatural nature of the narrative's events, and thus maintain their status as Fantastic. Laurel Lanner's monograph, *"Who Will Lament Her?": The Feminine and the Fantastic in the Book of Nahum* (LHBOTS 434; New York: T&T Clark, 2006), discusses Todorov's theory in more detail and applies it within the context of biblical studies.

16. Hans Walter Wolff's essay "The Kerygma of the Deuteronomistic Historical Work," in Walter Brueggemann and Hans Walter Wolff, *The Vitality of Old Testament Traditions*, second ed. (Atlanta: John Knox Press, 1982), 83–100, builds on Noth's theory of the Deuteronomistic History to discuss the purpose of the Deuteronomist, which for Wolff is to urge the people to return to right their relationship with YHWH. In this, Wolff sees the God of D as having clear and understandable commands, which the people have chosen to ignore.

17. But less so in 1–2 Samuel, which contemporary scholarship is more likely to view as consisting of older traditions than much of Noth's Deuteronomistic History. See, for example, Thomas Römer, *The So-Called Deuteronomistic History: A Sociological, Historical and Literary Introduction* (New York: T&T Clark, 2007); or the essays in Cynthia Edenberg and Juha Pakkala, eds., *Is Samuel Among the Deuteronomists?: Current Views on the Place of Samuel in the Deuteronomistic History* (Atlanta: SBL, 2013).

18. Amy Kalmanofsky's fascinating monograph *Terror All Around* explores YHWH as a monstrous figure in Jeremiah, but her work is primarily focused on God's overwhelming wrath and power. As Kalmanofsky demonstrates, the texts she discusses go to great lengths to portray God's violence as justified by the evil acts of Israel and the nations. God is monstrous because of God's power and violence, even though the text presents this violence as justified.

19. Exodus 2:22 announces that Moses and Zipporah have a son named Gershom, from the Hebrew גר (*ger*), "sojourner." In Exodus 4:20, Moses leaves for Egypt with his wife and sons, although the narrative has not informed the reader of the birth of additional children. Exodus 18:1–4 specifies Moses as having two sons; 18:4 identifies the second son as "Eliezer."

20. Exodus 3:1–4:17; the source-critical history of this text is challenging. See, for example, William Propp, *Exodus 1–18: A New Translation with Introduction and Commentary* (YAB 2A; New Haven, CT: Yale, 1999), 190–197; Boorer, *Vision of the Priestly Narrative*, 94–99, offers an argument for source-critical divisions with a particular emphasis on identifying the

portion of the text representing the narrative portion of P, what scholars frequently refer to as Pg.

21. The MT, frustratingly, only supplies a 3ms pronoun, leading some scholars to suggest that YHWH is attacking Moses's son rather than Moses himself. But the clear antecedent is Moses; Moses has, in fact, been the subject of the entire chapter, and nothing in the text indicates that this subject has changed.

22. The Hebrew accomplishes this with only two words: וירף ממנו.

23. The most thorough research history is provided by John T. Willis in *Yahweh and Moses in Conflict: The Role of Exodus 4:24–26 in the Book of Exodus* (Bible in History 8; New York: Peter Lang, 2010).

24. Recently, Thomas B. Dozeman, *Exodus* (Eerdmans Critical Commentary; Grand Rapids, MI: Eerdmans, 2009), 154–156, has argued for this reading.

25. B. Embry, "The Endangerment of Moses: Towards a New Reading of Exodus 4:24–26," *VT* 60 (2010): 177–196.

26. Propp, *Exodus 1–18*, 235. Propp continues: "Yahweh's problem is that he has two irreconcilable plans for Moses: he wants to dispatch him to Egypt to liberate the people, and he wants to punish him for his old crime . . . this impasse results in the Deity's bizarre behavior" (236). This would be highly convincing if the narrative bore any reference to Moses's murder of the Egyptian foreman. Lacking that reference, however, Propp's analysis reads like an attempt to justify YHWH's inexplicable behavior.

27. Willis, *Yahweh and Moses in Conflict*, 201–214. Willis sees this pericope as being one of many places where YHWH and Moses disagree. While Willis's argument is interesting, it still remains unclear why attempting to kill Moses seems like a reasonable mode of persuasion.

28. Christopher B. Hays, "'Lest Ye Perish in the Way': Ritual and Kinship in Exodus 4:24–26," *Hebrew Studies*, 48.1 (2007): 39–54, reads Zipporah's action in light of other ANE rituals of protection, and suggests that her statement "a bridegroom of blood by circumcision" is an attempt to appeal to YHWH's mercy through a claim of kinship.

29. Herbert Schmid, "Mose, der Blutbräutigam: Erwägungen zu Ex 4, 24–26," *Judaica* 22 (1966): 113–118 sees this as a Midianite tradition; Julian Morgenstern, "The 'Bloody Husband' (?) (Exod. 4:24–26) Once Again," *HUCA* 34 (1963): 35–70, esp. 38, argues it is from a Kenite source; John Gray, "Exodus," in *Interpreter's One Volume Commentary on the Bible*, ed. C. M. Laymon (London: Williams Collins Sons, 1971), 40, also sees a Kenite origin. In this way, both authors seek to distance this portrayal of YHWH from the YHWH of the Hebrew Bible as a whole.

30. Graybill, *Are We Not Men?*, 39–47.

31. An exception is David Pettit, "When the LORD Seeks to Kill Moses: Reading Exodus 4:24–26 in its Literary Context," *JSOT* 40.2 (2015): 163–177, who argues that this passage is part of YHWH's contest with Pharaoh over control of the Israelite people.

32. The Hebrew reads ויבקש המיתו. See Terence Fretheim, *Exodus* (Interpretation; Louisville, KY: John Knox, 1991), 78–82.

33. Ibid., 79; italics original.

34. Ibid., 81.

35. Römer, *Dark God*, 65. Römer explains further in a footnote: "Without doubt, this is what is behind Genesis 32. Compare Jacob's retrospective comment: 'I have seen God face to face, and my life is preserved'," 150, n. 11.

36. As does Walter Brueggemann, seeing the discovery of an explanation for the passage as an impossibility that points only towards YHWH's complete and total freedom. While this seems true to a point, Brueggemann downplays the shadow side of this freedom; in this passage, we are witnessing a very different type of freedom than YHWH's freedom to distribute unmerited grace, for example. Even with this disagreement, I find Brueggemann's focus on the character of God as the most important element in this passage to be very illuminating. See Walter Brueggemann, "Exodus," in *New Interpreter's Bible* (Nashville: Abingdon, 1994), 2:718–720.

37. See the brief discussion on the history of the satan in chapter 2, n. 52.

38. In a recent article, Samantha Joo, "Job, the Biblical Atlas," *CBQ* 74.1 (2012): 67–83, suggests that the satan is correct in his assessment of Job; Job understands that, as an outgrowth

of the relationship between deeds and consequences advanced by such traditions as found in Deuteronomy and Proverbs, Job would have naturally understood that fearing YHWH brings blessings. As such, Job as portrayed in the prologue is highly anxious about whether he fears YHWH enough.

39. See chapter 2, n. 54, for a discussion of ברך (*barak*) and the ambiguity as to whether it means "bless" or "curse" in this context.

40. This is not the first time in the Hebrew Bible that innocents have suffered so that God may prove a point; this theme runs throughout the first half of Exodus, where YHWH repeatedly "hardens Pharoah's heart" so that Pharaoh will not let the people go without a display of God's signs and wonders. In Ex 14:4, YHWH says this is explicitly so that "I will glorify myself over Pharaoh and all his army." This results in Pharaoh and his army chasing the Israelites, and drowning in the Red Sea. According to the biblical text, this violence was unnecessary, but desired by YHWH.

41. Philosopher Charles Taliaferro, "Is God Vain?" in *Questions About God: Today's Philosophers Ponder the Divine*, ed. Steven M. Cahn and David Shatz (New York: Oxford, 2002), 63–78, argues that the critique of God as vain is real and this criticism "may also stem from lack of appreciating the subtleties of the good" (77), particularly the creation and the incarnation. For Taliaferro, what might be perceived as vain is actually proper pride in God's creation. I find this unpersuasive; YHWH's not infrequent demands for acknowledgment of his greatness in the biblical text seem to indicate a need greater than pride. But as Taliaferro acknowledges, the distinction between vanity and pride is fine.

42. Nicholas Ansell, "'Fantastic Beasts and Where to Find The(ir) Wisdom': Behemoth and Leviathan in the Book of Job," in *Playing with Leviathan*, 90–114, esp. 94–95, argues that the satan exploits the permission of YHWH to touch "all that he has" in 1:11–12, extending it beyond Job's possessions and into his family, which would normally have been assumed to be part of Job's person, not simply possessions. In this reading, YHWH comes across as more benevolent, but easily duped; the implications of this are also troubling, and not easily reconciled with the grandeur of the theophanic speeches of 38–41.

43. Ps 88 is also comparable, as the psalmist blames YHWH for all of his ills; alone among the psalms, this psalm does not turn towards assurance of God's protection.

44. See, for example, Ansel, "'Fantastic Beasts,'" 90–114; cf. Fox, "The Meanings of the Book of Job," who argues for a less obscure, more benevolent deity in the theophanic speeches.

45. "Whoever fights monsters should see to it that in the process he does not become a monster. And when you look long into an abyss, the abyss also looks into you." Friedrich Nietzsche, *Beyond Good and Evil: Prelude to a Philosophy of the Future*, trans. Walter Kaufmann (New York: Vintage, 1966), 89.

46. Crouch, *War and Ethics*, 21–32. Certainly, there are instances where chaos and order are presented as this kind of a binary opposition. See the discussion of this dynamic in ch. 2, above.

47. Bernard Batto, *Slaying the Dragon*, asserts that *tehom* is cognate with the Akkadian *ti'amat* (76), although Tsumura strenuously disagrees.

48. Batto, *Slaying the Dragon*, finds a parallel to palace-building in both Genesis 1 and the closely related Ps 8, in which YHWH builds a "fortress" (78–79).

49. For overviews of this source division, see Norman Habel, *Literary Criticism of the Old Testament* (GBS; Philadelphia: Fortress, 1971), and David M. Carr, *Reading the Fractures of Genesis*. For an argument against this source-critical division, see Joshua A. Berman, *Inconsistencies in the Torah: Ancient Literary Convention and the Limits of Source Criticism* (New York: Oxford University Press, 2017), 236–268. While Berman's observations that these source divisions do not solve all of the textual problems with this passage are well noted, I find his rejection of the source-critical reading of Gen 6–9 to be unconvincing, as he is unable to offer a proposal that explains more of the discrepancies and doubling than the conventional source-critical solution.

50. See chapter 2, above, for further discussion of Marduk's ambiguous nature.

51. As Boorer and others have noted, this is a reworking of the non-P scene of Ex 4:2–4 in which YHWH gives a sign to Moses, transforming his staff into a snake. However, the non-P source refers to the נחש (*nahash*, snake), not the תנן (*tannin*) of Genesis 1:21; Exodus 7:8–13. See Boorer, *Vision of the Priestly Narrative*, 252–255.

52. The term for water here is מקוה (*mikveh*), literally a reservoir; the term is unusual, being used in the Penteteuch only here, in Leviticus 11:36, and when God gathers the waters together in Genesis 1:10 before naming the water מים (sea).

53. פיח, a different root than the אפר that the J narrative of Genesis 2:7 uses to describe YHWH's creation of humanity.

54. The plague of hail (Exodus 9:22–35) seems to stem primarily from the non-P source, and in this passage YHWH acts more like a storm god than a chaos monster in YHWH's use of weather for destructive purposes. For an overview of this motif in biblical and cognate literature, see Aloysius Fitzgerald, *The Lord of the East Wind* (CBQMS 34; Washington, DC: Catholic Biblical Association of America, 2002); Alberto R. W. Green, *The Storm-God in the Ancient Near East* (BJSUCSD 8; Winona Lake, IN: Eisenbrauns, 2003). Charlie Trimm discusses "nature weapons" in the context of the divine warrior motif in *"YHWH Fights for Them!": The Divine Warrior in the Exodus Narrative* (Gorgias Biblical Studies 58; Piscataway, NJ: Gorgias Press, 2014), 47–53.

Conclusion

THE CYCLES OF HORROR

After a rather moribund time, recent years have been good to horror. In various corners of the internet, there's been an ongoing debate over whether 2018 was the best year for horror movies ever, or just a really good one. The year saw concession profits take a hit during screenings of *A Quiet Place* because audiences were too afraid to disturb the silence with their crunching. The art-house horror tradition was carried forward when *Hereditary* became a major box-office and critical success. And Michael Myers (along with Jamie Lee Curtis) returned in the best *Halloween* film since the original, thirty years ago. (Not that there's much competition in this category.) The year 2019 is shaping up to be a banner year as well, with films such as *Us*, *Midsommar*, and *The Lighthouse* continuing the trend of horror that succeeds with critics and audiences alike. With Blumhouse continuing to crank out high-budget teen-horror fare, Jordan Peele showing signs of becoming a new horror auteur in the tradition of greats such as Wes Craven and John Carpenter, and the boom of television horror seeming to accelerate every year, it's a good time for horror.

When trends in horror are viewed in conjunction with the culture at large, this makes perfect sense. People are always drawn to horror in times of anxiety. The '60s and '70s were bull years for the horror market, as America and the rest of the world were swept up in rapid social change, along with imperialist wars that were being broadcast into our homes for the first time. And sliding into the early 80s, the anxieties shifted, but the conservative backlash made sure that the horror genre stayed strong. The popular subgenres shifted along with the winds of culture—instead of radical social critique,

American movie theaters (and home video rentals) were dominated by the reactionary slasher films.

As America started to settle into a period of relative comfort in the late '80s and through the early '90s, horror took a brief slumber as well. The end of history seemed to mean the end of horror as well.[1] There are only a handful of truly great horror films from that period, and even fewer that made a significant cultural impact. But during the early years of Bush II, something started to get unsettled in the American psyche, and it all rushed out in the wake of 9/11. This national trauma created another period where horror was relevant, in a wide variety of forms—not only did we see the rise of "torture porn"[2] in the wake of the Abu Ghraib scandal, but we saw more subtle expressions of unease with the increased popularity of ghost stories. While subgenres and trends have come and gone, this widespread popularity of horror continued through Obama's presidency, and into the era of Trump.[3]

So while horror might experience periods of dormancy, it never goes away for too long. Horror responds to the anxieties of the individual, and the anxieties of a culture; these anxieties are never too far below the surface. As I hope I've documented throughout this monograph, religion understands this deeply. And the Bible reflects this deep understanding.

THE DARK CORRIDORS OF THE BIBLE

There's a lot of darkness in the Bible—the passages mentioned here are just a sampling, and they've barely touched the New Testament. We've explored biblical ghosts, haunted places, chaos monsters, the monstrous within the community, the monstrous self, and the monstrous side of God. At each stop, we've taken some time to think about what this horror has to tell us about the text of the Bible, the culture from which it was produced, and the world we live in today.

There's darkness in the Bible because there's darkness in the world. While not pretending to be a comprehensive history of horror through the ages (that would be quite an undertaking!), there's enough in these pages to demonstrate that horror has been with us, in one form or another, for as long as people have been telling stories.[4] We've seen some ways in which cultures have adapted these narratives to their particular experiences, even taking the same monster and loading her or him with different metaphorical baggage, but the human fears at the core of these horror narratives are able to speak to people across times and cultures. We are all afraid for the end of our bodies, untimely or otherwise; we all fear that our world is falling apart; and we all fear that our life is, in the final reckoning, meaningless.

Horror gives us a vocabulary to talk about our struggles, our anxieties, and our fears. While we might not be able to articulate how traumatic experiences of violence linger in the psyche and resurface in unexpected ways, we can follow the journey of a fictional character as she is haunted by the murder of her friends thirty years ago (in the new *Halloween*). Sometimes, watching a family move into a new house and unravel the secrets of its past helps us to look at our own secrets in a different light. And while we might not know how we would respond if the societal structures we have all come to depend upon fell apart, we can explore possible ways to cope with this calamity through fictions of zombie apocalypses. Horror is one way that we can think through and process the deep, abiding struggles that are a part of everyday life.

Religion gives us a framework within which to place these struggles.

Like horror, religion is convinced that death is a serious problem for human life, and that we must wrestle with what this means. And like horror, religion understands that there is evil in the world, and that this is frightening not only for the evil itself, but for what this evil tells us about the world we live in. Both religion and horror help us to think through the same problems.

And the writers of the Hebrew Bible, slowly putting these scriptures together over generations, understood enough to know that for this collection of scriptures to be a true, authentic account of a meaningful religion, it couldn't simply turn its back on the darkness. So Job walks into the whirlwind to learn about the terrifying Leviathan, and emerges a different person. The psalmist speaks to God of the darkness of his own life and finds comfort in the reassurance that God is listening, and that God will act even if not in the psalmist's timeline. There are green pastures and a table with a wonderful banquet set before us. And there is also the valley of the shadow of death, which on some days seems to consume us. But we know that this valley is there because we've read about it in Psalm 23, so when we encounter it in our own lives we're not surprised. And we know that we can walk out the other side of it because our faith ancestors and our horror stories have shown us how.

NOTES

1. *The End of History and the Last Man* (New York: Free Press, 1992) is the title of Frances Fukuyama's much-discussed book arguing that the fall of the Berlin Wall and the collapse of the Soviet Union were indications of capitalism and democracy's final victories in the world's grand ideological struggle. With this victory, the world arrives at a place where historical struggle has come to an end. While many scholars vigorously disputed this thesis, the terrorist attacks of 9/11 put a definitive end to it.

2. As exemplified in films such as *Saw* (especially its sequels) and *Hostel*, with their focus on the prolonged suffering of characters as a way of eliciting audience response. Reynolds Humphries provides an overview of this much-maligned subgenre in "A (Post)modern Hour of Pain: *FearDotCom* and the Prehistory of the Post-9/11 Torture Film," in *American Horror Film: The Genre at the Turn of the Millennium*, ed. Steffan Hantke (Jackson: University of Mississippi Press, 2010), 58–74.

3. See, for example, the essays included in Victoria McCollum, ed. *Make America Hate Again: Trump-Era Horror and the Politics of Fear* (New York: Routledge, 2019), including my contribution on *The Witch* and *It Comes at Night*.

4. Literature scholar Paul A. Trout, *Deadly Powers: Animal Predators and the Mythic Imagination* (Amherst, NY: Prometheus Books, 2011), has gone as far as to suggest that the first tales of horror were campfire stories told by the cavemen to wrestle with the predatory beasts that were a part of their everyday world; these stories served as both tales of adventure and tales of caution. While a highly speculative thesis by necessity, it still offers an interesting insight into the ubiquity of horror narratives.

Bibliography

Aaron, David H. *Etched in Stone: The Emergence of the Decalogue*. London: T&T Clark, 2006.
Abasili, Alexander Izuchukwu. "Was It Rape?: The David and Bathsheba Pericope Re-Examined." *VT* 61.1 (2011): 1–15.
Aichele, George. "Film Theory and Biblical Studies." Pages 11–26 in *Close Encounters Between Bible and Film*. Edited by Laura Copier and Caroline Vander Stichele. SemSt 87. Atlanta: SBL Press, 2016.
Albright, William F. *Archaeology and the Religion of Israel*. Garden City, NY: Doubleday, 1969.
Anderson, Bernhard W. *Creation Versus Chaos: The Reinterpretation of Mythical Symbolism in the Bible*. New York: Association Press, 1967.
Anderson, Gary A. "What is Man That Thou Has Mentioned Him?: Psalm 8 and the Nature of the Human Person." *Logos: A Journal of Catholic Thought and Culture* 3.1 (2000): 80–92.
Ansell, Nicholas. "'Fantastic Beasts and Where to Find The(ir) Wisdom': Behemoth and Leviathan in the Book of Job." Pages 90–114 in *Playing with Leviathan: Interpretation and Reception of Monsters from the Biblical World*. Edited by Koert van Bekkum, Jaap Dekker, Henk van de Kamp, and Eric Peels. TBN 21; Leiden, NL: Brill, 2017.
Arden, Eugene. "How Moses Failed God." *JBL* 76 (1957): 50–52.
Ashley, Timothy. *The Book of Numbers*. NICOT. Grand Rapids, MI: Eerdmans, 1993.
Asma, Stephen T. *On Monsters: An Unnatural History of Our Worst Fears*. New York: Oxford, 2009.
Auld, A. Graeme. *I & II Samuel: A Commentary*. OTL. Louisville, KY: WJK, 2011.
Averbeck, Richard E. "The Three 'Daughters' of Baʾal and the Transformations of *Chaoskampf* in the Early Chapters of Genesis." Pages 237–256 in *Creation and Chaos: A Reconsideration of Hermann Gunkel's* Chaoskampf *Hypothesis*. Edited by JoAnn Scurlock and Richard H. Beal. Winona Lake, IN: Eisenbrauns, 2013.
Bachelard, Gaston. *The Poetics of Space*. Translated by Maria Jolas. Penguin Classics edition. New York: Penguin Books, 2014.
Baden, Joel S., and Candida R. Moss. "The Origin and Interpretation of ṣāraʿat in Leviticus 13–14." *JBL* 130.4 (2011): 643–662.
Badinter, Elisábeth. *Mother Love: Myth and Reality*. Translated by Francine du Plessix Gray. New York: McMillan, 1980.
Baecque, Antoine de, and Thierry Jousse. "Cinema and Its Ghosts: An Interview with Jacques Derrida." *Discourse: Journal For Theoretical Studies in Media and Culture* 37.1/2 (2015): 22–39.

Balanzategui, Jessica. "Haunted Nostalgia and the Aesthetics of Technological Decay: Hauntology and Super 8 in *Sinister*." *Horror Studies* 7.2 (2016): 235–251.

Ballentine, Debra Scoggins. *The Conflict Myth and the Biblical Tradition*. New York: Oxford, 2015.

Barsoti, Catherine M., and Robert K. Johnston. *Finding God in the Movies: 33 Films of Reel Faith*. Grand Rapids, MI: Baker, 2004.

Batto, Bernard F. "The Combat Myth in Israelite Tradition Revisited." Pages 217–236 in *Creation and Chaos: A Reconsideration of Hermann Gunkel's* Chaoskampf *Hypothesis*. Edited by JoAnn Scurlock and Richard H. Beal. Winona Lake, IN: Eisenbrauns, 2013.

―――. *Slaying the Dragon: Mythmaking in the Biblical Tradition*. Louisville, KY: WJK, 1992.

Beal, Timothy K. "Mimetic Monsters: The Genesis of Horror in *The Face of the Deep*." *Postscripts* 4.1 (2010): 85–93.

―――. *Religion and Its Monsters*. New York: Routledge, 2002.

Beardsworth, Sara. *Julia Kristeva: Psychoanalysis and Modernity*. Albany: SUNY University Press, 2004.

Bellin, Joshua David. *Framing Monsters: Fantasy Film and Social Alienation*. Cardondale, IL: Southern Illinois University Press, 2005.

Ben Zvi, Ehud. "Othering, Selfing, 'Boundarying' and 'Cross-Boundarying' as Interwoven with Socially Shared Memories: Some Observations." Pages 20–40 in *Imagining the Other and Constructing Israelite Identity in the Early Second Temple Period*. Edited by Ehud Ben Zvi and Diana V. Edelman. LHBOTS 456. New York: Bloomsbury T&T Clark, 2014.

Benz, Brendon C. "Yamm as the Personification of Chaos? A Linguistic and Literary Argument for a Case of Mistaken Identity." Pages 127–145 in *Creation and Chaos: A Reconsideration of Gunkel's* Chaoskampf *Hypothesis*. Edited by JoAnn Scurlock and Richard H Beal. Winona Lake, IN: Eisenbrauns, 2013.

Berman, Joshua A. *Inconsistencies in the Torah: Ancient Literary Convention and the Limits of Source Criticism*. New York: Oxford University Press, 2017.

Blake, Linnie. *The Wounds of Nations: Horror Cinema, Historical Trauma, and National Identity*. New York: Manchester University Press, 2008.

Blattenburger David E., III. *Rethinking I Corinthians 11:2–16 Through Archaeological and Moral-Rhetorical Analysis*. Lewiston, NY: Edward Mellen, 1997.

Blenkinsopp, Joseph. "Cityscape to Landscape: The 'Back to Nature' Theme in Isaiah 1–35." Pages 35–44 in *"Every City Shall be Forsaken": Urbanism and Prophecy in Ancient Israel and the Near East*. Edited by Lester L. Grabbe and Robert D. Haak. JSOTS 330. Sheffield, UK: Sheffield Academic Press, 2001.

―――. *Treasures Old and New: Essays in the Theology of the Pentateuch*. Grand Rapids, MI: Eerdmans, 2004.

Blouins: Michael J. "'A Growing Global Darkess': Dialectives of Culture in Goddard's *The Cabin in the Woods*." *Horror Studies* 6.1 (2015): 83–99.

Boorer, Suzanne. "The Place of Numbers 13–14* and Numbers 20:2–12* in the Priestly Narrative (Pg)." *JBL* 131.1 (2012): 45–63.

―――. *Vision of the Priestly Narrative: Its Genre and Hermeneutics of Time*. AIL 27. Atlanta: SBL, 2016.

Bosworth, David A. "Faith and Resilience: King David's Reaction to the Death of Bathsheba's Firstborn." *CBQ* 73.4 (2011): 691–707.

Bowler, Katie. *Blessed: A History of the American Prosperity Gospel*. New York: Oxford University Press, 2013.

Braudy, Leo. *Haunted: On Ghosts, Witches, Vampires, Zombies, and Other Monsters of the Natural and Supernatural Worlds*. New Haven, CT: Yale University Press, 2016.

Breifel, Aviva. "What Some Ghosts Don't Know: Spectral Incognizance and the Horror Film." *Narrative* 17.1 (2009): 95–110

Brenner, Athayla. "On 'Jeremiah' and the Poetics of (Prophetic?) Pornography." Pages 177–193 in *On Gendering Texts: Female and Male Voices in the Hebrew Bible*. Edited by Athalya Brenner and Fokkelien van Dijk-Hemmes. Leiden, NL: Brill, 1993.

Brown, William P. *Seeing the Psalms: A Theology of Metaphor*. Louisville, KY: WJK, 2002.

Bruce, Susan. "Sympathy For the Dead: (G)hosts, Hostilities, and Mediums in Alejandro Amenábar's *The Others* and Postmortem Photography." *Discourse* 27.2/3 (2005): 21–40.

Brueggemann, Walter. *David's Truth in Israel's Imagination*. Second edition. Minneapolis, MN: Fortress, 2002.

———. "Exodus." Page 2 in *New Interpreter's Bible*. Nashville: Abingdon, 1994.

———. *From Whom No Secrets Are Hid: Introducing the Psalms*. Edited by Brent A. Strawn. Atlanta: WJK, 2014.

———. "A Shape for Old Testament Theology II: Embrace of Pain." Pages 22–44 in *Old Testament Theology: Essays on Structure, Theme, and Text*. Edited by Patrick D. Miller. Minneapolis, MN: Fortress Press, 1992.

Buis, Pierre. "Qadesh, un Lieu Maudit?" *VT* 24 (1974): 268–285.

Bruner, Ron. "Harmony and Historiography: Genre as a Tool For Understanding the Differences Between Samuel-Kings and Chronicles." *Restoration Quarterly* 42.2 (2004): 79–93.

Bryan, David. *Cosmos, Chaos, and the Kosher Mentality*. JSPSup 12. Sheffield, UK: Sheffield Academic Press, 1995.

Budd, Philip J. *Numbers*. WBC 5. Nashville: Thomas Nelson, 1984.

Buell, Denise Kimber. "Hauntology Meets Posthumanism: Some Payoffs for Biblical Studies." Pages 29–56 in *The Bible and Posthumanism*. Edited by Jennifer L. Koosed. SemSt. 74. Atlanta: SBL, 2014.

Burnett, Joel S. "Forty-Two Songs for Elohim: An Ancient Near Eastern Organizing Principle in the Shaping of the Elohistic Psalter." *JSOT* 31.1 (2006): 81–101.

Bussing, Ilse M. "Complicit Bodies: Excessive Sensibilities and Haunted Space." *Horror Studies* 7.1 (2016): 41–59.

Butler, Judith. *Gender Trouble: Feminism and the Subversion of Identity*. New York: Routledge, 1990.

Byron, Glennis, ed. *Globalgothic*. London: Manchester University Press, 2013.

Carroll, Noël. "Afterword: Psychoanalysis and the Horror Film." Pages 257–270 in *Horror Film and Psychoanalysis: Freud's Worst Nightmare*. Edited by Steven Jay Schneider. New York: Cambridge University Press, 2004.

———. *The Philosophy of Horror: Or, Paradoxes of the Heart*. New York: Routledge, 1990.

Castello, Daniel. "The Fear of the Lord as Theological Method." *JTI* 2.1 (2008): 147–160.

Chisholm, Robert B., Jr. "Cracks in the Foundation: Ominous Signs in the David Narrative." *Biblio* 172 (2015): 154–176.

Cho, Paul Kang-Kul. "The Integrity of Job 1 and 42:11–17." *CBQ* 76.2 (2014): 230–251.

Cholewinski, Alfred. *Heiligkeitsgesetz und Deuteronomium*. AnBib 66. Rome: Biblical Institute Press, 1976.

Claassens, L. Juliana M. *Claiming Her Dignity: Female Resistance in the Old Testament*. Collegeville, MN: Liturgical Press, 2016.

Clanton, Dan, Jr. "The Divine Unsub: Television Procedurals and Biblical Sexual Violence." Pages 125–148 in *The Bible in Crime Fiction and Drama: Murderous Texts*. Edited by Caroline Blyth and Alison Jack. LHBOTS 678/STr 16. New York: T&T Clark, 2019.

Clines, David J. A. *Job 1–20*. WBC 18. Waco, TX: Word, 1988.

———. *Job 38–42*. WBC 18b. Grand Rapids, MI: Zondervan, 2015.

Clover, Carol. *Men, Women and Chain Saws: Gender in the Modern Horror Film*. Princeton, NJ: Princeton University Press, 1992.

Cogan, Mordechai. "The Road to En-Dor." Pages 319–326 in *Pomegranates and Golden Bels: Studies in Biblical, Jewish, and Near Eastern Ritual, Law, and Literature in Honor of Jacob Milgrom*. Edited by David P. Wright, David Noel Freedman, and Avi Hurvitz. Winona Lake, IN: Eisenbrauns, 1995.

Cohen, Jeffrey Jerome. "Monster Culture: Seven Theses." Pages 3–25 in *Monster Theory: Reading Culture*. Edited by Jeffrey Jerome Cohen. Minneapolis: University of Minnesota, 1996.

Collins, John. *The Bible After Babel: Historical Criticism in a Postmodern Age*. Grand Rapids, MI: Eerdmans, 2005.

Comaroff, Jean, and John L. Comaroff, eds. *Millennial Capitalism and the Culture of Neoliberalism*. Durham, NC: Duke University Press, 2001.

Conolly, Jez. *The Thing*. Devil's Advocates. Leighton Buzzard, UK: Auteur, 2013.
Conrich, Ian. "Before Sound: Universal, Silent Cinema, and the Last of the Horror Spectaculars." Pages 40–57 in *The Horror Film*. Edited by Stephen Prince. New Brunswick, NJ: Rutgers University Press, 2004.
Cook, Michael. *Detective Fiction and the Ghost Story*. London: Palgrave Macmillan, 2014.
Copan, Paul. *Is God a Moral Monster? Making Sense of the Old Testament God*. Grand Rapids, MI: Baker, 2011.
Copan, Paul, and Matthew Flanagan. *Did God Really Command Genocide?: Coming to Terms with the Justice of God*. Grand Rapids, MI: Baker, 2014.
Copier, Laura. *Preposterous Revelations: Visions of Apocalypse and Martyrdom in Hollywood Cinema 1980–2000*. Sheffield, UK: Sheffield Phoenix, 2012.
Crane, Jonathan Lake. *Terror and Everyday Life: Singular Moments in the History of the Horror Film*. Thousand Oaks, CA: Sage, 1994.
Cranz, Isabel. *Atonement and Purification: Priestly and Assyro-Babylonian Perspectives on Sin and Its Consequences*. FAT II/92. Tübingen, DE: Mohr Siebeck, 2017.
Creed, Barbara, *The Monstrous-Feminine: Film, Feminism, Psychoanalysis*. New York: Routledge, 1993.
Cross, Frank Moore. *Canaanite Myth and Hebrew Epic: Essays in the History of Israelite Religion*. New York: Harvard University Press, 1973.
Crouch, C. L. *War and Ethics in the Ancient Near East: Military Violence in Light of Cosmology and History*. BZAW 407. Berlin: de Gruyter, 2009.
Curtis, Barry. *Dark Places: The Haunted House in Film*. Locations. London: Reaktion Books, 2008.
Dahood, Mitchell. "Mišmār 'Muzzle' in Job 7:12." *JBL* 80:3 (1961): 270–271.
Davies, Eryl. "The Morally Dubious Passages of the Hebrew Bible: An Examination of Some Proposed Solutions." *CurBR* 3.2 (2005): 197–228.
Davis, Blair, and Kial Natale. "'The Pound of Flesh Which I Demand': American Horror Cinema, Gore, and the Box Office, 1998–2007." Pages 35–57 in *American Horror: The Genre at the Turn of the Millennium*. Edited by Steffen Hantke. Jackson: University of Mississippi Press, 2010.
Davis, Colin. "The Skeptical Ghost: Alejandro Amenábar's *The Others* and the Return of the Dead." Pages 64–75 in *Popular Ghosts: The Haunted Spaces of Everyday Culture*. Edited by María del Pilar Blanco and Esther Peeren. New York: Continuum, 2010.
Dawkins, Richard. *The God Delusion*. New York: Houghton Mifflin, 2006.
Day, John. *God's Conflict with the Dragon and the Sea: Echoes of a Canaanite Myth in the Old Testament*. UCOP 35. Cambridge, MA: Cambridge, 1985.
Dean-Jones, Lesley. *Women's Bodies in Classical Greek Science*. New York: Oxford, 1994.
Dekker, Jaap. "God and the Dragons in the Book of Isaiah." Pages 21–39 in *Playing with Leviathan: Interpretation and Reception of Monsters from the Biblical World*. TBN 21. Edited by Koert van Bekkum, Jaap Dekker, Henk van de Kamp, and Eric Peels. Leiden, NL: Brill, 2017.
Derrida, Jacques. *The Beast and the Sovereign*. 2 volumes. Translated by Geoffrey Bennington. Chicago: University of Chicago Press, 2009; 2011.
———. *Of Grammatology*. Translated by Gayatri Chakravorty Spivak. Baltimore: John Hopkins University Press, 1976.
———. *The Specters of Marx: The State of the Debt, the Work of Mourning, and the New International*. Translated by Peggy Kamuf. New York: Routledge, 1994.
———. *Writing and Difference*. Translated by Alan Bass. Chicago: University of Chicago Press, 1978.
Dever, William G. *Beyond the Texts: An Archaeological Portrait of Ancient Israel and Judah*. Atlanta: SBL, 2017.
Diewert, David A. "Job 7:12: *Yam*, *Tannim*, and the Surveillance of Job." *JBL* 106.2 (1987): 203–215.
Dika, Vera. *Games of Terror*. Madison, NJ: Farleigh Dickinson University Press, 1990.

Dillard, R. H. W. "*Night of the Living Dead*: It's Not Just Like a Wind That's Passing Through." Pages 14–29 in *American Horrors: Essays in the Modern American Horror Film*. Edited by Gregory A. Waller. Urbana, IL: University of Illinois Press, 1987.
Dixon, Wheeler Winston. *A History of Horror*. New Brunswick, NJ: Rutgers University Press, 2010.
Doak, Brian R. *Consider Leviathan: Narratives of Nature and the Self in the Book of Job*. Minneapolis, MN: Fortress, 2014.
———. *The Last of the Rephaim: Conquest and Cataclysm in the Heroic Ages of Ancient Israel*. Boston: Ilex Foundation, 2013.
Douglas, Mary. *Leviticus as Literature*. New York: Oxford University Press, 1999.
———. *Purity and Danger: An Analysis of Concept of Pollution and Taboo*. New York: Routledge & Kegan Paul, 1966.
Dozeman, Thomas B. *Exodus*. Eerdmans Critical Commentary. Grand Rapid, MI: Eerdmans, 2009.
Edenberg, Cynthia, and Juha Pakkala, eds. *Is Samuel Among the Deuteronomists?: Current Views on the Place of Samuel in the Deuteronomistic History*. Atlanta: SBL, 2013.
Elferen, Isabella van. *Gothic Music: The Sounds of the Uncanny*. Cardiff, UK: Wales University Press, 2012.
Embry, B. "The Endangerment of Moses: Towards a New Reading of Exodus 4:24–26." *VT* 60 (2010): 177–196.
Emerton, J. A. "Leviathan and LTN: The Vocalization of the Ugaritic Word for the Dragon." *VT* 32.2 (1982): 328–331.
Enns, Peter. *The Bible Tells Me So . . . : Why Defending Scripture Has Made Us Unable to Read It*. New York: Harper One, 2014.
Erwin, Elizabeth, and Dawn Keetley, eds. *The Politics of Race, Gender, and Sexuality in* The Walking Dead*: Essays on the Television Series and Comics*. London: McFarland, 2018.
Evans, Walter. "Monster Movies: A Sexual Theory." *Journal of Popular Film* 2.4 (Fall 1973): 353–365.
Faulkner, William. *Requiem for a Nun*. New York: Random House, 1951.
Feinstein, Eve Levavi. "The 'Bitter Waters' of Numbers 5:11–31." *VT* 62 (2012): 300–306.
———. *Sexual Pollution in the Hebrew Bible*. New York: Oxford University Press, 2014.
Feucht, Christian. *Untersuchungen zum Heiligkeitsgesetz*. Theologische Arbeiten XX. Berlin: Evangelische Verlagsanstalt, 1964.
Fishbane, Michael. "Accusations of Adultery: A Study of Law and Scribal Practice in Numbers 5:11–31." *HUCA* 45 (1974): 24–45.
———. *Biblical Interpretation in Ancient Israel*. New York: Oxford University Press, 1985.
———. "Jeremiah 4:23–26 and Job 3:3–13a: A Recovered Use of the Creation Pattern." *VT* 21.1 (1971): 151–167.
Fisher, Mark. *Ghosts of My Life: Writings on Depression, Hauntology and Lost Futures*. Winchester, UK: Zero Books, 2014.
———. "What Is Hauntology?" *Film Quarterly* 66.1 (2012): 16–24.
Fitzgerald, Aloysius. *The Lord of the East Wind*. CBQMS 34. Washington, DC: Catholic Biblical Association of America, 2002.
Forman-Brunell, Miriam. *Babysitter: An American History*. New York: New York University Press, 2009.
Fox, Michael V. "The Meanings of the Book of Job." *JBL* 137.1 (2018): 7–18.
Frayne, Douglas. "The Fifth Day of Creation in Ancient Syrian and Neo-Hittite Art." Pages 63–97 in *Creation and Chaos: A Reconsideration of Gunkel's* Chaoskampf *Hypothesis*. Edited by JoAnn Scurlock and Richard H. Beal. Winona Lake, IN: Eisenbrauns, 2013.
Freeland, Cynthia. "Horror and Art Dread." Pages 189–205 in *The Horror Film*. Edited by Stephen Prince. New Brunswick, NJ: Rutgers University Press, 2004.
Fretheim, Terrence. *Exodus*. Interpretation. Louisville, KY: John Knox, 1991.
Freud, Sigmund. "Analysis of a Phobia in a Five Year Old Boy." Pages 10.1–50 in *The Standard Edition of the Complete Psychological Works of Sigmund Freud*. Translated by James Strachey. London: Hogarth, 1953–1966.

Frevel, Christian. "Telling the Secrets of Wisdom: The Use of Psalm 104 in the Book of Job." Pages 157–168 in *Reading Job Intertextually*. Edited by Katherine J. Dell and Will Kynes. LHBOTS. New York: T&T Clark, 2012.

Frymer-Kensky, Tikva. "The Strange Case of the Suspected Sotah." *VT* 34 (1984): 11–26.

Fukuyama, Frances. *The End of History and the Last Man*. New York: Free Press, 1992.

Fyall, Robert S. *"Now My Eyes Have Seen You": Images of Creation and Evil in the Book of Job*. NSBT 12. Downers Grove, IL: Intervarsity, 2002.

Gaines, Jason M. H. *The Poetic Priestly Source*. Minneapolis, MN: Fortress, 2015.

Gammie, John G. "Behemoth and Leviathan: On the Didactic and Theological Significance of Job 40:15–41:26." Pages 217–231 in *Israelite Wisdom: Theological and Literary Essays in Honor of Samuel Terrien*. Edited by John G. Gammie, Walter A. Brueggemann, W. Lee Humphreys, and James M. Ward. Missoula, MT: Scholars Press, 1978.

Gencarella, Stephen Olbrys. "Thunder Without Rain: Fascist Masculinity in AMC's *The Walking Dead*." *Horror Studies* 7.1 (2016): 125–146.

Gilmore, David D. *Monsters: Evil Beings, Mythical Beasts, and All Manner of Imaginary Terrors*. Philadelphia: University of Pennsylvania Press, 2003.

Gilmour, Rachelle. "Saul's Rejection and the Obscene Underside of the Law." *Bible and Critical Theory* 15.1 (2019): 34–45. Web. Accessed 7 May, 2019. https://www.bibleandcriticaltheory.com/issues/vol15-no1-2019/vol-15-no-1-2019-sauls-rejection-and-the-obscene-underside-of-the-law/

Goldstein, Diane E., Sylvia Ann Grider, and Jeannie Banks Thomas, eds. *Haunting Experiences: Ghosts in Contemporary Folklore*. Logan, UT: Utah State University Press, 2007.

Goldstein, Elizabeth W. "Genealogy, Gynecology, and Gender: The Priestly Writer's Portrait of a Woman." Pages 74–86 in *Embroidered Garments: Priests and Gender in Biblical Israel*. Edited by Deborah W. Rooke. HBM 25. Sheffield, UK: Sheffield Phoenix, 2009.

———. *Impurity and Gender in the Hebrew Bible*. Lanham, MD: Lexington Books, 2015.

Gordon, Avery F. *Ghostly Matters: Haunting and the Sociological Imagination*. Minneapolis: University of Minnesota, 1997.

Grafius, Brandon R. "Apocalyptic Religions in *The Mist*." Blog Post. *Horror Homeroom*, December 26, 2017. Accessed May 24, 2018. http://www.horrorhomeroom.com/apocalyptic-religions-mist/

———. "Ideas of Motherhood in *Inside*." *Horror Studies* 6.1 (2015): 57–68.

———. "*Mama* and Kristeva: Matricide in the Horror Film." *Post Script: Essays in Literature and Film* 36:1 (2017): 52–64.

———. *Reading Phinehas, Watching Slashers: Numbers 25 and Horror Theory*. Lanham, MD: Lexington Books/Fortress Academic, 2018.

———. "Securing the Borders: Isolation and Anxiety in *The Witch*, *It Comes at Night*, and Trump's America." Pages 119–128 in *Make America Hate Again: Trump-Era Horror and the Politics of Fear*. Edited by Victoria McCollum. New York: Routledge, 2019.

———. "Single Moms in Horror: Progressive and Conservative Ideologies Beneath the Surface." Blog post. *Monstrous Times*, May 5, 2017. Accessed August 16, 2018. https://monstroustimes.wordpress.com/

———. "Text and Terror: Monster Theory and the Hebrew Bible." *CurBR* 16.1 (2017): 34–49.

Gray, George Buchanan. *Numbers: A Critical and Exegetical Commentary*. ICC. Edinburgh: T&T Clark, 1903.

Gray, John. *I & II Kings: A Commentary*. OTL. Philadelphia: Westminster, 1963.

———. "Exodus," pages 33–67. *Interpreter's One Volume Commentary on the Bible*. Edited by C. M. Laymon. London: Williams Collins Sons, 1971.

Graybill, Rhiannon. *Are We Not Men?: Unstable Masculinity in the Hebrew Prophets*. New York: Oxford, 2016.

———. "'Day of the Woman': Judges 4–5 as Slasher and Rape-Revenge Narrative." *Journal of Religion and Popular Culture* 30.3 (2018): 193–205.

Green, Alberto R. W. *The Storm-God in the Ancient Near East*. BJSUCSD 8. Winona Lake, IN: Eisenbrauns, 2003.

Gunkel, Hermann. *Creation and Chaos in the Primeval Era and the Eschaton: A Religio-Historical Study of Genesis 1 and Revelation 12*. Biblical Resource Series. Translated by K. William Whitney. Grand Rapids, MI: Eerdmans, 2006.

Gunn, David M. *The Fate of King Saul: An Interpretation of a Biblical Story*. JSOTSup 14. Sheffield, UK: JSOT Press, 1980.

Gunnell, Terry. "The Power in the Place: Icelandic *Álagablettir* Legends in a Comparative Context." Pages 27–41 in *Storied and Supernatural Places: Studies in Spatial and Social Dimensions of Folklore and Sagas*. Edited by Ülo Valk and Daniel Sävborg. Studia Fennica Folkloristica 23. Helsinki: Finnish Literature Society, 2018.

Gutiérrez, Gustavo. *On Job: God-Talk and the Suffering of the Innocent*. Translated by Matthew J. O'Connell. Maryknoll, NY: Orbis, 1987.

Habel, Norman C. *Job: A Commentary*. OTL. Louisville, KY: WJK, 1985.

———. *Literary Criticism of the Old Testament*. GBS. Philadelphia: Fortress, 1971.

Hagan, Harry. "Deception as Motif and Theme in 2 Sm 9–20; 1 Kgs 1–2." *Bib* 60.3 (1979): 301–326.

Hagglund, Mark. *Radical Atheism: Derrida and the Time of Life*. Redwood City, CA: Stanford University Press, 2008.

Halbertal, Moshe, and Stephen Holmes. *The Beginning of Politics: Power in the Biblical Book of Samuel*. Princeton: Princeton University Press, 2017.

Hamori, Esther J. "The Prophet and the Necromancer: Women's Divination for Kings." *JBL* 132.4 (2013): 827–843.

———. *Women's Divination in Biblical Literature: Prophecy, Necromancy, and Other Arts of Knowledge*. AYBRL. New Haven, CT: Yale University Press, 2015.

Haralambakis, Maria. "'I Am Not Afraid of Anybody, I Am the Ruler of this Land': The Portrayal of Job in the *Testament of Job*." Pages 127–144 in *Men and Masculinity in the Hebrew Bible and Beyond*. Edited by Ovidiu Creanga. Sheffield, UK: Sheffield Phoenix, 2010.

Harrington, Erin. *Women, Monstrosity and Horror Film: Gynaehorror*. Film Philosophy at the Margins 2. New York: Routledge, 2018.

Harrington, Thea. "The Speaking Abject in Kristeva's *Powers of Horror*." *Hypatia* 13.1 (1998): 138–157.

Hays, Christopher B. *A Covenant with Death: Death in the Iron Age II and Its Rhetorical Uses in Proto-Isaiah*. Grand Rapids, MI: Eerdmans, 2015.

———. "'Lest Ye Perish in the Way': Ritual and Kinship in Exodus 4:24–26." *Hebrew Studies*, 48.1 (2007): 39–54.

Hearn, Lafcadio. *Kwaidan: Stories and Studies of Strange Things*. Clarendon, VT: Tuttle, 2015.

Heiser, Michael S. "Co-regency in Ancient Israel's Divine Council as the Conceptual Backdrop to Ancient Jewish Binitarian Monotheism." *BBR* 26.2 (2016): 195–225.

Hetherington, Marc J., and Jonathan D. Weiler. *Authoritarianism and Polarization in American Politics*. New York: Cambridge University Press, 2009.

Hills, Matt. "An Event-Based Definition of Art Horror." Pages 137–156 in *Dark Thoughts: Philosophic Reflections on Cinematic Horror*. Edited by Steven Jay Schneider and Daniel Shaw. Lanham, MD: Scarecrow, 2003.

Hogan, David J. *Dark Romance: Sexuality in the Horror Film*. London: McFarland, 1986.

Holland, Timothy. "Ses Fantômes: The Traces of Derrida's Cinema." *Discourse: Journal For Theoretical Studies in Media and Culture* 37.1/2 (2015): 40–62.

Horowitz, Gad. *Repression: Basic and Surplus Repression in Psychoanalytic Theory: Freud, Reich, Marcuse*. Toronto: University of Toronto Press, 1977.

Hoschschild, Arlie Russell. *Strangers in Their Own Land: Anger and Mourning on the American Right*. New York: The New Press, 2016.

Houck-Loomis, Tiffany. "When Fast-Held God Images Fail to Meet Our Needs: A Psychoanalytic Reading of Job Chapters 6 and 7." *Pastoral Psychology* 64.2 (2015): 195–203.

Houston, Walter. *Purity and Monotheism: Clean and Unclean Animals in Biblical Law*. JSOTSup 140. Sheffield, UK: Sheffield Academic Press, 1993.

Humphreys, W. Lee. "From Tragic Hero to Villain: A Study of the Figure of King Saul and the Development of 1 Samuel." *JSOT* 7.1 (1982): 95–117.

———. *The Tragic Vision and the Hebrew Tradition*. OBT 18. Philadelphia: Fortress, 1985.

Ingebretsen, Edward J. *At Stake: Monsters and the Rhetoric of Fear in Popular Culture*. Chicago: University of Chicago Press, 2001.

Jack, Alison. "Tartan Noir and Sacred Scripture: The Bible as Artefact and Metanarrative in Peter May's *Lewis Trilogy*." Pages 29–40 in *The Bible in Crime Fiction and Drama: Murderous Texts*. Edited by Caroline Blyth and Alison Jack. LHBOTS 678; STr 16. London: T&T Clark, 2018.

Jackson, Shirley. *The Haunting of Hill House*. New York: Penguin, 1984.

Janzen, David. "The Condemnation of David's 'Taking' in 2 Samuel 12:1–14." *JBL* 131.2 (2012): 209–220.

Janzen, J. Gerald. "Another Look at God's Watch Over Job (7:12)." *JBL* 108.1 (1989): 109–116.

Jarrard, Eric. "'Now You're in the Sunken Place: Constructed Monsters in Daniel 7 and *Get Out*." *Biblical Reception* 6 (2019): forthcoming.

Jeffers, Ann. *Magic and Divination in Ancient Palestine and Syria*. Studies in the History and Culture of the Ancient Near East 8. Leiden, NL: Brill, 1996.

Jeon, Jaeyoung. "Two Laws in the Sotah Passage (Num. v 11–31)." *VT* 57 (2007): 181–207.

Jobling, David. *1 Samuel*. Berit Olam. Collegeville, MN: Liturgical Press, 1998.

Joffe, Laura. "The Answer to the Meaning of Life, the Universe, and the Elohistic Psalter." *JSOT* 27.2 (2002): 223–235.

Johnson, Kenneth. "The Point of View of the Wandering Camera." *Cinema Studies* 32.2 (1993): 49–56.

Joo, Samantha. "Job, the Biblical Atlas." *CBQ* 74.1 (2012): 67–83.

Joosten, Jan. *People and Land in the Holiness Code: An Exegetical Study of the Ideational Framework of the Law in Leviticus 17–26*. VTSup LXVII. Leiden, NL: Brill, 1996.

Joseph, Allison. *Portrait of the Kings: The Davidic Prototype in Deuteronomistic Poetics*. Minneapolis, MN: Fortress, 2015.

———. "Who Is Like David? Was David Like David?: Good Kings and the Book of Kings." *CBQ* 77.1 (2015): 20–41.

Judis, John B. *The Populist Explosion: How the Great Recession Transformed American and European Politics*. New York: Columbia Global Reports, 2016.

Kalat, David. *J-Horror: The Definitive Guide to* The Ring, The Grudge, *and Beyond*. New York: Vertical, 2007.

Kalmanofsky, Amy. *Dangerous Sisters of the Hebrew Bible*. Minneapolis, MN: Fortress, 2014.

———. "Israel's Baby: The Horror of Childbirth in the Hebrew Prophets." *BibInt* 16.1 (2008): 60–82.

———. "The Monstrous-Feminine in the Book of Jeremiah." *Lectio Difficilior*, edition 1/2009. Accessed August 29, 2018. http://www.lectio.unibe.ch.

———. *Terror All Around: The Rhetoric of Horror in the Book of Jeremiah*. LHBOTS 390. London: T&T Clark, 2008.

Kazen, Thomas. "Purity and Persia." Pages 435–462 in *Current Issues in Priestly and Related Literature: The Legacy of Jacob Milgrom and Beyond*. Edited by Roy E. Gane and Ada Taggar-Cohen. RBS 82. Atlanta: SBL, 2015.

Kazuhiko, Komatsu. *An Introduction to Yōkai Culture: Monsters, Ghosts, and Outsiders in Japanese History*. Translated by Hiroko Yoda and Matt Alt. Tokyo: Japan Publishing Industry Foundation for Culture, 2017.

Keesey, Pam. "*The Haunting* and the Power of Suggestion: Why Robert Wise's Film Continues to 'Deliver the Goods' to Modern Audiences." Pages 305–316 in *Horror Film Reader*, eds. Alain Silver and James Ursini. New York: Limelight Editions, 2000.

Keetley, Dawn. "*127 Hours*: Geological Horror." *Horror Homeroom*, Sept. 11, 2015. http://www.horrorhomeroom.com/geological-horror-of-rocks-and-danny-boyles-127-hours-2010/

Kelle, Brad E. *Ezekiel: A Commentary in the Wesleyan Tradition*. New Beacon Bible Commentary. Kansas City, MO: Beacon Hill Press, 2013.

Kelly, Casey Ryan. "Camp Horror and the Gendered Politics of Screen Violence: Subverting the Monstrous-Feminine in *Teeth* (2007)." *Women's Studies in Communication* 39.1 (2016): 86–106.

Kilker, Robert. "All Roads Lead to the Abject: The Monstrous Feminine and Gender Boundaries in Stanley Kubrick's *The Shining*," *Literature/Film Quarterly* 34.1 (2006): 54–63.

Kim, Uriah Y. "Postcolonial Criticism: Who Is the Other in the Book of Judges?" Pages 161–182 in *Judges & Method: New Approaches in Biblical Studies*. Second edition. Minneapolis, MN: Fortress, 2007.

Kinder, Marsha, and Beverle Houston. "Seeing is Believing: *The Exorcist* and *Don't Look Now*. Pages 44–61 in *American Horrors: Essays on the Modern American Horror Film*. Edited by Gregory A. Waller. Chicago: University of Illinois Press, 1987.

King, Stephen. *Skeleton Crew*. New York: Scribner, 2016.

Klawans, Jonathan. *Impurity and Sin in Ancient Judaism*. Oxford: Oxford University Press, 2000.

Klein, Ezra, and Alvin Chang. "Political Identity is Fair Game for Hatred: How Republicans and Democrats Discriminate." *Vox*, Dec. 7, 2015. https://www.vox.com/2015/12/7/9790764/partisan-discrimination.

Knauf, Ernst Axel. "The Glorious Days of Manasseh." Pages 164–188 in *Good Kings and Bad Kings*. Edited by Lester L. Grabbe. LHBOTS 393. London: T&T Clark, 2005.

Knight, Douglas A. *Law, Power, and Justice in Ancient Israel*. LAI. Louisville, KY: WJK, 2001.

Knohl, Israel. *The Sanctuary of Silence: The Priestly Torah and the Holiness School*. Translated by Jackie Feldman and Peretz Rodman. Minneapolis, MN: Fortress, 1995.

Koehler, Ludwig, and Walter Baumgartner. *Hebrew and Aramaic Lexicon of the Old Testament*. Subsequently revised by Walter Baumgartner and Johann Jakob Stamm. Translated and edited under the supervision of M. E. J. Richardson. Study Edition. 2 volumes. Leiden, NL: Brill, 2001.

Koski, Kaarina. "The Sacred and the Supernatural: Lutheran Church Buildings in Christian Practice and Finnish Folk Belief Tradition." Pages 54–79 in *Storied and Supernatural Places: Studies in Spatial and Social Dimensions of Folklore and Sagas*. Edited by Ülo Valk and Daniel Sävborg. Studia Fennica Folkloristica 23. Helsinki: Finnish Literature Society, 2018.

Korpel, Marjo, and Johannes de Moor. "The Leviathan in the Ancient Near East." Pages 3–20 in *Playing with Leviathan: Interpretation and Reception of Monsters from the Biblical World*. Edited by Koert van Bekkum, Jaap Dekker, Henk van de Kamp, and Eric Peels. TBN 21. Leiden, NL: Brill, 2017.

Kreitzer, Larry J. *Gospel Images in Fiction and Film*. Sheffield, UK: Sheffield Academic Press, 2002.

Kristeva, Julia. *Black Sun: Depression and Melancholia*. Translated by Leon S. Rudiez. New York: Columbia University Press, 1989.

———. *Powers of Horror: An Essay on Objection*. Translated by Leon S. Roudiez. New York: Columbia University Press, 1982.

Kryzwinska, Tanya. "Demon Daddies: Gender, Ecstasy, and Terror in the Possession Film." Pages 247–267 in *Horror Film Reader*. Edited by Alian Silver and James Ursini. New York: Limelight Editions, 2000.

Kugler, Robert. "Urim and Thummim." Pages 5:719–721 in *NIDB*. Edited by Katherine Doob Sakenfeld. Nashville: Abingdon, 2009.

Kugler, Robert A., and Richard L. Rohrbaugh. "On Women and Honor in the *Testament of Job*." *JSP* 14:1 (2004): 43–62.

Kwon, Jiseong James. *Scribal Culture and Intertextuality: Literary and Historical Relationships between Job and Deutero-Isaiah*. FAT II/85. Tübingen, DE: Mohr Siebeck, 2016.

Laclau, Ernesto. "Time Is Out of Joint." *Diacritics* 25.2 (1995): 85–96.

Lakey, Michael. *Image and Glory of God: 1 Corinthians 11:2–16 as a Case Study in Bible, Gender and Hermeneutics*. LNTS. New York: T&T Clark, 2010.

Lanner, Laurel. *"Who Will Lament Her?": The Feminine and the Fantastic in the Book of Nahum*. LHBOTS 434. New York: T&T Clark, 2006.

Lapsley, Jacqueline E. *Can These Bones Live?: The Problem of the Moral Self in the Book of Ezekiel.* BZAW 301. Berlin: de Gruyter, 2000.

Lefebvre, Henri. *The Production of Space.* Translated by D. Nicholson-Smith. Malden, MA: Blackwell, 1991.

LeMon, Joel M., and Kent Harold Richards, eds. *Method Matters: Essays on the Interpretation of the Hebrew Bible in Honor of David L. Peterson.* RBS 56. Atlanta: SBL, 2009.

Lemos, T. M. *Marriage Gifts and Social Change in Ancient Palestine, 1200 BCE to 200 CE.* New York: Cambridge University Press, 2010.

———. "Were Israelite Women Chattel? Shedding New Light on an Old Question." Pages 227–241 in *Worship, Women and War: Essays in Honor of Susan Niditch.* Edited by John J. Collins, T. M. Lemos, and Saul M. Olyan. BJS 357. Providence, RI: Brown Judaic Studies, 2015.

Leshem, Yossi. "'And David Was Sitting in Jerusalem': The Accounts in Samuel and Chronicles." *HUCA* 87 (2016): 49–60.

Levenson, Jon L. *Creation and the Persistence of Evil: The Jewish Drama of Divine Omnipotence.* Second edition. Princeton, NJ: Princeton University Press, 1994.

Levine, Baruch A. "Leviticus: Its Literary History and Location in Biblical Literature." Pages 11–23 in *The Book of Leviticus: Composition and Reception.* Edited by Rolf Rentdorff and Robert A. Kugler. VTSup XCIII. Leiden, NL: Brill 2003.

———. *Numbers 1–20: A New Translation with Introduction and Commentary.* AB 4A. New York: Doubleday, 1993.

Lewis, Theodore J. *Cults of the Dead in Ancient Israel and Ugarit.* HSM 39. Atlanta: Scholars Press, 1989.

Linafelt, Tod. "Taking Women in Samuel: Readers/Responses/Responsibility." Pages 99–113 in *Reading Between Texts: Intertextuality and the Hebrew Bible.* Edited by Danna Nolan Fewell. Literary Currents in Biblical Interpretation. Louisville, KY: WJK, 1992.

———. "The Undecidablity of ברך in the Prologue to Job and Beyond." *BibInt* 4.2 (1996): 154–172.

———. "The Wizard of Uz: Job, Dorothy, and the Limits of the Sublime." *BibInt* 14.1–2 (2006): 94–109.

Lindow, John. "Nordic Legends of the Churchyard." Pages 42–53 in *Storied and Supernatural Places: Studies in Spatial and Social Dimensions of Folklore and Sagas.* Edited by Ülo Valk and Daniel Sävborg. Studia Fennica Folkloristica 23. Helsinki: Finnish Literature Society, 2018.

Lipton, Diana. "Feeding the Green-Eyed Monster: Bitter Waters, Flood Waters, and the Theology of Exile." Pages 102–118 in *Embroidered Garments: Priests and Gender in Biblical Israel.* Edited by Deborah W. Rooke. HBM 25. Sheffield, UK: Sheffield Phoenix, 2009.

Longman, Tremper, III. *Job.* Baker Commentary on the Old Testament and Wisdom. Grand Rapids, MI: Baker, 2012.

Luckhurst, Roger. "Corridor Gothic." *Gothic Studies* 20:1–2 (2018): 295–310.

Lutz, John. "From Domestic Nightmares to the Nightmare of History: Uncanny Eruptions of Violence in King's and Kubrick's Versions of *The Shining*." Pages 161–178 in *The Philosophy of Horror.* Edited by Thomas Fahy. Lexington: University Press of Kentucky, 2010.

———. "Zombies of the World, Unite: Class Struggle and Alienation in *Land of the Dead*." Pages 121–136 in *The Philosophy of Horror.* Edited by Thomas Fahy. Lexington: University Press of Kentucky, 2010.

Maccoby, Hyam. *Ritual Morality: The Ritual Purity System and Its Place in Judaism.* New York: Cambridge University Press, 1999.

Machinist, Peter. "How Gods Die, Biblical and Otherwise: A Problem of Cosmic Restructuring." Pages 189–240 in *Reconsidering the Concept of Revolutionary Monotheism.* Edited by Beate Pongratz-Leisten. Winona Lake, IN: Eisenbrauns, 2011.

Macumber, Heather. "A Monster without a Name: Creating the Beast Known as Antiochus IV in Daniel 7." *JHS* 15 (2015): 1–26.

Maier, Cristl M. *Daughter Zion, Mother Zion: Gender, Space, and the Sacred in Ancient Israel.* Minneapolis, MN: Fortress, 2008.

———. "Zion's Body as a Site of God's Motherhood in Isaiah 66:7–14." Pages 225–242 in *Daughter Zion: Her Portrait, Her Response*. Edited by Mark J. Boda, Carol J. Dempsey, and LeAnn Snow Flesher. AIL 13. Atlanta: SBL 2012.
Malley, Brian. *How the Bible Works: An Anthropological Study of Evangelical Biblicism*. Lanham, MD: AltaMira Press, 2004.
Marcus, David. "David the Deceiver and David the Dupe." *Prooftexts* 6 (1986): 163–171.
Marcuse, Herbert. *Eros and Civilization: A Philosophical Inquiry into Freud*. Translated by Jeremy J. Shapiro. Boston: Beacon, 1966.
Martin, Daniel. *Extreme Asia: The Rise of Cult Cinema From the Far East*. Edinburgh: Edinburgh University Press, 2017.
Marzouk, Safwat. *Egypt as a Monster in the Book of Ezekiel*. FAT II/76. Tübingen, DE Mohr Siebeck, 2015.
Maxwell-Stuart, P. G. *Ghosts: A History of Phantoms, Ghouls & Other Spirits of the Dead*. Gloucestershire, UK: Tempus Publishing Limited, 2006.
Mayr, Suzette. "'House of Mirrors': The Sentinel House as Homosocial Space in Andrew Pyper's *The Guardians*." *Horror Studies* 8.1 (2017): 97–114.
McAfee, Noëlle. "Abject Strangers: Towards an Ethics of Respect." Pages 116–134 in *Ethics, Politics, and Difference in Julia Kristeva's Writing*. Edited by Kelly Oliver. New York: Routledge, 1993.
McCollum, Victoria, ed. *Make America Hate Again: Trump-Era Horror and the Politics of Fear*. New York: Routledge, 2019.
McKenzie, Steven L. *King David: A Biography*. New York: Oxford, 2000.
———. "The So-Called Succession Narrative in the Deuteronomistic History." Pages 123–135 in *Die sogenannte Thronfolgegeschichte Davids*. Edited by A. de Pury and Thomas Römer. OBO 176. Freiburg, DE: Universitätsverlag, 2000.
McKenzie, Steven L., and John Kaltner, eds. *New Meanings for Ancient Texts: Recent Approaches to Biblical Criticism and Their Applications*. Louisville, KY: WJK, 2013.
Mee, Laura. *The Shining*. Devil's Advocates. Leighton Buzzard, UK: Auteur Publishing, 2017.
Milgrom, Jacob. "The Case of the Suspected Adulteress, Numbers 5:11–31: Redaction and Meaning." Pages 69–79 in *The Creation of Sacred Literature*. Edited by R. E. Friedman. Berkeley: University of California Press, 1981.
———. "The Dynamics of Purity in the Priestly System." Pages 29–32 in *Purity and Holiness: The Heritage of Leviticus*. Edited by M. J. H. M. Poorthuis and J. Schwartz. Leiden, NL: Brill, 2000.
———. *Leviticus 1–16: A New Translation with Introduction and Commentary*. AB 3. New York: Doubleday, 1991.
———. *Leviticus 17–22: A New Translation with Introduction and Commentary*. AB 3A. New York: Doubleday, 2000.
———. *Numbers*. JPS Torah Commentary. Philadelphia: Jewish Publication Society, 1990.
Miller, Patrick D. *The Hand of the Lord: A Reassessment of the Ark Narrative in 1 Samuel*. New York: John Hopkins, 1977.
Miller, Robert D., II. *The Dragon, the Mountain, and the Nations: An Old Testament Myth, Its Origins, and Its Afterlives*. EANEC 6. University Park, PA: Eisenbrauns, 2018.
———. "Tracking the Dragon Across the Ancient Near East." *ArOr* 82.2 (2014): 225–245.
Mishra, Pankaj. *The Age of Anger: A History of the Present*. New York: Farrar, Straus, and Giroux, 2017.
Mobley, Gregory. *Return of the Chaos Monsters: And Other Backstories of the Bible*. Grand Rapids, MI: Eerdmans, 2012.
Moore, Meghan Bishop, and Brad Kelle. *Biblical History and Israel's Past: The Changing Study of the Bible and History*. Grand Rapids, MI: Eerdmans, 2011.
Moore, Michael S. "Bathsheba's Silence (1 Kings 1:11–31)." Pages 336–346 in *Inspired Speech: Prophecy in the Ancient Near East*. Edited by John Kaltner and Louis Stulman. JSOTSup 378. London: T&T Clark, 2004.
———. "Big Dreams and Broken Promises: Solomon's Treaty With Hiram in Its International Context." *BBR* 14.2 (2004): 205–221.

Moore, Stephen D., and Yvonne Sherwood. *The Invention of the Biblical Scholar: A Critical Manifesto*. Minneapolis, MN: Fortress.

Morgenstern, Julian. "The 'Bloody Husband' (?) (Exod. 4:24–26) Once Again." *HUCA* 34 (1963): 35–70.

Morrow, William S. *Protest Against God: The Eclipse of a Biblical Tradition*. HBM 4. Sheffield, UK: Sheffield Phoenix, 2006.

Moses, Robert. "'The Satan' in Light of the Creation Theology of the Book of Job." *HBT* 34.1 (2012): 19–34.

Moughtin-Mumby, Sharon. *Sexual and Marriage Metaphors in* Hosea, Jeremiah, Isaiah, *and* Ezekiel. Oxford Theological Monographs. New York: Oxford University Press, 2008.

Mulder, Michael. "Leviathan on the Menu of the Messianic Meal: The Use of Various Images of Leviathan in Early Jewish Tradition." Pages 117–130 in *Playing with Leviathan: Interpretation and Reception of Monsters from the Biblical World*. TBN 21. Edited by Koert van Bekkum, Jaap Dekker, Henk van de Kamp, and Eric Peels. Leiden, NL: Brill, 2017.

Mullen, E. Theodore. *Assembly of the Gods: Divine Council in Canaanite and Early Hebrew Literature*. HSM 24. Chico, CA: Scholars Press, 1980.

Murphy, Kelly J. "The End Is (Still) Around: The Zombie and Contemporary Apocalyptic Thought." Pages 469–495 in *Apocalypses in Context: Apocalyptic Currents Through History*. Edited by Kelly J. Murphy and Justin Jeffcoat Schedtler. Minneapolis, MN: Fortress, 2015.

Murray, Stephen Butler. *Reclaiming Divine Wrath: A History of a Christian Doctrine and Its Interpretation*. Studies in Theology, Society, and Culture 8. New York: Peter Lang, 2011.

Neal, Steve. "*Halloween*: Suspense, Aggression, and the Look." Pages 331–345 in *Planks of Reason: Essays on the Horror Film*. Edited by Barry Keith Grant. Lanham, MD: Scarecrow Press, 1984.

Newkirk, Matthew. "Reconsidering the Role of Deception in Solomon's Ascent to the Throne." *JETS* 57.4 (2014): 703–713.

Newsom, Carol. *The Book of Job: A Contest of Moral Imaginations* (New York: Oxford University Press, 2003).

Nietzsche, Friedrich. *Beyond Good and Evil: Prelude to a Philosophy of the Future*. Translated by Walter Kaufmann. New York: Vintage, 1966.

Nihan, Christophe. *From Priestly Torah to Pentateuch: A Study in the Composition of the Book of Leviticus*. FAT II/25. Tübinge, DE: Mohr Siebeck, 2007.

Nikolchina, Miglena. *Matricide in Language: Writing Theory in Kristeva and Woolf*. New York: Other Press, 2004.

Nolan, Amy. "Seeing Is Digesting: Labyrinths of Historical Ruin in Stanley Kubrick's *The Shining*." *Cultural Critique* 77 (2011): 180–204.

Noth, Martin. *Numbers: A Commentary*. Translated by James D. Martin. OTL. Philadelphia: WJK, 1969.

Nussbaum, Martha. *For Love of Country?* Boston: Beacon Press, 1996.

O'Kane, Martin. "The Flight Into Egypt: Icon of Refuge for the H(a)unted." Pages 15–60 in *Borders, Boundaries, and the Bible*. Edited by Martin O'Kane. JSOTSup 313. London: Sheffield Academic Press, 2002.

Oliver, Kelly. *Reading Kristeva: Unravelling the Double-Bind*. Bloomington: Indiana University Press, 1993.

Oliver, Mary Beth, and Meghan Sanders, "The Appeal of Horror and Suspense." Pages 242–259 in *The Horror Film*. Edited by Stephen Prince. New Brunswick, NJ: Rutgers University Press, 2004.

Olson, Dennis. "The Book of Judges." In *The New Interpreter's Bible*, vol. 2, 721–888. Nashville, TN: Abingdon, 1998.

Olyan, Saul M. *Disability in the Hebrew Bible: Interpreting Mental and Physical Differences*. Cambridge, MA: Cambridge University Press, 2008.

Otto, Rudolph. *The Idea of the Holy*. Translated by John W. Harvey. Second edition. New York: Oxford, 1950.

Pandzic, Maja. "Female 'Madness' as the Driving Force in the *Insidious* Film Series." *Outskirts* 35 (2016): 1–20.

Parker, Rozsika. *Torn in Two: The Experience of Maternal Ambivalence*. New and Revised edition. London: Virago Books, 2005.
Perdue, Leo. "Job's Assault on Creation." *HAR* 10 (1986): 295–315.
Peterson, Christopher. "Derrida's Ouija Board." *Qui Parle* 17.2 (2009): 85–101.
Pettit, David. "When the LORD Seeks to Kill Moses: Reading Exodus 4:24–26 in its Literary Context." *JSOT* 40.2 (2015): 163–177.
Pew Research Center. "Partisanship and Political Animosity in 2016." http://www.people-press.org/2016/06/22/partisanship-and-political-animosity-in-2016.
Pheasant-Kelly, Fran. "Cinematic Cyborgs, Abject Bodies: Post-Human Hybridity in *T2* and *Robocop*." *Film International* 53: 54–63.
Phillip, Tarja. "Priestly Matters: Priestly Writing on Impurity." Pages 40–59 in *Embroidered Garments: Priests and Gender in Biblical Israel*. Edited by Deborah W. Rooke. HBM 25. Sheffield, UK: Sheffield Phoenix, 2009.
Pikkety, Thomas. *Capital in the Twenty-First Century*. Translated by Arthur Goldhammer. Cambridge, MA: Belknap Press, 2014.
Poe, Edgar Allan. "The Fall of the House of Usher." Pages 177–191 in *Complete Stories and Poems of Edgar Allan Poe*. New York: Doubleday, 1966.
Poole, W. Scott. *Monsters in America: Our Historical Obsession with the Hideous and the Haunting*. Waco, TX: Baylor, 2011.
———. *Wasteland: The Great War and the Origins of Modern Horror*. Berkeley, CA: Counterpoint, 2018.
Poorthuis, Marcel, and Joshua Schwartz. "Introduction." Pages 3–26 in *Purity and Holiness: The Heritage of Leviticus*. Edited by M. J. H. M. Poorthuis and J. Schwartz. Jewish and Christian Perspectives 2. Leiden, NL: Brill, 1999.
Pope, Marvin H. *Job: A New Translation with Introduction and Commentary*. AB 18. New York: Doubleday, 1966.
Prince, John Dyneley. "Notes on Leprosy in the Old Testament." *JBL* 38.1 (1919): 30–34.
Prince, Stephen. "Dread, Taboo, and *The Thing*: Toward a Social Theory of the Horror Film. Pages 118–130 in *The Horror Film*. Edited and Introduction by Stephen Prince. New Brunswick, NJ: Rutgers University Press, 2004.
Propp, William. *Exodus 1–18: A New Translation with Introduction and Commentary*. YAB 2A. New Haven, CT: Yale, 1999.
Regenspan, Barbara. *Haunting and the Educational Imagination*. Boston: Sense, 2014.
Richardson, Judith. *Possessions: The History and Uses of Haunting in the Hudson Valley*. Cambridge, MA: Harvard, 2003.
Ricouer, Paul. *Interpretation Theory: Discourse and the Surplus of Meaning*. Fort Worth: Texas Christian University Press, 1976.
Rindge, Matthew S. "Lars von Trier's *Dogville* as a Cinematic Parable." Pages 260–269 in *T&T Clark Companion to the Bible and Film*. Edited by Richard Walsh. London: T&T Clark, 2018.
Roberts, Robin. *Subversive Spirits: The Female Ghost in British and American Popular Culture*. Jackson: University of Mississippi Press, 2018.
Römer, Thomas. *Dark God: Cruelty, Sex, and Violence in the Old Testament*. Mahwah, NJ: Paulist Press, 2013.
———. "Lilith. I. Ancient Near East and Hebrew Bible/Old Testament." *Encyclopedia of the Bible and Its Reception*. Volume 16. Berlin: de Gruyter, 2018.
———. *The So-Called Deuteronomistic History: A Sociological, Historical and Literary Introduction*. New York: T&T Clark, 2007.
Ruane, Nicole J. *Sacrifice and Gender in Biblical Law*. New York: Cambridge, 2013.
Scherer, Elisabeth. "Well-Travelled Female Avengers: The Transcultural Potential of Japanese Ghosts." Pages 61–82 in *Ghost Movies in Southeast Asia and Beyond: Narratives, Cultural Contexts, Audiences*. Edited by Peter J. Bräunlein and Andrea Lauser. Leiden, NL: Brill, 2016.
Schiffendecker, Kathryn. *Out of the Whirlwind: Creation Theology in the Book of Job*. HTS 61. Cambridge, MA: Harvard University Press, 2008.
Schmid, Herbert. "Mose, der Blutbräutigam: Erwägungen zu Ex 4, 24–26." *Judaica* 22 (1966): 113–118.

Schmidt, Brian B. *Israel's Beneficent Dead: Ancestor Cult and Necromancy in Ancient Israelite Religion and Tradition*. Winona Lake, IN: Eisenbrauns, 1994.

———. "The 'Witch' of En-Dor, 1 Samuel 28, and Ancient Near Eastern Necromancy." Pages 109–129 in *Magic and Ritual in the Ancient World*. Edited by Paul Mirecki and Marvin Meyer. Religions in the Graeco-Roman World 129. Leiden, NL: Brill, 2015.

Schneider, Steven Jay. "Introduction." Pages 1–15 in *Horror Film and Psychoanalysis: Freud's Worst Nightmare*. Edited by Steven Jay Schneider. New York: Cambridge University Press, 2004.

———. "Monsters as (Uncanny) Metaphors: Freud, Lakoff, and the Representation of Monstrosity in Cinematic Horror." Pages 167–192 in *The Horror Reader*. Edited by Alain Silver and James Ursini. New York: Limelight Editions, 2000.

———. "Toward an Aesthetics of Cinematic Horror." Pages 130–149 in *The Horror Film*. Edited by Stephen Prince. New Brunswick, NJ: Rutgers University Press, 2004.

———, ed. *Horror Film and Psychoanalysis: Freud's Worst Nightmare*. New York: Cambridge University Press, 2004.

Schreiner, Thomas R. "Head Coverings, Prophecies, and the Trinity: 1 Corinthians 11:2–16." Pages 124–139 in *Recovering Biblical Manhood and Womanhood: A Response to Evangelical Feminism*. Edited by John Piper and Wayne Grudem. Wheaton, IL: Crossway Books, 1991.

Schroeder, Joy A. *Dinah's Lament: The Biblical Legacy of Sexual Violence in Christian Interpretation*. Minneapolis, MN: Fortress, 2007.

Schwartz, Baruch J. "The Bearing of Sin in the Priestly Literature." Pages 3–21 in *Pomegranates and Golden Bells: Studies in Biblical, Jewish, and Near Eastern Ritual, Law, and Literature in Honor of Jacob Milgrom*. Edited by David P. Wright, David Noel Freedman, and Avi Hurvitz. Winona Lake, IN: Eisenbrauns, 1995.

———. "Israel's Holiness: The Torah Traditions." Pages 47–59 in *Purity and Holiness: The Heritage of Leviticus*. Edited by M. J. H. M. Poorthuis and J. Schwartz. Jewish and Christian Perspectives 2. Leiden, NL: Brill, 1999.

Schwartz, Baruch J., David P. Wight, Jeffrey Stackert, and Naphtali S. Meshel, eds. *Perspectives on Purity and Purification in the Hebrew Bible*. LHBOTS 474. New York: T&T Clark, 2008.

Schwáb, Zoltán. "Is Fear of the Lord the Source of Wisdom, or Vice Versa?" *VT* 63 (2013): 652–662.

Scurlock, JoAnn. "*Chaoskampf* Lost—*Chaoskampf* Regained: The Gunkel Hypothesis Revisited." Pages 258–268 in *Creation and Chaos: A Reconsideration of Hermann Gunkel's* Chaoskampf *Hypothesis*." Edited by JoAnn Scurlock and Richard H. Beal. Winona Lake, IN: Eisenbrauns, 2013.

———. *Magico-Medical Means of Treating Ghost-Induced Illnesses in Ancient Mesopotamia*. Ancient Magic and Divination III. Leiden, NL: Brill, 2006.

Seibert, Eric. *Disturbing Divine Behavior: Troubling Old Testament Images of God*. Minneapolis, MN: Fortress, 2009.

———. *The Violence of Scripture: Overcoming the Old Testament's Troubling Legacy*. Minneapolis, MN: Fortress, 2012.

Seow C. L. *Job 1–21: Interpretation and Commentary*. Illuminations. Grand Rapids, MI: Eerdmans, 2013.

Ska, Jean-Louis. *Introduction to Reading the Pentateuch*. Translated by Sr. Pascale Dominique. Winona Lake, IN: Eisenbrauns, 2006.

Sloane, Andrew. "Aberrant Textuality? The Case of Ezekiel the (Porno) Prophet." *TynBul* 59.1 (2008): 53–76.

Smith, Christian. *The Bible Made Impossible: Why Biblicism is Not a Truly Evangelical Reading of Scripture*. Grand Rapids, MI: Brazos, 2011.

Smith, Greg. "'Real Horrorshow': The Juxtaposition of Subtext, Satire, and Audience Implication in Stanley Kubrick's *The Shining*." *Literature/Film Quarterly* 25.4 (1997): 300–306.

Smith, Mark S. *The Early History of God: Yahweh and the Other Deities in Ancient Israel*. Second edition. Grand Rapids, MI: Eerdmans, 2002.

———. *God in Translation: Deities in Cross-Cultural Discourse in the Biblical World*. FAT 57. Tübingen, DE: Mohr Siebeck, 2008.
———. *The Priestly Vision of Genesis 1*. Minneapolis, MN: Fortress, 2010.
———. *Where the Gods Are: Spatial Dimensions of Anthropomorphism in the Biblical World*. AYBRL. New Haven, CT: Yale University Press, 2016.
Solimar, Otero. "'Fearing Our Mothers': An Overview of the Psychoanalytic Theories Concerning the Vagina Dentata Motif." *American Journal of Psychoanalysis* 56.3 (1996): 269–288.
Sonik, Karen. "From Hesiod's Abyss to Ovid's *rudis indigestaque moles*: Chaos and Cosmos in the Babylonian 'Epic of Creation'." Pages 1–25 in *Creation and Chaos: A Reconsideration of Hermann Gunkel's* Chaoskampf *Hypothesis*. Edited by JoAnn Scurlock and Richard H. Beal. Winona Lake, IN: Eisenbrauns, 2013.
Sparks, Kenton L. "Enuma Eliš and Priestly Mimesis: Elite Emulation in Nascent Judaism." *JBL* 126 (2007): 629–632.
Stade, D. B. "Beiträge zur Pentateuchkritik." *ZAW* 15 (1895): 166–175.
Sternberg, Meir. *The Poetics of Biblical Narrative: Ideological Literature and the Drama of Reading*. Bloomington: Indiana University Press, 1985.
Stokes, Ryan E. "Satan, YHWH's Executioner." *JBL* 133.2 (2014): 251–270.
Stone, Allison. "Against Matricide: Rethinking Subjectivity and the Maternal Body." *Hypatia* 27.1 (2012): 118–138.
Stone, Ken. "Animal and Sexual Difference, and the Daughter of Jephthah." *BibInt* 24 (2016): 1–16.
———. *Reading the Hebrew Bible with Animal Studies*. Stanford, CA: Stanford University Press, 2018.
———. *Sex, Honor, and Power in the Deuteronomistic History*. JSOTSup 234. Sheffield, UK: Sheffield Academic Press, 1996.
Stoneman, Ethan, and Joseph Packer. "No, Everything is Not All Right: Supernatural Horror as Pessimistic Argument." *Horror Studies* 8.1 (2017): 147–163.
Subissati, Andrea, and Alexandra West. "All Work and No Play: Stanley Kubrick's *The Shining* (1980)." *Faculty of Horror*. Podcast audio, Dec. 21, 2015.
Sunderland, Paul. "The Autonomous Camera in Stanley Kubrick's *The Shining*." *Sydney Studies in English* 39 (2013): 58–85.
Sweeney, Marvin A. *I & II Kings*. OTL. Louisville, KY: WJK, 2008.
Taliaferro, Charles. "Is God Vain?" Pages 63–78 in *Questions About God: Today's Philosophers Ponder the Divine*. Edited by Steven M. Cahn and David Shatz. New York: Oxford, 2002.
Tamber-Ross, Caryn. "Biblical Bathing Beauties and the Manipulation of the Male Gaze: What Judith Can Tell Us About Bathsheba and Susanna." *JFSR* 33.1 (2017): 55–72.
Todorov, Tzvetan. *The Fantastic: A Structural Approach to a Literary Genre*. Translated by Richard Howard. Ithaca, NY: Cornell, 1975.
Trimm, Charlie. *'YHWH Fights for Them!': The Divine Warrior in the Exodus Narrative*. Gorgias Biblical Studies 58. Piscataway, NJ: Gorgias Press, 2014.
Tsumura, David S. *Creation and Destruction: A Reappraisal of the* Chaoskampf *Theory*. Winona Lake, IN: Eisenbrauns, 2005.
Tucker, Gene M. "Rain on a Land Where No One Lives." *JBL* 116.1 (1997): 3–17.
Valk, Ülo. "Ghostly Possession and Real Estate: The Dead in Contemporary Estonian Folklore." *Journal of Folklore Research* 43.1 (2006): 31–51.
van Bekkum, Koert. "'Is Your Rage Against the Rivers, Your Wrath Against the Sea?': Storm-God Imagery in Habakkuk 3." Pages 55–76 in *Playing with Leviathan: Interpretation and Reception of Monsters from the Biblical World*. TBN 21. Edited by Koert van Bekkum, Jaap Dekker, Henk van de Kamp, and Eric Peels. Leiden, NL: Brill, 2017.
Vance, J. D. *Hillbilly Elegy: A Memoir of a Family and Culture in Crisis*. New York: Harper, 2016.
van de Kemp. "Leviathan and the Monsters in Revelation." Pages 167–175 in *Playing with Leviathan: Interpretation and Reception of Monsters from the Biblical World*. TBN 21.

Edited by Koert van Bekkum, Jaap Dekker, Henk van de Kamp, and Eric Peels. Leiden: Brill, 2017.

van Der Toorn, Karel. *Family Religion in Babylonia, Ugarit, and Israel: Continuity and Change in the Forms of Religious Life*. Leiden, NL: Brill, 1996.

van Houwelingen, Rob. "The Air Combat between Michael and the Dragon: Revelation 12:7–12 in Relation to Similar Texts from the New Testament." Pages 151–166 in *Playing with Leviathan: Interpretation and Reception of Monsters from the Biblical World*. TBN 21. Edited by Koert van Bekkum, Jaap Dekker, Henk van de Kamp, and Eric Peels. Leiden, NL: Brill, 2017.

van Seters, John. *The Biblical Saga of King David*. Winona Lake, IN: Eisenbrauns, 2009.

van Werven, Ben. "As a Fish on Dry Land: Some Remarks on Tannîn in Ezekiel." Pages 40–54 in *Playing with Leviathan: Interpretation and Reception of Monsters from the Biblical World*. TBN 21. Edited by Koert van Bekkum, Jaap Dekker, Henk van de Kamp, and Eric Peels. Leiden, NL: Brill, 2017.

Vidler, Anthony. *The Architectural Uncanny: Essays in the Modern Unhomely*. Cambridge, MA: MIT Press, 1992.

Volf, Miroslav. *Free of Charge: Giving and Forgiving in a Culture Stripped of Grace*. Grand Rapids, MI: Zondervan, 2005.

Wada-Marciano, Matsuyo. "J-horror: New Media's Impact on Contemporary Japanese Horror Cinema." Pages 15–38 in *Horror to the Extreme: Changing Boundaries and Asian Cinema*. Edited by Jinhee Choi and Mitsuyo-Wada Marciano. Aberdeen, UK: Hong Kong University Press, 2009.

Wakeman, Mary K. *God's Battle with the Monster: Study in Biblical Imagery*. Leiden, NL: Brill, 1973.

Walker, Michael. *Modern Ghost Melodramas: What Lies Beneath*. Film Culture in Translation. Amsterdam: Amsterdam University Press, 2017.

Walsh, Richard. "On the Harmony of the (Asocial) Gospel: *Intolerance*'s Crosscut Stories." Pages 43–77 in *Close Encounters Between Bible and Film: An Interdisciplinary Engagement*. Edited by Laura Copier and Caroline Vander Stichele. SemSt 87. Atlanta: SBL, 2016.

Waltke, Bruce K., and M. O'Connor. *An Introduction to Biblical Hebrew Syntax*. Winona Lake, IN: Eisenbrauns, 1990.

Wardlaw, Terrence R., Jr. *Elohim Within the Psalms: Petitioning the Creator to Order Chaos in Oral-Derived Literature*. LHBOTS 602. New York: Bloomsbury T&T Clark, 2015.

Warning, Wilfred. *Literary Artistry in Leviticus*. BibInt 35. Leiden, NL: Brill, 1999.

Waterhouse, Ruth. "*Beowulf* as Palimpsest." Pages 26–36 in *Monster Theory: Reading Culture*. Edited by Jeffrey Jerome Cohen. Minneapolis: University of Minnesota Press, 1996.

Watson, Rebecca S. *Chaos Uncreated: A Reassessment of the Theme of "Chaos" in the Hebrew Bible*. BZAW 341. Berlin: de Gruyter, 2005.

Watts, James W. *Ritual and Rhetoric in Leviticus: From Sacrifice to Scripture*. New York: Cambridge, 2007.

Watts, John D. W. *Isaiah 34–66*. WBC 25. Waco, TX: Word Books, 1987.

Wee, Valerie. *Japanese Horror Films and Their American Remakes: Translating Fear, Adapting Culture*. Routledge Advances in Film Series 27. New York: Routledge, 2014.

Weems, Renita. *Battered Love: Marriage, Sex, and Violence in the Hebrew Prophets*. OBT. Minneapolis, MN: Fortress, 1995.

Weiss, Gail. "The Abject Borders of the Body Image." Pages 41–59 in *Perspectives on Embodiment: The Intersections of Nature and Culture*. Edited by Gail Weiss and Honi Fern Haber. New York: Routledge, 1999.

Westbrook, April D. *"And He Will Take Your Daughters . . .": Woman Story and the Ethical Evaluation of the Monarchy in the David Narrative*. LHBOTS 610. New York: Bloomsbury T&T Clark, 2015.

Westermann, Claus. *Genesis 1–11*. Translated by John J. Scullion. Continental Commentaries. Minneapolis: Fortress, 1994.

Wetmore, Kevin J., Jr., ed. *The Streaming of* Hill House: *Essays on the Haunting Netflix Adaptation*. Jefferson, NC: McFarland, 2020.

Whitney, K. William. *Two Strange Beasts: Leviathan and Behemoth in Second Temple and Early Rabbinic Judaism*. Winona Lake, IN: Eisenbrauns, 2006.
Wiggins, Steve A. "Good Book Gone Bad: Reading Phinehas and Watching Horror." *HBT* 41.1 (2019): 93–103.
———. *Holy Horror: The Bible and Fear in Movies*. Jefferson, NC: McFarland, 2018.
———. *Nightmares with the Bible*. Horror and Scripture. Lanham, MD: Lexington Books/Fortress Academic, 2020 (forthcoming).
Williams, David. *Cain and Beowulf: A Study in Secular Allegory* (Toronto: University of Toronto Press, 1982).
Williams, Delores S. *Sisters in the Wilderness*. Maryknoll: Orbis, 1995.
Williams, Tony S. *George A. Romero: Knight of the Living Dead*. Second edition. New York: Columbia University Press, 2015.
———. *Hearths of Darkness: The Family in the American Horror Film*. Updated edition. Jackson: University of Mississippi Press, 2014.
Willis, John T. *Yahweh and Moses in Conflict: The Role of Exodus 4:24–26 in the Book of Exodus*. Bible in History 8. New York: Peter Lang, 2010.
Wolff, Hans Walter. "The Kerygma of the Deuteronomistic Historical Work." Pages 83–100 in *The Vitality of Old Testament Traditions*. Walter Brueggemann and Hans Walter Wolff. Second edition. Atlanta: John Knox Press, 1982.
Wood, Robin. *Hollywood From Vietnam to Reagan . . . and Beyond*. Revised and Expanded Edition. New York: Columbia University Press, 2003.
Yamasaki, Gary. *Insights from Filmmaking for Analyzing Biblical Narrative*. Reading the Bible in the 21st Century: Insights. Minneapolis, MN: Fortress, 2016.
Yee, Gail. *Poor Banished Children of Eve: Women as Evil in the Hebrew Bible*. Minneapolis, MN: Fortress, 2003.
Zanger, Jules. "A Sympathetic Vibration: Dracula and the Jews." *English Literature in Transition, 1880–1920* 34.1 (1991): 33–44.
Zappia, Dominic. "Demythologizing the Satan Tradition of Historical-Criticism: A Reevaluation of the Old Testament Portrait of שָׂטָן in Light of Old Testament Pseudepigrapha." *SJOT* 29.1 (2015): 117–134.
Zimran, Yisca. "'Look! The King is Weeping and Mourning': Expressions of Mourning in the David Narratives and Their Interpretive Contribution." *JSOT* 42.4 (2018): 491–517.

FILMOGRAPHY

127 Hours. Film. Directed by Danny Boyle. 2010; Paris: Pathé Films.
Abbott and Costello Meet Frankenstein. DVD. Directed by Charles Barton. 1948; Los Angeles: Universal, 2008.
Alien. Blu-Ray. Directed by Ridley Scott. 1979; Burbank, CA: 20th Century Fox, 2011.
The Amityville Horror. DVD. Directed by Stuart Rosenberg. 1979; Los Angeles: MGM Studios, 2014.
The Birth of a Nation. DVD. Directed by D. W. Griffith. 1915; New York: Kino Lorber, 2002.
Black Christmas. DVD. Directed by Bob Clark. 1974; Oaks, PA: Eclectic, 2006.
The Bride of Frankenstein. DVD. Directed by James Whale. 1935; Los Angeles: Universal, 2001.
The Brood. Blu-Ray. Directed by David Cronenberg. 1979; Chicago, IL: Criterion, 2015.
Cabin in the Woods. Blu-Ray. Directed by Drew Goddard. 2011; Santa Monica, CA: Lions Gate, 2012.
Carrie. Blu-Ray. Directed by Brian de Palma. 1976; Eugene, OR: Shout! Factory, 2016.
The Cat People. DVD. Directed by Jacques Tourneur. 1942; Atlanta: Turner Home Entertainment, 2005.
The Changeling. DVD. Directed by Peter Medak. 1980; Los Angeles: HBO Studios, 2005.
The Conjuring. Film. Directed by James Wan. 2013; Los Angeles: New Line Cinema.
Crimson Peak. Film. Directed by Guillermo del Toro. 2015; Burbank, CA: Legendary Pictures.

Dawn of the Dead. DVD. Directed by George A. Romero. 1979; Beverly Hills, CA: Anchor Bay Entertainment, 2001.
Day of the Dead. DVD. Directed by George A. Romero. 1983; Beverly Hills, CA: Anchor Bay, 2001.
The Devil's Backbone. Film. Directed by Guillermo del Toro. 2001; Madrid: El Deseo.
The Exorcist. DVD. Directed by William Friedkin. 1973; Los Angeles: Warner Home Video, 2011.
The Fall of the House of Usher. DVD. Directed by Jean Epstein. 1928; Los Angeles: Image Entertainment, 2001.
The Fall of the House of Usher. DVD. Directed by Roger Corman. 1960; Los Angeles: MGM, 2001.
The Fly. DVD. Directed by David Cronenberg. 1986; Los Angeles: 20th Century Fox, 2005.
Frailty. Film. Directed by Bill Paxton. 2001; Los Angeles: David Kirschner Productions.
Frankenstein. DVD. Directed by James Whale. 1931; Universal City, CA: Universal Studios, 2004.
Ghost Dance. Directed by Ken McMullen. 1983; London: Channel Four Films.
A Ghost Story. Film. Directed by David Lowery. New York: A24 Films.
Halloween. DVD. Directed by John Carpenter. 1978; Troy, MI: Anchor Bay Entertainment, 2003.
Halloween. Film. Directed by David Gordon Greene. 2018; Los Angeles: Miramax.
The Haunted Mansion. Film. Directed by Rob Minkoff. 2003; Burbank, CA: Walt Disney Pictures.
The Haunting. DVD. Directed by Robert Wise. 1963; Los Angeles: Warner Brothers, 2003.
The Haunting. Film. Directed by Jan de Bont. 1999. Los Angeles: Dreamworks.
The Haunting of Hill House. TV Series. Directed by Michael Flanagan. 2018. Los Angeles: Paramount Television.
The Hills Have Eyes. DVD. Directed by Wes Craven. 1977; Chatsworth, CA: Image Entertainment, 2011.
The Innkeepers. Film. Directed by Ti West. 2011; Orland Park, IL: Dark Sky Films.
The Innocents. Blu-Ray. Directed by Jack Clayton. 1961; Chicago: Criterion, 2014.
Inside (À l'intérieur). DVD. Directed by Alexandre Bustillo and Julien Maury. 2007; New York: Dimension Extreme, 2008.
Insidious. Film. Directed by James Wan. 2010. Los Angeles: Sony.
Ju-On: The Grudge. Film. Directed by Tikashi Shimizu. 2002; Tokyo: Pioneer LDC.
King Kong. DVD. Directed by Merian C. Cooper and Ernest B. Schoedsack. 1933; Burbank, CA: Warner Home Video, 2005.
Kuroneko (The Black Cat). DVD. Directed by Kaneto Shindô. 1968; Chicago: Criterion, 2011.
Kwaidan. Blu-Ray. Directed by Masaki Kobayashi. 1964; Chicago: Criterion, 2015.
Last Year at Marienbad. Blu-Ray. Directed by Alain Resnais. 1961; Chicago, Criterion, 2009.
Land of the Dead. Blu-Ray. Directed by George A. Romero. 2005; Los Angeles: Universal.
The Legend of Hell House. Blu-Ray. Directed by John Hough. 1973; Eugene, OR: Shout! Factory, 2014.
Leviathan. Blu-Ray. Directed by George P. Cosmatos. 1989; Eugene, OR: Shout! Factory, 2014.
Lights Out. Film. Directed by David F. Sandberg. 2016; Los Angeles: New Line Cinema.
Mama. Film. Directed by Andy Muschietti. 2013; Los Angeles: Universal.
The Mist. Film. Directed by Frank Darabondt. 2007; Los Angeles: Dimension.
The Mist. TV Series. Created by Christian Torpe. 2017; Los Angeles: Paramount Network.
Night of the Living Dead. Blu-Ray. Directed by George A. Romero. 1968; Chicago: Criterion, 2017.
The Omen. DVD. Directed by Richard Donner. 1978; Burbank, CA: Warner Home Video, 2001.
Ouija. Film. Directed by Stiles White. 2014; Los Angeles: Universal Pictures.
Peeping Tom. DVD. Directed by Michael Powell. 1959; Chicago: Criterion, 1999.
Poltergeist. DVD. Directed by Tobe Hooper. 1982. Los Angeles: Warner Home Video, 2008.

Psycho. DVD. Directed by Alfred Hitchcock. 1960; Universal City, CA: Universal Studios, 2000.
A Quiet Place. Film. Directed by John Krasinski. 2018; Los Angeles: Platinum Dunes.
The Ring. Film. Directed by Gore Verbinski. Los Angeles: Dreamworks, 2002.
Ringu. DVD. Directed by Hideo Nakata. 1998; Los Angeles: Dreamworks, 2003.
Rosemary's Baby. DVD. Directed by Roman Polanski. 1968; Chicago: Criterion, 2012.
Scream. DVD. Directed by Wes Craven. 1996; Los Angeles: Dimension, 1998.
The Shawshank Redemption. Blu-Ray. Directed by Frank Darabont. 1994; Los Angeles: Warner Home Video, 2008.
The Shining. Blu-Ray. Directed by Stanley Kubrick. 1980; Los Angeles: Warner Home Video, 2007.
The Silence of the Lambs. DVD. Directed by Jonathan Demme. 1991; Chicago: Criterion, 1999.
The Sixth Sense. Film. Directed by M. Night Shyamalan. 1999; Los Angeles: Hollywood Pictures.
Sleepaway Camp. Blu-Ray. Directed by Robert Hiltzik. 1983; Eugene, OR: Shout! Factory, 2014.
South Park: Bigger, Longer, and Uncut. Directed by Trey Parker. 1999; New York: Scott Rudin Productions.
Star Wars, Episode IV: A New Hope. Blu-Ray. Directed by George Lucas. 1977; Los Angeles: 20th Century Fox, 2015.
Teeth. Film. Directed by Mitchell Lichtenstein. 2007; New York: Pierpoline Films.
The Thing. Blu-Ray. Directed by John Carpenter. 1982; Los Angeles: Universal, 2008.
The Thing from Another World. DVD. Directed by Christian Nyby. 1951; Burbank, CA: Warner Home Video, 2010.
Ugestsu Monogatari. DVD. Directed by Kenji Mizoguchi. 1953; Chicago: Criterion, 2005.
The Uninvited. Blu-Ray. Directed by Lewis Allen. 1944; Chicago: Criterion, 2013.
Urban Legend. Film. Directed by Jamie Blanks. 1998; Los Angeles: Phoenix Pictures.
When a Stranger Calls. DVD. Directed by Fred Walton. 1979; Los Angeles: Sony, 2006.
The Witch. Film. Directed by Robert Eggers. 2015; Brooklyn: Parts and Labor Films.
The Woman in Black. Film. Directed by James Watkins. 2012; London: Hammer Films.

General Index

127 Hours, 17–18

Aaron, 67, 126, 135
abject, 10, 104, 114–117
Abraham, 6
Absalom, 88–89, 110
Adonijah, 91
adultery, 110–114
Ahithophel, 89
Aichele, George, 16
Alien, 102–103, 108
Amnon, 88–89
anxiety, 5, 18–19, 21, 67–68, 79, 102–106, 108, 109, 113, 143
Asherah, 68
Ashley, Timothy, 111
audience response, 3–4, 17–18, 65

Ba'al, 68
Ba'al Cycle, 34–35, 134
Babylon, 8, 31, 84, 87
Bachelard, Gaston, 81
Bathsheba, 87–92
Batto, Bernard, 34, 134
Beal, Timothy, 36, 133
Beowulf, 30
Bible and film, 16–17
Black Christmas, 101
The Blair Witch Project, 5, 56
Blenkinsopp, Joseph, 65

boundaries, 17, 22, 30–32, 36, 39–40, 44–45, 65, 105–106, 109, 114, 117, 128, 135–136
The Brood, 103, 113–114

Carrie, 103–104, 108, 112–113
Carroll, Noël, 4, 17, 22, 102, 106
Chaoskampf, 16, 33–37, 39–42, 133–138
Clines, David, 43
Clover, Carol, 103
Cohen, Jeffrey Jerome, 17, 30–31
control, 1, 18, 34, 57, 86, 104, 108–111
Copier, Laura, 16–17
Creed, Barbara, 103
Crouch, C. L., 133
Curtis, Barry, 79

David, 6, 10, 45, 62–64, 77, 86–92, 109–110, 126
dawn, 40, 42–43
Day, John, 34
De Moor, Johannes, 35
death, 1–2, 9, 55–56, 61–64, 66, 68, 77–79, 83, 86, 88, 91, 105–106, 110, 128, 145
decalogue, 66–67, 114–115
Derrida, Jacques, 57–59, 60, 65, 68
Deuteronomistic History, 60, 86, 88, 89–90, 129
Deuteronomy, 60, 66–68, 129
The Devil's Backbone, 56
différance, 58

Dinah, 109
disease, 85
disgust, 18, 102–103, 107–108
Douglas, Mary, 22, 106
Dracula, 30
dragon. *See* Leviathan
dread, 5, 68, 137–138

Elohistic source, 85
Endor, 62
Enns, Peter, 125
Enuma Elish, 33–35, 36, 133–134
evil, 4, 10, 30, 33–36, 44–45, 90, 145
Exodus, 11, 67, 134, 135–137
The Exorcist, 1, 9–10, 35, 103, 108

"The Fall of the House of Usher," 78
fear, 2–6, 11, 17, 18–21, 37, 39, 44, 62–64, 66–68, 83, 89, 104, 107, 126–127, 131, 138, 144
Final Girl, 101
Fishbane, Michael, 40, 111
folklore, 83
Frailty, 127, 137
Frankenstein, 30, 128
Freeland, Cynthia, 4, 5
Fretheim, Terence, 130–131
Freud, Sigmund, 19, 21, 65, 92

Gammie, John, 44
gender, 57, 101–117
Genesis, 11, 33–35, 36, 40, 133–137
A Ghost Story, 58–59, 64
Ginger Snaps, 104
Gray, George Buchanan, 111
Graybill, Rhiannon, 130
Grendel, 30, 83
Gunkel, Hermann, 33–34
Gunnell, Terry, 83
Gutiérrez, Gustavo, 37

Hagglund, Martin, 58
Halloween (1978), 18, 101
Halloween (2018), 143, 145
Hamori, Esther, 60–61
Hardy Boys, 7
Harrington, Erin, 103
The Haunting, 77–78, 82

The Haunting of Hill House, 77–78, 84–86, 90
The Haunting of Hill House (Television), 85
hauntology, 57–58
Hereditary, 143
Hills, Matt, 17
Hiram, 90
Hoffmann, E. T. A., 19
Holiness Code, 102, 115–116
House of David, 10, 77, 86–92

impurity. *See* purity/impurity
Inside, 29–30, 45

J source, 134–135
Jacob, 109, 131
Jesus, 6
Joab, 87
Job, 6, 11, 16, 30, 32–46, 129, 131–133
Jobling, David, 60
Joshua, 6
Judges, 6, 129
justice, 6, 38, 55–57, 60, 65, 68, 91, 126, 132

Kalmanofsky, Amy, 83–84, 102
Kierkegaard, Søren, 5
King Kong, 30
Kings, Book of, 86, 91, 129
Korpel, Marjo, 35
Kreitzer, Larry, 16
Kristeva, Julia, 114

Lefebvre, Henri, 81
Lethal Weapon, 1
Levenson, Jon, 35
Leviathan, 31
Leviathan, 10, 30, 32–46, 145
Lewton, Val, 5
Lights Out, 57
Lindow, John, 83
Lipton, Diana, 111

Mama, 56
Marcuse, Herbert, 21
Marduk, 33–36, 133–134
Marx, Karl, 57, 60
Marzouk, Safwat, 36, 133

General Index

Maxwell-Stuart, P. G., 56
mediums, 61–64
menstruation, 103–104, 106–107, 112–113
Meribah, 126
Midian, 68, 117, 129
Milgrom, Jacob, 105
Miller, Robert III, 34
The Mist, 127–128, 137
Mobley, Gregory, 33
Monster House, 79
monsters, 10–11, 17–22, 29–46, 101–117, 125–138, 144
monstrous feminine, 103, 107–108, 117
Moses, 8, 10, 45, 115, 126–131, 136
Murphy, Kelly J., 20

Nathan, 88–91, 109
necromancers, 60–61, 66
Nietzsche, Frederick, 133
Night of the Living Dead, 20, 31, 35
Nightmare on Elm Street, 2–3
normality, 22–23, 109
numinous, 105–106, 129

offering, 63, 85, 110–111
Oliver, Mary Beth, 3
Olyan, Saul, 85
The Omen, 1–2, 4
The Orphanage, 55
other, 20, 30–32, 35–36, 38–39, 101–102, 116
other gods, 10, 59, 65–68
The Others, 56, 64
Otto, Rudolph, 126–127

P source, 102, 105–108, 133–136
Peterson, Christopher, 65
Phinehas, 109
Pliny the Younger, 83
Poltergeist, 80, 91
prosperity gospel, 8, 11
psychoanalytic theory, 19–23, 114
purity/impurity, 105–108, 117

A Quiet Place, 143

race, 20
Rahab. *See* Leviathan
Re and Apophis, 36

Reagan revolution, 18
repression, 8–9, 21–22, 45, 68, 78–79, 92
Revelation, Book of, 32, 37
The Ring, 57
Roberts, Robin, 57
romantic comedy, 7–8
Römer, Thomas, 131
Ruane, Nicole, 104, 106
ruins, 77, 83–84

Samuel, 10, 59–65
Sanders, Meghan, 3
satan, 37–39, 131–132
Saul, 6, 59–65, 90
Schiffendecker, Katherine, 42
Schneider, Steven Jay, 19
Schwartz, Joshua, 105
Scurlock, JoAnn, 60
Sea of Reeds, 11, 133, 135–136, 137
Seibert, Eric, 6
serpent, 32, 35
sex, 81
sexual violence, 22, 88–91
The Shining, 80–83, 89, 91
The Sixth Sense, 5, 56, 64
slasher films, 5, 18, 101–102, 104, 109, 143
Smith, Mark, 34, 68
social-scientific, 21–22
Solomon, 88, 91
Something Wicked This Way Comes, 3
Sonik, Karen, 34
sotah, 110–114
South Park, 103
Sparks, Kenton, 34
Stir of Echoes, 57
Stone, Ken, 110
structuralism, 36, 58
Superman, 1

taboo, 22
Teeth, 104
Tel Dan Stele, 86
The Thing, 31
The Thing from Another World, 31
Tiamat, 33–36, 133–135
trace, 38–39, 58, 65, 91
trauma, 18, 21, 56–59, 64, 79–84, 88–92, 103, 144–145

uncanny, 19, 78–81
The Uninvited, 56, 79
Urban Legend, 101–102
urban legends, 101
Uriah, 87–91, 109
Uzzah, 126

Vagina Dentata, 103
vampires, 19
van der Toorn, Karel, 66
Vidler, Anthony, 79
Volf, Miroslav, 126

Wakeman, Mary, 33–34

The Walking Dead, 20
Westermann, Claus, 34
When a Stranger Calls, 101
White Zombie, 20
wilderness, 6, 66, 68
Woman in Black, 57, 82, 89
Wood, Robin, 8–9, 19–21

yam, 33, 35, 39–40, 42
YHWH, 10–11, 32–46, 62–68, 90, 91, 107, 109, 110, 112–116, 125–138

Zipporah, 129–131
zombies, 4, 18, 20, 31, 35, 145

Scripture Reference Index

Genesis:
1, 33–36, 40, 133, 136
1:1, 84
1:1-2:4, 137
1:2, 34, 133
1:7, 134
1:9-10, 136
1:21, 135
1:22, 135
2:4-3:24, 137
6-9, 36, 134–135, 137
6:5-8, 134
6:9-13, 134
7:4, 135
7:12, 135
8:2, 135
32, 131
34:2, 109
34:7, 109

Exodus:
4:21, 126
4:22-23, 129
4:24-26, 129–131
7:3, 126
7:8-13, 135
7:17-18, 135
7:19, 136
7:21, 136
8:20, 136
9:8-12, 136
14, 136–137
14:4, 126
14:16, 136
14:22, 136
14:29, 136
19:11, 115
20:1-17, 114
20:17, 115
32, 67

Leviticus:
13:45-46, 85
14, 85–86
15, 106–107, 115–116
15:19, 107
18:1-5, 116
18:19, 107
18:22, 107
18:23, 116
18:24, 116
18:28, 107
20, 116
20:10, 110, 112
20:15-16, 107
20:18, 107

Numbers:
5:11-31, 110–112
13, 30
17:16, 110
19:15, 110

171

20:2-13, 126
25, 67
35:30, 110–112

Deuteronomy:
5, 114
6:14, 66
11:16, 66
13:7, 67
17:6, 110–112
19:15, 110–112
22:22-27, 110–112

Judges:
2:11, 67
2:12, 67

1 Samuel:
3, 61
6:19, 126
7:7, 62–63
12:14, 62
12:24, 62
13:8-14, 63
15:25, 63
15:30, 63
16:14-23, 90
17:11, 63
17:24, 63
18:10-11, 90
18:12, 63
18:13, 63
18:29, 63
19:9-10, 90
20:16, 86
21:5, 86
25, 61
25:1, 62
28, 61–65
28:3, 62
28:5, 62
28:6, 62, 64
28:10, 62
28:12-13, 62
28:15, 64
28:16, 64
28:20, 62
31:1-2, 65

2 Samuel:
2:1-11, 86, 90
3:1, 86
3:6, 86
5:11-13, 90
6:7, 126
7, 88
7:16, 87
11:1, 87
11:5, 87
11:13, 87
12, 88, 109
12:11, 88, 109
13, 88
16:20-23, 109–110
16:22, 88

1 Kings:
1:15, 91
6-7, 91
11:1-8, 91

Isaiah:
8:19, 65
8:20, 42–43
13:19-22, 84
19:3, 66
27, 32
27:1, 39
29:1-4, 84
29:6, 84
30:7, 32
34:8-15, 84
51:9, 39
58:8, 42

Jeremiah:
4:7, 83
4:23-26, 84
9:10, 84

Ezekiel:
20, 67
23, 67
23:3, 67
29:1-7, 39
29:3, 32
32:1-10, 39
32:2, 32

Hosea:
2:8, 39
6:3, 42

Psalms:
8, 132
23, 9, 145
74:13-14, 32, 39
82, 66, 68
89:10, 32
89:11, 32, 39
104:26, 32, 41, 45
139:9, 42–43

Job:
1:1, 37
1:6, 37
1:9, 37
1:9-10, 39
1:11, 37, 131–132
2:12, 44
3:3, 40
3:4-7, 40
3:6, 40
3:8, 37, 38, 40, 41, 44, 45
3:9, 40, 43
3:23, 39
4-5, 39
6:4, 132
6:12, 43
7:12, 37–41, 44
7:17, 39, 132
7:18-20, 132
9:13, 37, 38
9:16, 132
9:19, 132
10:9, 44

10:16, 132
11:3, 42
15:20-35, 83
15:21, 83
15:24, 83
16:9, 132
16:12-13, 132
17:16, 44
18:13, 42
20:11, 44
26:12, 37, 38
26:13, 37
30:19, 44
32-37, 38
38-39, 41
38:8, 39, 41
40:3-5, 41
40:25-26, 44
40:25, 41
40:27, 41
40:29, 44
40:31, 42
41, 37
41:2, 41, 44
41:3, 41–42
41:4, 42
41:5, 42–43
41:7-9, 43
41:10, 42–43
41:11-13, 44
41:25, 43–44
42:7, 44
42:7-17, 38

Song of Songs:
6:10, 42

About the Author

Brandon R. Grafius is assistant professor of biblical studies at Ecumenical Theological Seminary in Detroit. He holds a PhD in Bible, culture, and hermeneutics from Chicago Theological Seminary. His first book, *Reading Phinehas, Watching Slashers: Horror Theory and Numbers 25*, was published by Lexington Books/Fortress Academic in 2018, and his essays on horror and/or Bible have appeared widely in academic journals and edited volumes. He is currently working on a monograph on *The Witch* and Puritan religious anxieties for the Devil's Advocates series.

www.ingramcontent.com/pod-product-compliance
Lightning Source LLC
Chambersburg PA
CBHW020830020526
44115CB00029B/97